JOHN BARNES

The Autobiography

JOHN BARNES

The Autobiography

HEADLINE

First published in 1999
by HEADLINE BOOK PUBLISHING

10 9 8 7 6 5 4 3 2 1

British Library Cataloguing in Publication Data

Barnes, John, 1963–
  John Barnes : the autobiography
  1.Barnes, John, 1963– 2.Soccer players – England –
  Biography 3.Soccer players – England – Liverpool –
  Biography
  I.Title
  796.3'34'092

ISBN 0 7472 2194 4

Typeset by Palimpsest Book Production Limited,
Polmont, Stirlingshire

Printed and bound in Great Britain by
Mackays of Chatham plc, Chatham, Kent

HEADLINE BOOK PUBLISHING
A division of the Hodder Headline Group
338 Euston Road
London NW1 3BH

www.headline.co.uk
www.hodderheadline.com

contents

acknowledgements

I would like to thank all those who have helped me in my career and supported me throughout, especially my mother and father, family and friends, who have been such a big part of my life.

I am particularly grateful to Henry Winter for his involvement in the writing of this book, and to Marion Paull and Ian Marshall.

But thanks mostly to my wife Suzy and the four Js – Jamie, Jordan, Jemma and Jasmin.

chased

S hort of size and breath, the policeman kept about twenty yards behind me, trailing me for all his worth. As I continued on my way through the streets of London, I knew what was going through the policeman's mind. He was convinced this black boy was heading down Wigmore Place intent on burglary. Rich pickings could be found in Wigmore Place, a cul de sac off Wigmore Street lined with smart mews houses. The situation was all too familiar to me, funny even in its predictability. Policemen would see my tracksuit, the sweat on my brow and smell criminal activity. I was actually out training.

I was only young, still a few years away from professional football with Watford, but I pushed myself through long runs late at night, pounding the pavements of London to prepare me for matchday. I ran up Harley Street, through Regent's Park and panted up Primrose Hill, such a steep climb but worth it for the spectacular view over London. I turned, belted down the hill and re-traced my steps back into the centre of town. I wore a tracksuit and looked fit enough to be someone in serious training but the police saw only a black boy out at midnight. Nearing the end of my run in an expensive part of the capital where police proliferated, I slowed down whenever they were about. If I'd carried on running, the night would have been pierced by sirens and blue lights, so I walked; but they still watched.

Being followed by the police after dark became part of my life. While I kept along Wigmore Street, a relatively busy thoroughfare, the police ignored me. In their eyes, this little black boy could just have been looking for a bus-stop to take him home to a rougher part of London. But the moment I turned into Wigmore Place, they reached for their radios, reporting a suspicious black boy who had no legitimate business entering a prosperous dead end. I had to turn down Wigmore Place – I lived there.

My father was Jamaica's military attaché to London in the late 1970s and early 1980s and one of the perks of the posting was this great home. The only drawback was that the Metropolitan Police could not comprehend a black boy living there. Our house was at the far end of Wigmore Place, so I carried on walking, occasionally glancing back and seeing this policeman whispering into his walkie-talkie. I prepared for my normal routine in such situations. I would put my key in the door, open it, turn round and say, 'Good night, officer.' I had it all sussed. As I reached my front door, the policeman was within ten yards of me. 'No problem,' I thought, 'I've been followed to my door so many times before.' I walked up to the door, slid the key into the lock, turned it and pushed – and pushed. The door opened only three inches. My mother, forgetting I was out running, had put the security chain on. I kept pushing, harder and harder as the policeman drew closer, I burst out laughing because I realised how ridiculous it must look.

'Listen, officer,' I said, turning to face him, 'my mother has locked me out accidentally.' But as soon as I turned round, he backed away.

'Now listen, son,' he shouted, 'I've radioed for back-up so don't start causing problems.'

'No, no, you don't understand,' I replied. 'I live here.' The policeman looked at me as if I was some dangerous animal, not the son of a visiting diplomat.

'Don't try anything stupid,' he yelled from the safety of thirty yards away. Fortunately, one of my sisters heard the commotion. She came running downstairs and opened the door to find me and a policeman glaring at each other. Unfortunately, she shouted up to my parents, 'Daddy, Daddy, Johnny's been brought home by a policeman.'

Dad thought I was in trouble. As a military man, my father lives and breathes respect for authority so he immediately assumed the worst.

'What have you been doing?' he barked at me. Before I could reply, the policeman intervened, having finally realised that I was not a burglar but in fact a resident of Wigmore Place.

'Sorry, sir,' the policeman said, 'he wasn't actually doing anything wrong.'

Rather than ticking the policeman off for harassing his son, my father replied, 'Very well done, officer, you can't be too careful these days.' If I hadn't been his son, I would have been guilty in my father's eyes. Such a law-abiding figure as my father believes that if a policeman stops someone, it's because the person has committed an offence.

'Well done, officer,' he said again. 'Do you want to come in and have a drink?'

'No thank you, sir,' said the policeman. 'Good night, sir.' With that he turned round and left, probably to shadow another black boy whom he thought had ventured into too smart a part of town. For me, it was a case of another night, another police officer eyeing me suspiciously. This was racism pure and simple. When the 1999 report into the Stephen Lawrence murder spoke of institutionalised racism in the Metropolitan Police, I thought to myself, 'It's not the police force, it's the English generally.'

I kept being stopped by policemen. At one point, my family spent four months in an apartment at the top of the Jamaican High Commission on St James's, off Piccadilly. The building was near the Ritz and was easy to spot because of the huge Jamaican flag hanging outside. The police always kept an eye on the building but they never believed anyone actually lived there. The Barnes family did. I even had a key to the big front door of the High Commission. If the police saw a black boy running down St James's at 2 a.m., they followed me. If they saw me enter the closed High Commission building, they rushed across to accost me. Luckily, once the front door was open, the security guard would be sitting there. The police would leave when they realised I was known to the High Commission staff. The inconvenience aside, the continual stopping never really bothered me because I understood the reasons for it. It must have been more frustrating for the police. They never realised their actions were driven by innate racism.

Even when I became well-known, having established myself with Watford and been capped by England, I still encountered problems. One spring day in 1984, just before Watford faced Everton in the FA Cup final, I arranged to meet my father outside Lillywhites sports shop on Piccadilly Circus. Dad wanted to see me, to wish me well because he was going to miss my special day at Wembley. Duty called him back to the Caribbean. He was head of the West Indian peace-keeping forces in Grenada, having led them in the previous year, so he had to return. It was good to meet up, however briefly. Lillywhites was our traditional rendezvous. My father adored sports stores, walking around them and looking particularly at the squash and tennis racquets. He loved sport. I arrived early and stood in the foyer; I had just come from training at Watford and was still in my club tracksuit.

A white security guard kept looking at me. After I had waited a couple of minutes, the guard said, 'You can't stand here, please leave.' Apparently a shoplifter had just been working Lillywhites over and the guard thought I might be his accomplice.

'I'm waiting for my father,' I told him.

'You still can't wait here,' the guard replied. 'Go outside.' As he said it, he recognised me. You might have thought that a current England international and FA Cup finalist standing in the foyer of Lillywhites would count for something, but he looked me up and down and said, 'I told you not to stand around here.' I went outside and waited for my father on the pavement. I was livid.

Racism is a way of life for black people. The majority of motorists stopped by Merseyside Police are black. When I played for Liverpool, my car was often flagged down. Once they saw it was John Barnes inside, they would say, 'Sorry, John, we've only stopped you because we've had a report that a car like yours has been stolen. It's an easy mistake to make, sir.' Mistake? They were simply targeting black people. I wished I had the nerve to reply, 'Well, officer, there's a car like mine in front. But because it belongs to a white person you don't stop him.' Police always throw this get-out line at me, that my car could have been stolen, that they were just doing their job. The implication was that I should be grateful they were keeping an eye out for possible stolen cars. Although it is so obvious I have been stopped because of the colour of my skin, I always remain polite. I am lucky I am a footballer. Friends of mine who own nice cars but are not footballers are forever having their cars searched. But then that's the racist society we live in.

jamaican born and bred

I suppose I am not a real Englishman. I was raised in Jamaica, which had a profound influence on me. My birthplace was the capital, Kingston, in an army camp called Up Park, a name redolent of Jamaica's colonial past. When the British West Indies Regiment was stationed in Kingston, all its brigadiers, colonels and generals were quartered in fabulous houses at Up Park Camp. These buildings were beautiful, two or three storeys high, often seven-bedroomed and each surrounded by an acre or more of manicured garden. When Jamaica gained independence, all the local army officers moved into Up Park, taking over the very English homes of the sons of Surrey and Suffolk who were returning across the Atlantic. My father was a colonel, who rose to become number two in the Jamaican army, and we lived well at Up Park. A maid and a cook looked after us; labour is so cheap in Jamaica that anyone with a decent job employs staff.

Up Park was idyllic for children, particularly a boy like me who loved sport. Sport has always formed a central part of my life. When I was born, on 7 November 1963, my mother placed a football in my crib. My father insisted I be christened John Charles Bryan Barnes because of his admiration for John Charles, the great Welsh footballer. Up Park catered for a growing boy's passion for all sorts of sports. The place resembled a village, eight square miles in size and full of swimming pools, squash courts and tennis courts. For my schooling, I travelled into Kingston, which has never been a safe place to walk around. But back at Up Park, we roamed where we liked, playing football, hanging around after dark, just fooling about and laughing with friends.

They were happy times. Memories of Up Park come flooding back whenever I return to Jamaica to visit my parents, who now run a country club which houses the Squash Racquets Association. Back in Jamaica, I occasionally bump into old friends from Up Park; or old soldiers, who march up to me and declare, 'Barnes, I remember you growing up in Up Park Camp; you were always playing football.' They never mention my professional career in England, restricting themselves to, 'You are the son of Colonel Barnes.' In Jamaica, my father is more famous than me. Everyone recognises Colonel Ken Barnes. High-ranking army officers are prominent figures in Jamaica, on a par with politicians. Jamaicans know that I left Kingston and ended up playing for the great Liverpool and for England and have since gone on to become head coach of Celtic, but each one knows more about Ken Barnes. Every Jamaican I meet tells me, 'Your father used to play football for Jamaica.'

Dad loves his sport. He was born in Trinidad and played cricket for their Second XI before moving to Jamaica aged eighteen to join the British West Indies Regiment. My father was so versatile at sport. He represented Jamaica at football and squash, and at Sandhurst he became heavyweight boxing champion and a first-team rugby man despite never having run with a ball before. His athleticism ensured he was swiftly noticed by the rugby selectors. But a passion for football beat strongest within him. He went to Wembley to watch the 1960 FA Cup final when Wolves beat Blackburn 3–0.

As a player, Dad was possibly not a particularly good centre-half. I remain convinced the reason why Jamaica's selectors picked him was because of his army background. Jamaican people have a problem with discipline but, as an army officer, Dad inspired respect. His job was mainly to keep the other players in line and aware of the team tactics. My father eventually managed Jamaica, although it proved a short-term commission because of the players' indiscipline. My father could not stand or understand footballers who did tricks and took risks with the ball which clearly undermined the team cause. He soon resigned.

Jamaica overflows with footballing talent. Kingston is far more prolific in producing gifted players than Trinidad or Tobago, which have nurtured stars such as Dwight Yorke. It is just this indiscipline that holds them back. Jamaican footballers used to have a terrible attitude. They believed they were the biggest and the best. Jamaicans still call all the other islanders 'Smallies', as in small islanders. This superiority complex spills into an over-arrogance which tempers teams' strength. I have played in Jamaica for various invitational sides and the locals' behaviour was shocking; it was complete anathema to someone with a professional or team-conscious approach. They would not pass to anyone they felt should not be in the team. Swearing at the manager and walking off the pitch were not uncommon.

Their attitude improved enough for them to reach the 1998 World Cup finals held in France, an unheard-of achievement for a team from that part of the world. Haiti managed a similar success but they were French-speaking. For an English West Indian island, Jamaica's qualification was unprecedented. For Jamaicans like myself, it was little short of a miracle because I know about the internal problems. Traditionally, Jamaicans' disposition has been bad and my father could not handle that. As well as being manager of the national side, he sat on the disciplinary committee of the Jamaican Football Association. Farce reigned. Few of the players sent off or otherwise in trouble actually presented themselves before the disciplinary committee. Those who did would charge into the committee room and swear at the officials or threaten to shoot them. My father resigned from that post as well.

The importance of law and order was paramount with my father. If a riot broke out, he admired the policeman in the middle hitting everyone with a stick. I can just imagine him jokingly shouting, 'That's it, officer, they all need a good beating, keep going.' Never mind the ins and outs of the situation, a beating would knock some sense into them was my father's approach. Dad's view of life and the way he conducted himself were so different from those Jamaicans he played with and then managed. My father is the most ethical person in the whole world. As I grew up, I realised no one could be more truthful and honest. I thought that nobody else existed who would always do the right thing like him. He is a real gentleman, a model Sandhurst graduate. For instance, if a woman enters the room, my father always gets up; and even though his army days are over, he stands to attention if the British national anthem is played. Dad comes from the old school of West Indian families who love everything British, like the Royal Family. He reminds me of the classic English gentleman.

I wanted to be my father, to copy his every move and live my life by his principles, saying and doing the right thing. I have failed even to come close. My father is someone I respect more than anyone in the world. I have watched, admired and even met Nelson Mandela. I have read and learned from Martin Luther King. I know so much about their lives, about the sacrifices they made, the punishment they took for their beliefs. My father shares their strength of character; I know he would die for his beliefs if he had to.

Although I admire my father enormously, I do not feel as close to him as I do to my mother. An air of reserve governs Dad's demeanour. His own father was a Trinidadian civil servant and although the family was a loving one, expressions of emotion were rare. Dad dislikes arguments. He just wants to keep the peace and be happy. He would never become confrontational with my mother. 'OK, go on,' he will say. Anything for a quiet life. His family was not as outwardly warm as the Hills, my mother's family. A gathering of the Hills is always a loud affair. When my mother, Jean, and her three sisters congregate, the women gabble away while the husbands stay quiet. The Hills have always been exotic. My mother's father and his brother started the trade unions in Jamaica. They were imprisoned because trade unions were illegal at the time. The Hills were a very political family, very outspoken, always in the newspapers. They grew up with the Manleys, whose son Michael became Prime Minister. There is even a road named after my grandfather, Ken Hill, because of his fame as a politician. They were sporty, too. My uncle, Anthony Hill, was a teenage prodigy at football. At eighteen, people were calling him the best centre-forward Jamaica had ever had. But he was ingrained with that Hill political streak and became ambassador to Washington and then to the UN in Geneva.

My mother is a remarkable lady, a personality known throughout Jamaica. She is always busy, always involved in new ventures. She was the Sue Lawley of Jamaican television, presenting all sorts of programmes for the Jamaican Broadcasting Corporation. She even hosted a show in England which ran on Channel Four for six weeks. I remember her interviewing Annie Lennox before she was famous with the Eurythmics. Variety spices my mother's life. She has been an executive for the National Trust. At sixty-three, she completed a law degree. If I run into any problems, I go to my mother rather than my father. Even now, if I ring home and my father picks up the phone, I'll say, 'Hi, Dad, how are you doing?' We trade small talk briefly. And then I'll chat for an hour with my mother about life and everything. I know my father takes great pride in what I do. He just doesn't show it, although he is mellowing. When Jamaicans became excited about how well I was doing at Liverpool, my father insisted they calmed down. 'Stop making such a fuss,' he said. 'John's rubbish.' My father was always dismissive about me in public but I knew that deep down he welled up with pride. He is not the type to show those feelings and I don't want him to. It would embarrass me. I don't want my father to think of me as a successful footballer. I want to be acknowledged as having become a successful person. The sportsman who scored a great goal in Brazil, who won cups and championships with Liverpool, is not the real John Barnes.

My attitude stems from my mother and the values she instilled in me. She thinks deeply about life; always has. Because of her, I've read extensively about Buddhism. Combined with my mother's advice, Buddhism taught me to ignore the trappings of fame. If a man is stripped of all he has, divested of clothes, money, home and cars, he reveals his true self. This tenet dominates my life. When I look in the mirror, I don't see John Barnes The Football Celebrity. I see John Barnes The Person. And I like what I see, not because of the trappings of a football career, but because of the way I am. I wish people could see me for who I am, not what I am. The public's appreciation of me as a gifted footballer is great but it really means nothing to me. If my playing career had been marked by failure, I would still be the same person.

This desire to be myself, not some star, stems from my mother's words and examples. She lectured on 'Science of the Mind', a celebration of positive thinking, asserting that those who do the right thing receive reward. I believe in fate although not in the extreme sense of standing in front of buses convinced I will walk away unscathed. Fate dominates my life and career, from transfers and injuries to simple things like finding the right house to live in. My mother drummed into me that if I live a good life, good things will happen to me. As a young footballer, scarcely older than fifteen, I was surrounded by team-mates who were more skilful than me. We played on Sunday mornings and some had come straight from all-night parties. These players possessed more talent than me and often shone on the Sunday, despite their clubbing, but it was me who turned professional. Fate dictated that I was rewarded for being tucked up in bed on a Saturday night. A scout spotted me on a day when I happened to play brilliantly.

My mother taught me that fate ordains my every move. During my time at Newcastle United, where I went from Liverpool, hotel life began to depress me. I hunted for a house but found nothing, until I heard of one at Hepscott, near Morpeth, which is quite a way north of Newcastle. 'I'm never going to go up to Hepscott,' I thought, but out of desperation, I said to my family, 'Let's go and look at this godforsaken house in godforsaken Morpeth which is miles away.'

The house turned out to be just ten minutes' drive away from good schools, and there were thirteen other children of my own kids' age in the neighbouring five houses. It was perfect.

As I listened to my mother talking away in our old house at Up Park, I learned that fate can also be bad but that situations can be influenced if your attitude is right. If I had partied every Saturday night, I would have struggled on the pitch the next morning. When I couldn't get in the Newcastle side, I always tried to do the right thing, being punctual for training and working really hard, even though I knew Newcastle's manager, Ruud Gullit, wanted me to leave. Some of my friends said to me, 'What's the point you going to training? Gullit's not going to pick you.' But my mother's teachings about fate made me know something good would happen to me if I carried on doing the right thing. If I adopted a bad attitude, maybe I would be denied the opportunity of succeeding in management or television when my playing days were over. In the summer of 1999, I was rewarded with Celtic's offer of the head coaching position.

My mother's philosophy demands doing the right things now, taking care of the present. She also made me believe in reincarnation, in karma. If I live a good life, I believe I will be reincarnated as a higher being. If I live a bad life, I believe I will be reincarnated as a lower being. Because I have experienced a prosperous, healthy and happy existence, I must have been a decent person in a past life. When people tell me my views on fate and reincarnation are illogical, I always produce one image as a riposte: I find it impossible to accept that a still-born baby, who took nine months to nurture but then had its life snuffed out, will never come back. Life after death must exist.

Buddhism and rival religions fascinate me. I spend so long in the car, driving from home to the training ground, stadium or airport, that I decided to use the time constructively. I stopped playing my funk and soul CDs and started reflecting on which religion carries the greatest authority. My parents raised me as a Christian. I believe in Jesus Christ, that he was a great man and a prophet like Mohammed. I believe in prophets and psychics, men who possess powers. I wondered what happened before Jesus was born, two thousand years ago. Have all those people burned in hell because they were not Christians? I don't accept that. Christianity cannot be the only true religion. Leading your life as a Roman Catholic may have been fine fifteen hundred years ago but it is impossible to follow such an outdated path now. I have read the Koran but find the Muslim faith too awkward. Buddhism offers most relevance. It pertains to everyday life. I used to tease Newcastle's chaplain about me being a Buddhist. 'If Jesus came back from the dead,' I would say to him, 'why did no one recognise him?'

If my mother had heard that, she would have scolded me for being flippant to a chaplain. My mother always worried about me and wanted to make sure I grew up the right way. I was never academically minded which troubled her, particularly because my two sisters, Tracy and Gillian, are both very bright. Tracy worked very hard. She spent a long time at university and became a lawyer in Jamaica. She is now married and works in Washington. Sport has brought out Tracy's competitive side. She swam for Jamaica and even played squash internationally, despite not picking up a racquet until she was eighteen. When Tracy sets her mind to something, she invariably excels. Gillian doesn't work as hard as Tracy but is naturally intelligent so she does fine in life. Gillian won a tennis scholarship to America and played semi-pro after graduating in International Relations. My academic career was less illustrious. I attended a grammar school and managed five O-levels but I was never in my sisters' league. They were racking up ten O-levels while I was always a tearaway. I was never in real trouble but I never paid much attention at school. My mother worried what was going to become of me.

My mother meditates at 5 a.m. and when I was ten she started meditating with me. She impressed on me the importance of proper behaviour. During our meditation, I wished she would hurry up or shut up. I used to sit down, close my eyes and breathe really heavily to make her believe I was meditating. I was there under sufferance. I kept thinking, 'Oh no, not again,' whenever my mother summoned me to meditate. But, slowly, I absorbed her words of advice. Those morning meditations moulded the way I lead my life.

During my time at Watford, our manager Graham Taylor sent the players to a hypnotist – an exotic woman somewhere in Watford. As with my mother's meditation, I didn't want to be there. I just hoped this hypnotist would hurry up so I could go off and do something interesting. We had to do it to keep Graham Taylor happy. The hypnotist kept saying, 'Your hand is getting lighter.' Eventually my hand floated up in the air. Her words sank in just as my mother's had.

My mother was a real disciplinarian. As a child, I was always naughty, messing around, getting into fights and scrapes. She shouted at me and beat me. Whenever my mother caught me doing something wrong, she screamed at me to get a switch from the nearest tree and struck me with it. If we were in the house, she took off her belt and hit me with that. But it wasn't abuse, as one British newspaper disgracefully claimed in 1990. Beatings from parents were the norm in Jamaica. British people simply do not appreciate how disciplined Jamaican children are. Black kids born in Britain have it easy compared with a Jamaican's strict upbringing, although many Jamaicans rebel as my father discovered with his football teams.

Discipline is lax across Europe. My father's cousin got married and took her family to live in Sweden. It didn't work out and she got divorced. When the children returned to Trinidad, they were swearing and smoking. One of them even had a pipe! These were habits they picked up in Sweden. No one stopped them. No one dared to and I soon discovered why.

'How do you get away with everything?' I asked my cousin.

'My parents would not risk hitting us,' he replied. 'In Sweden, there's a commercial on TV giving a number to call if you've got a complaint about your parents. I could have my father arrested.' It's crazy. Swedish children misbehave without anyone being allowed to control them. Sweden consequently suffers a desperately high suicide rate among teenagers. They need discipline, not tolerance.

Parents wouldn't need to beat them hard, just the odd smack to keep their kids in line.

I started rebelling against the strictness of my Jamaican upbringing only when I arrived in Europe. The English boys I hung around with stayed out at nightclubs until 2 a.m. I desperately wanted to go with them but my mother refused. I went anyway, although never on the eve of games. She once came to a nightclub to drag me home. My mother never worried back at Up Park. Army camps are safe, even late at night. Only when we moved to England, did she begin to be alarmed. I hated her over-protective nature but now I thank her for making me understand the importance of discipline. When I started my professional career at Watford, I coped comfortably with Graham Taylor's obsession with discipline. He was so strict that some players grumbled and even fell by the wayside but I was used to the heavy hand. I survived and prospered because of my strict childhood.

My parents sent me to be taught by priests at St George's College, Kingston, where, needless to say, discipline was strict. I learned mainly about sport there. St George's backed on to Sabina Park, the Test cricket ground, and we took short cuts across the outfield when heading for our playing fields. It was the closest I got to cricket at school. I come from the West Indies, so everyone is convinced my first love must have been cricket, but football obsessed me. I did eventually become a good left-handed bowler but really football was the only sport for me. Cricket has never been as big as football in Jamaica. It is not like Guyana and Barbados where cricket is king. Football rules in Jamaica, always has done, although basketball is growing rapidly in popularity now.

The success of the Reggae Boyz in qualifying for France '98 has led the outside world to think football is a new phenomenon in Jamaica. But as a kid, all I talked about with my friends was football. My first love was Germany. Their football has fascinated me ever since my father went to the Munich Olympics in 1972 and brought me back some Gerd Müller adidas boots. I was so excited. I had always wanted a pair of them. I've loved German football ever since.

Although Pele became my favourite player of all time, my idols as a child were Wolfgang Overath, Franz Beckenbauer, Gunther Netzer and Gerd Müller. Overath was the one I most admired: he was left-footed like me, playing left-side of midfield. I loved him.

I vividly remember the 1974 World Cup. I was ten at the time and when the West Germans played Holland in the final in Munich, my father took me to watch the match on a huge screen at the National Stadium, Jamaica's equivalent of Wembley. Of the two thousand people there, I was the only one who wanted West Germany to win. In fact, I was the only person in the whole of Jamaica who wanted the Germans to win. Jamaicans supported the Dutch because of their elegant style of football. They revelled in the skill of Johan Cruyff and Johan Neeskens, and loved their sense of imagination and adventure. Jamaicans began following Dutch fortunes when Holland beat Brazil, who experienced a nightmare of a tournament. Jamaicans instinctively want Brazil to win because of their flair but everyone was impressed by the way Holland defeated them in Dortmund, particularly their brilliant second-half display. Jamaicans prayed the Dutch would humiliate West Germany. I got a terrible teasing from my friends when Neeskens scored after only eighty seconds. All around me at the National Stadium, people went wild with delight but West Germany didn't let me down. Paul Breitner equalised and then Müller, wearing those magical boots, turned cleverly to hit the winner.

Watching players like Müller and Overath doubled my desire to kick a ball about whenever I could. Before I started playing competitively, I swam most days. My sister Tracy swam for Jamaica at the time so I trained with her. The main pool in Jamaica was right by Up Park. On the way over to swimming. I always stopped to play football with friends. My father quickly noticed.

'If you are going to play football every day, you will have to stop the swimming,' he said. 'You have to be more devoted to be a swimmer. But you are being distracted by football so I think you should go and do that instead.' At the age of nine, my swimming career was over. My life in football began.

With my friends at Up Park, I formed a team called Bartex. The 'Bar' part came from the first three letters of Barnes. That was only right – I was captain and best player. Also it was my ball. We played a few matches against other teams but nothing too serious. Scrimmage was our main pursuit, a small-sided game with rocks about three feet apart for goalposts. The narrowness of the goal made it impossible to shoot from twenty yards; passing the ball into the net was the best way of scoring. Scrimmage's popularity among kids explains why Jamaicans and some South American teams are excellent at getting into the box but cannot shoot from range. Jamaicans can play one-twos all day but few of them can thump in a thirty-yarder. I remember playing for England against Colombia at Wembley once and Carlos Valderrama's team dripped with exquisite technique. The Colombians kept conjuring wonderful passing triangles but none of them was prepared to let fly from twenty-five yards. Colombia's history of scrimmage made them work the ball into the box. Scrimmage prepared me for Liverpool, where most of the training involved small-sided games. Scrimmage formed such a large portion of my day that if I left my ball at home, I kicked a discarded milk carton about.

The most skilful schoolboy footballers are revered in Jamaica. The island's best football is seen at schoolboy level. At seventeen or eighteen, the top players leave Jamaica on football scholarships to America. Many settle in the States, and these erstwhile schoolboy stars never graduate to Jamaican Major League teams. So Jamaicans flock to schoolboy matches to see the bright lights before they disappear. The national final for sixth-formers, the Manning Cup, is an enormous event. Schools are given the day off and everyone packs into the National Stadium, invariably heaving with a 30,000 full house. The Manning Cup final is such a celebrated occasion, such a landmark in the life of any schoolboy footballer, that I still feel a sense of disappointment at having left Jamaica before I was old enough to play in it. I was advanced for my age, playing midfield for the Under-15s at twelve, but not enough to make Manning Cup selection.

In January 1976, my father was sent on a four-year posting to London. Leaving Kingston was difficult for me. I loved Up Park, my friends, my football. Jamaica will always be special to me. Jamaican people were very proud when I represented England. They knew then, in the 1980s, that the Reggae Boyz had no chance of ever achieving any prominence in world football so they were just pleased I found an opportunity elsewhere, particularly when I became the first Jamaican to appear on the World Cup stage. Jamaicans did not mind that I was representing England. So many of their relatives emigrated to England that no one took offence. Changing allegiances would trigger a different reaction now. The Reggae Boyz have a chance of success and so Jamaicans frown on anybody choosing to play under another flag. But in the 1980s, they derived great pleasure from my success. I was even invited to meet the Prime Minister.

Such recognition happens to all successful Jamaican sportsmen. Trevor Berbick, the heavyweight boxer who went to America and fought Mike Tyson, returned to a huge parade. Many Jamaicans head overseas to play sport or represent other countries. The reaction to Ben Johnson's drugs scandal irritated me. When Johnson sprinted to gold at the Seoul Olympics he was hailed as a Canadian role model and everyone loved him; but the moment he was exposed as a drugs cheat and stripped of his medal, he was described as 'Jamaican-born Ben Johnson'. I laughed when I read how English papers changed their tune, from praising a Canadian to villifying a Jamaican-born cheat. Journalists seemed to imply that Johnson must be guilty because of his Jamaican roots which was ridiculous.

I resent this view of Jamaicans, who have habitually proved great achievers. Because of their innate arrogance, Jamaicans survive and succeed wherever they live. Many of the leading sportsmen in America boast Jamaican origins. English sport is the same; Linford Christie and Ian Wright are of Jamaican stock. We are an island of people who make the most of our situation and thrive anywhere, even in the unlikeliest places. I have met Jamaicans in Russia. I toured China with Watford once and all of a sudden heard a

Jamaican voice. It is an extraordinary world where a poor boy from Kingston ends up in Peking. He was getting by, selling reggae music and Bob Marley hats. In Scandinavia, I found countless African students all corralled in the same area, and one Jamaican living in the middle of Gothenburg among all the affluent whites. He was unemployed but he somehow scratched together a living. If a Jamaican moves somewhere, he looks for the most important people, attaches himself to them and becomes someone.

Jamaicans always want something from you; give them some sports shoes or shorts and they are beside themselves with delight. Their approach is different from the English.

'Can I have a shirt?' say fans in England.

'I'm sorry, I haven't got a spare on me now,' I reply. 'How about tomorrow?'

'Fine,' they say, and I never see them again. Jamaicans are far more persistent. I was in Jamaica once, about a four-hour bus ride from Kingston, when a guy strolled up.

'Have you got any spare kit?' he asked.

'Sorry,' I said. 'I don't have anything on me and I'm going back to Kingston today.'

'Don't worry,' he replied, 'I'll come and get something from you in Kingston tomorrow.'

'Fine, fine, see you tomorrow,' I said, rather irritated by now. He seemed happy with that and walked away. Back in Kingston the next day, the doorbell rang and there he was.

'I was just passing,' he said, matter-of-factly. I gave him a pair of shorts and he was so happy. He deserved them.

Ian Wright and I always laugh about this Jamaican trait. The pair of us were in Kingston once when a guy came up. We went through the usual routine.

'Have you got anything?' he asked me and Wrighty. We apologised that we hadn't and explained we were heading back to England soon. Our new friend appeared unperturbed.

'No problem,' he said, 'I'll come and find you.' He had no inkling of which road, which city. He would have gone to London, which is the only city Jamaicans know. This would have narrowed down his search for Wrighty but not me. Jamaicans have heard of Liverpool but they probably think it is a London suburb. 'Don't worry,' he said, 'I will find you.'

'Sure, sure,' I said as he walked off. I turned towards Wrighty and we both started laughing at the ridiculous thought of this man crossing the Atlantic for a free pair of Liverpool or Arsenal socks.

'You think I won't find you?' the man shouted back at us, clearly having seen Wrighty and myself giggling away. He was serious. One day, there will be a knock at my door and there he will be, probably having walked from the airport.

Another national characteristic is that Jamaicans accomplish things. Unfortunately, many succeed through foul means rather than fair. For instance, it is not unusual for Jamaicans to encounter problems with American immigration, being deported one week and returning illegally the next. My sister Gillian has lived in America for fifteen years legally, working on a student visa while applying for her Green Card. Gillian is still waiting. Yet other Jamaicans enter America illegally and somehow acquire a Green Card within six months. The backdoor opens if you push it hard and often enough.

Historically, life was tough for Jamaicans. The slavery system was very harsh on the island, by far the worst in the West Indies. In Barbados, slavery was gentler, if such a description can be applied to a life of servitude. One of my best friends, Charlie, whom I met in Liverpool, is a typical Bajan, always smiling. Barbados is a beautiful island, known as Little England. Tourism flourishes and visitors never get murdered as they do in Jamaica. Because of the particularly brutal slavery system in force in Jamaica, people were brought up very roughly, desensitised even. Slavery's legacy means Jamaicans know how to survive hardship.

The island of my youth is still affected by slavery. Many Jamaican men sire children with different women. It happens in England, too. They consider it a show of power. In fact, it stems from slavery. Slaves were encouraged to breed so the master had more hands to exploit or sell. Male slaves were discouraged from exhibiting any responsibility towards their offspring so the family ethos was totally destroyed. The master took charge of the children. In London nowadays, there are so many black teenaged girls known as 'baby mothers' who bear children to different men. Switch on any black television comedy and there will be a skit on black men who each have five baby mothers. The man walks around proudly, saying, 'I breed her and her.' They never pay maintenance because they are unemployed. They consider it funny to have a cluster of children, a sign of virility and power without responsibility. They do not understand their actions are simply a sad echo of the days of slavery.

For all its problems, I love Jamaica. Unfortunately, my wife, Suzy, could never go and live there because she is obsessed with punctuality and Jamaicans are terrible at time-keeping. If I book a table in a Kingston restaurant for 9 p.m., I do not expect to sit down before 10.30. My aunt, a lawyer in America, once called a meeting of colleagues in Kingston.

'Meet at 2 p.m.,' she told them. My aunt arrived on time to find an empty room. People were still walking in at 3.30. 'Why are you late?' she asked each one as they ambled in.

'What is the problem?' they replied. 'When you said 2 p.m. I thought you meant around 2 p.m., which could mean 3 p.m. or 3.30.' Jamaicans can be very frustrating.

But it is still my birthplace, where I feel most at home. Flying out of Kingston in 1976, leaving behind everything I knew, was a painful experience for a child. I had no idea what awaited in England.

london life

I had never seen snow before. Tropical Jamaica seemed another planet away, let alone another continent, when we arrived in freezing England on 26 January 1976. As our plane came in to land at Heathrow, I stared out of the window and saw all the white roofs. My heart sank. I could not imagine living in such a cold climate. But beyond the white roofs, I caught sight of what seemed like countless football pitches and my spirits lifted. There was row upon row of pitches, game after game involving teams all wearing proper kit. I was amazed. Jamaicans had kit for school matches but not Sunday-morning league games like this. Organised youth leagues did not exist in Jamaica. I pushed my face up to the window, hoping to see more. They had linesmen! For kids' matches! 'This is great,' I thought. Although I hated the cold and went through customs shivering, that glimpse of all those boys playing proper football excited me. On the journey into London, I promised myself I would soon be playing for one of those teams. Within a week of stepping off that plane, I had my club.

My family lived in a variety of places in London, from St James's to Hampstead. We settled first into a flat on York Street, just off Baker Street, in central London. My father had already been in London for some time, living in the Selfridge Hotel, doing his work as military attaché and preparing for our arrival. My sister Tracy quickly became involved in sport in London. As an international swimmer, Tracy needed to maintain her training. She looked around the Baker Street area and found the Mermaid and Marlin Swim Team, who were based just off Lisson Grove. Tracy got talking to one of the swimmers who said her brother played football for Stowe Boys Club. Tracy told Dad and we went to have a look. Stowe Boys Club was just under the Westway fly-over where the A40 leaves London at Paddington. My dad met Joe Lowney, who ran Stowe, and immediately liked him and the club. I joined on the spot.

Most of Stowe's boys came from Paddington. My team contained two white lads, Gary Marsh and Gary Smith, both very good footballers, but it was mainly black kids, all of them fit and strong. The standard was high. Richard Cadette, who went on to Brentford, starred in the Stowe side below mine. Other Stowe boys eventually knocked around the non-league scene. Silvester Williams and Derek Brown turned out for Wembley. Derek even played for Woking against Everton in the FA Cup. Many Stowe boys had the talent to make the professional grade, but enjoyed the nightlife too much.

Sundays could never come soon enough for me. We clambered into our little Stowe Boys Club bus, full of chatter and excitement, for the short journey to Regent's Park. Every time I climbed from the bus and ran through the gates into the park, all those feelings I experienced as we flew into Heathrow came flooding back. Here I was, with a proper team and kit, passing by pitch after pitch, each one staging its own match, its own dramas. Regent's Park was heaven on earth to me. We kicked a ball all the way to our pitch in the middle of the park; that was our warm-up. We did not need much more as we were rarely extended. The Regent's Park Sunday League was not particularly exacting; Stowe won most games 10–0.

Everyone in the team wanted to attack. The moment Stowe gained possession would be a signal for a mass charge. Back in Kingston, I played upfront or midfield. At Stowe, all the kids wanted to fool around, to score a hat-trick apiece, but no one wanted to defend. Someone had to show responsibility. After I had been made captain, I thought it had better be me. So I spent my three and a half years with Stowe at centre-half. I was the only one with the necessary discipline. Occasionally, I dribbled out of defence. If I had wanted to I could have gone around all the opposing players and scored. But I preferred to give the ball to the other centre-back, Micky Edmonds, who loved dribbling. 'Go on Micky,' I told him. 'Off you go. I'll stay here.' Even at thirteen, I was very team-orientated, aware of the need for shape and discipline. This sense of self-restraint, of sacrificing personal desire for the good of the collective meant I was well prepared for the life of a professional. When Graham Taylor told me to stop dribbling down the wing and to man-mark Ray Wilkins during one Manchester United – Watford match, I could do it. From my Stowe days, I understood the importance of placing the team before myself.

Stowe actually taught me very little, apart from about winning. We had a great year in the 1978–79 season, dominating the West London, London and then the national five-a-side competition in Bradford, where we beat a team from Newcastle in the final. Stowe's approach to five-a-sides was similar to our tactics in Regent's Park – I held the fort while the others ran all over the place.

My life revolved around Stowe and school. I went to Marylebone Grammar School which was 400 yards away from home. I was lucky with Marylebone. Tracy and Gillian had a terrible time with their first school, an appalling comprehensive which some girls eventually burned down. My sisters lasted two weeks there before Mum and Dad rescued them and sent them to Henrietta Barnet, an excellent school in Golders Green. I had no such teething problems, quickly settling into Marylebone. Even though it was close to Paddington, which had some really rough schools, Marylebone was good academically. Although they came from poor areas, many of the boys at Marylebone were bright. They were street-wise, too, which helped me acclimatise to London life.

The Marylebone boys teased me at first, making fun of my

huge duffle-coat that I was too cold to take off. But I soon made friendships that have lasted to this day. One of the first guys I met was Antony Demetriou, who was best man at my wedding. Antony and I speak every day. He works in sales for a big printing company. My best friend at Marylebone was Mark Pembroke, whose parents emigrated from Guyana. Mark and I were very close although we have fallen out of touch. At Marylebone, Mark, Antony and I began hanging out with a guy called Lenny Hutchins and then Tony Mason, who has worked for Sky. Lofty Belot was another of our group. He designs clothes. Wherever I have lived – Liverpool, Newcastle, Glasgow – Lofty, Tony, Antony and Lenny always come up for a night out. They still behave like teenagers. As I am the only one married with children, I try to keep them on the straight and narrow.

We grew up together at the same school and nightclubs, loving the same music. When I was not training down at Stowe, I went round to my friends' houses and soon started hanging out in nightclubs with them. It was not expensive. All we needed was enough for the bus-fair and the admission. Pocket money covered my nights out. We knock back the wine nowadays but our drinking then was limited to juice, Coke or water. The culture of that time was to sip water and dance all night. I never tried to impress girls by standing at the bar and drinking beer. I never needed to buy girls drinks to persuade them to dance with me.

I love dancing. Reggae is fine but my main passion has always been dancing to soul music and R and B. Hip-hop came along later but by then I was too old for that. My era was soul and funk. We would go out to concerts, dancing to Cameo and The Commodores. Earth, Wind and Fire always set me off. They still do. I bought all their records, which I never stop listening to. I own all the albums of Parliament, Funkadelic, Bootsy Collins, Slave and Steve Arrington. When I was still thirteen, we frequented the 100 Club on Oxford Street on a Saturday afternoon. The star turn was Ronnie, a venerable white DJ obsessed with soul music. Ronnie was brilliant at filling the dance-floor. We thought we were so grown up going into 'a nightclub' but it was just for teenagers. It was a black club, although some white kids came in because they were into the black scene. When we fancied a different venue, we went to Crackers, at the top of Wardour Street, which kids used to go to at 3 p.m. on weekdays. I didn't go that often because I refused to bunk off school.

On turning fifteen, I started to go out regularly at night, particularly to a club called Giovanni's in Belsize Park. I could have gone off the rails but my parents ensured I didn't. They always kept an eye on me. Curfew was set at midnight. Unfortunately, on one occasion I was enjoying myself too much at Giovanni's. At 12.15, I suddenly realised the time and rushed out just as my mother, in her dressing-gown, charged across the car park. Luckily, I caught her before she went into the club. That could have been so humiliating, for both of us. I could just imagine my mum asking everyone in there, 'Have you seen my son, John Barnes? He was supposed to be home by midnight.'

Sometimes it was difficult to meet the curfew because I would walk home. We used to walk miles in those days and thought nothing of it. During my Giovanni's period, my family lived in Highgate so I regularly walked home from Belsize Park. It was only two miles. I once emerged from a club in Harlesden having missed the last bus. We couldn't afford taxis so there was nothing for it but to walk. It wasn't a problem. Even if the walk lasted a couple of hours, it was fun. I was young, strolling through town with my friends, talking and just messing around. My father was a great walker. The two of us once walked from Wembley to Highgate, which is at least five miles. My dad even trekked from Crystal Palace to Golders Green, one side of London to the other. He loved athletics and had been to see a meeting at Crystal Palace. He couldn't be bothered to get the train home so he walked. It took him five hours.

Staying out late, hanging around nightclubs with friends, often walking home at night – that was the way I spent my evenings when I wasn't training. We never got in any trouble with the police. They hassled me occasionally on the way home, particularly on my training nights when I ran around London. But there was not a bad one among us Marylebone boys. There was no drinking, no fighting, just a group of guys having a good time. It was girls who caused me trouble. My friends' parents were quite liberal in allowing them to go to parties and not come home. My parents were far stricter. One night, I told Mum I would be staying at Mark's house and she rang to find out how I was. Mrs Pembroke answered the phone.

'John and Mark have gone to a party,' she said.

'When are they coming home?' Mum asked.

'They are not,' said Mark's mother. My father was listening in and he went mad because I was only fourteen. It wasn't quite a party either. Mark and I were down in Streatham, south London, with two girls. The parents of one girl were away so we had headed over to her house. Mum got the phone number off Mrs Pembroke and called us in Streatham.

'I am coming to collect you now,' she said. 'Where in Streatham are you?'

'Mum, I honestly don't know,' I replied. 'We walked miles to get here, over a bridge and along different roads. Don't worry about me.' I was desperately trying to prevent an embarrassing situation. Mum was having none of it.

'We are coming to get you,' she said. 'Just give me the address.' One of the girls told me the name of the road which I passed on to my mother, without giving her the house number. Three hours later, my parents' car pulled up in the road.

Mum and Dad stayed in the car for about half an hour. They did not know the number so they just sat there, listening for music because they thought Mark and I were at a party. There was no party, just Mark, me and two girls with the music and lights down low. Suddenly the doorbell rang. I was marched out by my parents, which was humiliating in front of the girls. There was I thinking I was a big man, then my mum and dad arrive to drag me home.

'How did you know which house it was?' I asked on the way home.

'We saw the curtains twitch when you were trying to sneak a look outside,' Dad answered.

Incidents like that occurred a lot. My friends were all staying up late, impressing girls and I was always making excuses to go because I had to get home. I told fibs to my parents, saying I was in one place when I was really in another. My friends were staying out, enjoying themselves so why shouldn't I? Mark used to sneak his dad's car out. He would push it down the road so it was quiet and then jump in and start it. We drove around London, having a laugh, looking at the girls. To us, it was harmless fun.

I was quite naive, though. Because my friends all went out, I thought they didn't study. Mark was the leader. 'Don't worry about homework,' Mark would say. 'Let's go out.' But Mark always fitted in his studying and passed all his O-levels and A-levels. All my friends eclipsed me academically. I did one year of A-levels but dropped out because of football whereas they all completed their A-levels. Mark, Tony and the others were all bright boys. I needed to put in the hours to keep up but never did. I hated schoolwork although I loved being at school. I was never disruptive in class. Whenever reports came home, they never read: 'John's a problem; he just makes a noise in class and refuses to try.' My reports were always quite positive, focusing on my keenness to participate. My hand always shot up when the teacher said, 'Put your hand up if you know the answer.' I rarely knew the answer. I just wanted to be involved.

My friends and I never messed around at school. We signed up for all the school trips the geeky guys went on. We even went boating on the Norfolk Broads. I could hear people saying, 'Why the hell do that lot want to go to the Norfolk Broads? They normally go clubbing.' But Mark, Antony, Tony, Lenny, Lofty and I just loved being together, whether boating or partying. The highlight of the year was school camp near Dorking, all of us in tents talking and joking. A prize was awarded at the end of the week for the best tent, judged on our cooking, orienteering and cross-country running. We always tried to win the prize, although we messed around at night.

School was great. Although I wasn't clever like the others, I still paid attention in class, enough to manage five O-levels – English language and literature, history, maths and French. I enjoyed French the most. I love languages. In Jamaica, the second language is Spanish so I know some of that. Whenever I meet someone from another country, I ask them to teach me some words in their language. During my time at Newcastle United, I spoke a lot to Nol Solano, the Peruvian. We discussed Brazilian football and he gave me some tips in Portuguese. It just sounds so intelligent to speak another language, although I know it does not mean you are bright. I have met multi-lingual Europeans who are as thick as anything. I preferred English language to literature. William Shakespeare never inspired me but English language seemed quite simple as subjects go; I am not sure whether it is actually possible to fail the English language exam. Maths left me cold. I enjoyed history, although I found the way it was taught to me focused too much on politics and people like Disraeli and Gladstone. European history was more about wars, which I found fascinating. The Crimean War captivated me for a whole term.

Marylebone Grammar School actually closed when I was there. The school wanted to become a comprehensive but because it had been a grammar school for so long the authorities refused permission. So I spent a year at Haverstock Comprehensive near Hampstead. But most of my schooling was at Marylebone. The main sport was not football but rugby. I love rugby and have sent my two sons to rugby-playing schools. When I arrived in England, rugby was an alien activity to me, but Marylebone insisted on it. My class had thirty boys, enough for two sides. I was new and untested so I was put in the B team, which was pretty humiliating. I was in with all the fatty and weedy boys. My teacher obviously thought a boy from Jamaica was never going to be able to play rugby. The rules were incomprehensible but I had the speed to run round everyone and score tries. Within a couple of weeks, I was playing centre for the class side and then for the full school team.

Marylebone used to compete with all London's real rugby schools like Teddington and Latymer Upper. I started to make a name for myself and my elusive running brought me an invitation for a trial for Middlesex Schools. I suddenly found myself surrounded by dedicated rugby players. They were so serious. 'If this is what rugby is all about,' I said to my father, 'then it isn't for me.' I stopped playing.

I spent a lot of time playing racquet sports, particularly squash. My father was outstanding at squash and I grew up trying to emulate him. I was left-handed and I always thought left-handed people who play racquet sports look good. Tennis stars like John McEnroe and Rod Laver had a great feel for the ball, a special touch. Tennis never excited me as much as squash, which thrilled me with its emphasis on explosiveness and working out angles. I love squash's test of concentration as well as stamina.

My father often took me on at squash. He was brilliant for a sports-mad son, constantly taking me to football matches, watching me play for Stowe, a lone supportive father on the touchline. Dad encouraged me to develop my potential. When we lived in Wigmore Place, Dad and I would run over to Primrose Hill and sprint up it. The steepness momentarily sapped my legs of strength but if I faltered, Dad barked, 'If you want to play football properly, you have to be fit.' I became so used to the run that I would do it at night as well, although the police occasionally delayed the finish. After we moved to Hampstead Way, Dad and I nipped over the road to the Heath extension where he worked on my ball skills, passing the ball to me or kicking it high and demanding I control it instantly. When we lived on Broadland Road in Highgate, the house backed on to a football pitch which was convenient for training.

My father was forever coaching me. Every Sunday, my sisters swam in Potters Bar. While they ploughed up and down, Dad and I practised on a nearby pitch. Dad threw the ball up and shouted 'trap it on your chest' or 'trap it on your head'. Boredom would eventually seize me.

'Dad? Can't we just play?' I asked, knowing the answer. My father was too committed to the training ethos to slacken off.

'No,' he replied, 'we've got to train.' As a player himself, my father was very disciplined and he wanted me to be the same. Every Jamaican kid wants to backheel the ball, flick it up, execute the type of tricks they see Brazilians doing. Dad wasn't into the clever stuff. He insisted on practice and discipline which is why I accepted the defensive responsibilities at Stowe.

I stayed at Stowe until September 1980. In my final season there, in the Under-16s, my coach was Ray Sullivan. He was also involved with Sudbury Court, a good non-league club based in Wembley. Brian Stein played for them before going on to Luton Town. So did Philip DeFreitas, the cricketer. Sudbury Court enjoyed a good reputation. They were recognised regulars of the Middlesex League, playing against decent non-league sides like Yeading. Ray would take some of Stowe's better players up to Sudbury Court for a trial. I liked Sudbury Court and was keen to play for them. I had outgrown Stowe, who had no Under-17s side. It was time to move on.

Sudbury Court were careful to protect me. They just wanted me to go out and enjoy myself. It was similar to when I reached Watford and the older players ensured there was no pressure on the youngsters. Sudbury Court's dressing-room was full of experienced campaigners who knew the non-league scene could be intimidating for a teenager. The Middlesex League had enough 6ft 4in ex-pros who could scar a callow centre-back fresh from Regent's Park. I am not sure I would have coped in defence, so I was relieved when Sudbury Court used me on the left wing for my debut on 13 September 1980. Des Lawlor, the manager, was aware that I would come to little harm out there. 'Don't worry about tactics,' Lawlor said, 'just go out and run at them.' So that's how I became such an attacking left-winger. At Stowe, I had been the most responsible. At Sudbury Court, it was the opposite. I was surrounded by mature players so I just focused on my own game.

I quickly settled, even scoring on my second outing, a 5–3 win at Hillingdon, one of the better non-league teams around. It was a new experience playing at clubs that had their own stands and grounds. We never had that at Sudbury Court, which is basically a social club with pitches alongside, but we were never over-awed because we were good. Sudbury Court brought in a lot of players from other clubs and our motley crew lost only three of thirty-three games that season. Everyone said it was a fairytale for Sudbury Court just to be in the Premier Division but we went and won it. The Harrow Charity Cup was also taken back to our modest club-house, thanks to a goal from me. I should have been voted Player of the Year but instead the honour went to the centre-forward, Pat Collins. Pat scored twenty-six goals and had been there a while.

I was disappointed because I had a good season. Scouts from professional clubs kept coming down to Sudbury Court to watch me. Fulham checked me over but decided against pursuing any interest. They reckoned they already had a similar player to me in Leroy Rosenior. Des Lawlor rang Arsenal about me but they proved too bureaucratic, wanting all sorts of forms filled in. They obviously were not bothered about me. A huge club like Arsenal must have so many people phoning in saying, 'there is this brilliant boy playing non-league.' When Ipswich Town sent a scout along, I became very excited because Bobby Robson's side were causing a stir in the League and in Europe, but nothing came of it.

Queens Park Rangers wanted to sign me the moment they saw me running at defenders. I was flattered because Rangers were my team. As a Marylebone boy, I became mesmerised by that Stan Bowles side. For all my support for Rangers, there was something in their attitude that made me cautious. Anyway, I wanted to finish the season with Sudbury Court. But I did agree to go training on Rangers' astroturf pitch just behind the Loft. Rangers had some talented youngsters there including David Kerslake, Gary Cooper and Wayne Fereday but it still did not feel right. Watford also invited me training and they seemed far friendlier than Rangers. I will never forget Chris Geilor, the youth coach at Rangers. He gave me a fiver on expenses to come down training, saying one day, 'There's no training tonight, come back next season.' This was in April. That was it. My mind was made up. I was going to Watford, where they would never be so offhand. The youth man at Vicarage Road, Tom Walley, made me feel wanted. Tom was always ringing up, asking me to come training, picking me up and just generally showing how much the club cared about me. Watford felt right.

Watford heard about me through one of their fans, who contacted Tom. 'I've just seen this winger play for Sudbury Court,' he told Tom. 'His name is John Barnes and he is definitely worth a look.' I never found out who the fan was and Watford never revealed his identity. Watford's curiosity was certainly whetted. The great Bertie Mee, who was looking after the apprentices for Graham Taylor, drove over to Sudbury Court with a scout to see me for himself. Bertie stayed only ten minutes but made sure his scout got my phone number and address. That night Bertie called my father and arranged to come and see us. My family were impressed with Watford's courteous but serious attitude. The fact that Bertie Mee, the famous double-winner with Arsenal, was coming to our house delighted my father.

They had met before when Arsenal visited Kingston. A riot broke out at the stadium and Mee and his players were helped to safety by my father, whose soliders had been deployed there in case of trouble. My dad and Bertie shared similar traits. Whenever I dealt with Bertie at Watford, it was like talking to my father. Bertie was very serious, always upright and doing the right thing. He was a 'yes sir, no sir' person. Bertie's insistence on discipline, which echoed Graham Taylor's, inevitably found favour with my father, who warmly welcomed Bertie when he arrived to talk about my future.

'Do not worry about John,' Bertie said. 'He will be in good hands at Watford. We will make sure he is well looked after.'

I doubt if my parents would have let me go to any other club. My father's posting was over and the family was heading back to Jamaica the moment Gillian and Tracy finished their exams. The thought of leaving me behind troubled my parents. Their worry was more on a personal than professional level. I was only seventeen. Would I fall by the wayside? But we all knew that I could always come home to Kingston. My parents realised what a great opportunity I was being offered by Watford. My father believed greatly in my footballing potential. He and I both thought I would go on to do great things. But every young player thinks that and how many do? One per cent? It was a gamble, but we had to take it.

Cynics often question whether footballers from comfortable backgrounds like myself, Ashley Ward and Graeme Le Saux possess a deep, burning hunger. A crazy perception persists that a footballer must have suffered a deprived childhood, not knowing where his next meal or pair of boots was coming from, to acquire the desire to turn football into a career. That is nonsense. My passion to succeed matches anybody's. My commitment to football may even be stronger because alternative career paths would have opened up for me. The players who come from impoverished homes may have thought of football as their only avenue to a good living. Players like myself, Ward and Le Saux had other options but chose football because we love it so much.

My parents did not think sport was necessarily a good career, although they realised it might prove the best for a son who was not desperately academically inclined. Dad never really talked about what I should do for a living. When my friends visited, he sat them down and told them the benefits of joining the army, of becoming an engineer or a pilot. But he never spoke to me about enlisting. He knew army life would not suit me. Maybe my father thought I was too soft or indisciplined. It never even crossed my mind to join the army, although I knew many people who did. My cousin, Jamie, whose father was a colonel, has risen to the rank of captain. Friends of mine are in the army, having wanted to sign up since they were kids.

I was never sure what I wanted to do. Just as Watford were showing interest, I was offered a football scholarship to Washington University. This would have entailed doing an undemanding degree and, on graduating, dropping out of football because America lacked a proper professional set-up. But at least I would have had a degree and a start in the States. But then came the phone-call and visit from Bertie Mee. Mee and Taylor invited me to train with Watford's youth squad for the last three weeks of the 1980–81 season. Watford agreed with Sudbury Court that if they did not have a game, I could turn out for Watford youth. One night I played for Watford at QPR and got a very frosty reception, which merely confirmed to me that I had chosen well. I smiled broadly when we beat Rangers.

In July, my family returned to Jamaica. I stayed with a friend of Mum's for two weeks before moving into digs in Watford when pre-season started. The move was completed with Watford paying Sudbury Court a fee in the form of a set of kit. My first pre-season proved almost brutal in the impact it had on my body. Cross-country appeared to be the main element of Graham Taylor's training. I arrived at Vicarage Road weighing 10st 5lb and within a year was two stones heavier, all through gym work.

After surviving pre-season, I settled quickly at Watford. A planned business studies course at college in September was scrapped because I was already a regular in Watford's first team by then. My promotion was swift. Watford fielded me in three youth-team games, the last one being at Brisbane Road when Graham Taylor looked on. Graham saw me control the ball and then send a left-footed volley flying past Orient's goalkeeper. 'That's all I need to see,' Graham said to those around him and left. After giving me four reserve matches to prepare me, Graham decided I was ready for my Watford debut.

taylor-made

Without Graham Taylor, I would never have made it as a professional footballer, never have represented England seventy-nine times. A demanding man, Graham Taylor has proved by far the most important figure in my career, providing the discipline and momentum I needed to reach the top. I both respect and fear him. I have never sworn in his ear-shot. I just would not dare. Even now when I see Graham or speak to him, I call him 'Boss'. It's ridiculous. I am a grown man and stopped playing for him years ago. I am even a coach in my own right now. But before picking up the phone to call Graham, I conduct the same old debate with myself. 'Right,' I think, 'this time, I'm not going to call him Boss, I'm going to call him Graham.' As I dial the number, I tell myself, 'What is this Boss rubbish anyway? Just call him Graham.' But when I hear that familiar voice answering the phone, my first words are always, 'Hiya, Boss, it's me!' I just cannot help it.

Graham Taylor gave me the confidence to succeed. He was a motivator, the best I have worked with. His achievement in leading Watford into the top division in 1982, and then to second place, Europe and an FA Cup final, indicate Graham's inspirational abilities. That he took Watford up again in 1999 confirmed his talent for coaxing the best out of players. Graham can convince a player he can run through a brick wall. If I faced the most respected right-back in the world, Graham would say, 'John, you are better than him. Now go and beat him.'

Graham probably caught me at the right time. I was young and eager to be moulded. I was not like Pat Rice, a double-winner with Arsenal who came to Watford as a thirty-one-year-old pro. The innocence of youth is what got me by at Watford. If I had been more experienced, I might have questioned Graham's belief that I had the beating of a right-back with fifty England caps. But I was only seventeen and hung on every one of Graham's words.

A tough man, Graham expected us to give a hundred per cent in everything we did. The physical preparation for matches was exhausting. No one dared jog during the cross-country. We had to run it and run it hard. Graham was obsessed with cross-country and relished racing over the course himself. When I arrived at Watford, Graham always finished among the top four. When we were out running, he shouted at us, cajoling us to improve our times. We were so scared of him we never thought about easing up. During my six years of running that three-mile course every other week, I always finished within fifteen seconds of my best time, around twenty-one minutes. Graham demanded the optimum every time. I was similarly consistent in my 'doggy' times, those shuttle sprints between cones; I was never more than two seconds off my best. Nowadays, footballers do all sorts of times, depending on how they feel.

At Watford, we never outwardly questioned training or the commitment Graham demanded. If we went into the gym for some work with weights we were expected to lift to our maximum every time. I would never dream of putting a lighter weight on. None of the younger players would. Some of the older pros had the nous to cheat or cut corners when Graham was not looking. Kenny Jackett hated long-distance running. Graham would stand there yelling at Kenny when he came round. Occasionally, Graham ran alongside Kenny to make sure he clocked a decent time. When we ran up and down the terrace steps at Vicarage Road, Graham resembled a sergeant-major the way he screamed in Kenny's ear. 'Push yourself harder,' Graham shouted. Kenny just shrugged his shoulders.

They both knew he would deliver on matchdays; when he heard that first whistle, Kenny ran around more than anyone else. He was the archetypal midfield dynamo, charging from end to end. Kenny could get away with cheating at training. Everyone else gave maximum effort.

There were times when I moaned inwardly about the cross-country and Graham's fixation with discipline but, like the other players, I acquiesced because it was for my own good. I am similarly strict with my children, who probably wish hurtful things on me. I felt the same resentment when my parents or Graham Taylor disciplined me. But however much it hurt, I appreciated it in the long run. And there were a lot of long runs with Graham!

Feelings of awe characterised my view of Graham, although he never treated me as a little boy. He understood what I was capable of. At times, Graham asked me to perform duties which I thought were way out of my league, like man-marking Ray Wilkins when Watford met Manchester United in the FA Cup. In the team meeting beforehand, Graham said, 'John, Ray Wilkins is United's playmaker and you are to follow him all game.' My fitness encouraged Graham to believe I could do it. His confidence was good enough for me. I shadowed Ray everywhere, snapping away at his heels. Ray's not a big strong guy but I still harried away at him, blocking and tackling so he could not spray those passes around. Ray never resented my close presence, although he was probably surprised to find a left-winger hounding him. Every now and again, Graham told me to mark an opponent out of the game. He did it against Liverpool when I trailed John Wark. Unfortunately, Warky sneaked in and scored from one of his typical late runs.

Graham used me in a range of positions, from the occasional man-marking role to centre-forward and initially and primarily as a left-winger. After watching my youth-team performance against Orient, Graham toughened me up quickly in the reserves before blooding me as a substitute against Oldham Athletic on 5 September 1981. Luther Blissett was suspended so they needed a spare striker on the bench. I came on for fifteen minutes and did enough to win my first start a week later at Stamford Bridge. Chelsea's fans greeted with me with the inevitable abuse about my colour, but, because of the track around the pitch, all the racists in the Shed seemed a long way away.

Watford, a Division Four side as recently as 1978, were at the start of a special period, the most memorable in an unfashionable club's history. I revelled in being part of Graham's great adventure. After Chelsea, games against Rotherham and Wrexham followed before I scored my first professional goal in a 3–1 win over Barnsley at Vicarage Road. It was only a tap-in from Luther's cross but I felt I had arrived. The game that really thrust me into the limelight was a televised match at Carrow Road. Watford had been in the Second Division for a couple of years, never at the forefront. Then came the fixture with an ambitious Norwich City and suddenly the debate was whether Watford were ready for promotion. Norwich were a decent side with good players like Willie Donachie and Steve Walford so our credentials were going to be examined. The challenge brought the best out of me. I scored against Chris Woods, a future England goalkeeper, and also hit the crossbar with a free kick, which bounced down for Luther to head in. I had a good game against Donachie, a former Scotland international, and because it had been on television people began talking about me. Television lifted me into the public's consciousness.

In post-match interviews, Graham kept saying positive things about me, about what I could achieve in football. He was always urging me on. We often talked about what he termed 'my laid-back attitude'. When I reached twenty-one and was representing England, Graham still impressed on me the need to keep developing. 'Rise, rise, rise,' was his mantra to me. 'You can become the best player in the world.' Despite all that encouragement, I did level off when I could have pushed myself more. Being laid-back is part of my West Indian upbringing and that frustrated Graham. Sometimes, when a game turned nasty, Graham wanted me to fight my way out of the situation, not physically but through mental strength. If a full-back got the better of me, Graham shouted, 'Keep going at him.' But I rarely produced that bit extra he wanted. Maybe there wasn't any more in me. Most of the time I didn't have to push myself because I normally had the beating of the full-back. On the odd occasion when I was second-best, Graham could never understand why I wouldn't fight my way through. He would have done. Graham's upbringing demanded that reaction. He was a modest player who sweated for everything he got, whether it was at Scunthorpe, Grimsby or Lincoln. I wasn't made that way.

Some people suggested Graham may have been envious of my skills, but that was untrue. He possessed no skills, so Graham would have been envious of everyone at Watford! He just believed that anyone can achieve anything if they put their mind to it. Graham was completely different from Terry Venables, who succeeded him as England coach. Terry man-managed in a different way. He put his arm around some players but bollocked others. Graham was hard with everyone. Graham's philosophy was simple. 'If you aren't strong enough for criticism,' he said, 'you are not the man I want in my team.'

Watford sounded like heaven to my father; all that discipline and 1950s way of playing. Like Graham, my father would not tolerate square passing or the concept that a team might have to go back to build an attack. Occasionally, we speak about football on the phone. 'Don't start on about the right way of playing, Dad!' I tell him. 'Your idea of perfect football is to get the ball forward quickly and fight them on the beaches.' He loves gung-ho, attack-obsessed football, a Charge of the Light Brigade in boots. He knows how I feel about the sanctity of passing, and how sometimes, to build the right move, a team must be slower and more methodical.

Watford were anathema to my personal view of the need for patience in football. But I was happy to fit into Watford's style because I was young, on the way up and in fear of Graham Taylor. I did what I was told. Graham's game-plan was to propel the ball forward quickly to Ross Jenkins and Luther Blissett. To accomplish this, Graham gave every player a plan which had to be rigidly adhered to. Watford's ethos was that the team came ahead of personal satisfaction or glory. My job was to stay on the left-wing and not come infield too much except to get into the box. Graham drilled our responsibilities into us and mine involved whipping in crosses to Ross and Luther. It was simple – get the ball, beat the right-back and cross from the byeline. The full-back knew my intentions but could do little about it. A quick and tricky winger is difficult to stop legally.

Bertie Mee likened me to Tom Finney, the Preston and England winger of the forties and fifties. 'It's partly because you don't get angry,' said Bertie, 'but mostly because of the way you play on the wing.' Being of a certain generation and culture, Bertie loved out-and-out wingers, dribblers in the mould of Finney and Stanley Matthews. Encouraged by Bertie, Graham was determined to use out-and-out wingers at Watford. It was a brave move, against the prevailing trend. In the early eighties, tactics were changing. Wingers disappeared, many managers preferring wide midfielders in the Steve Coppell or Trevor Steven mould, who operated wide, got crosses in and worked back. Football was becoming increasingly defensive. The 4–2–4 formation was largely consigned to the history books – except at Vicarage Road.

My duties were primarily attacking, although Graham gave me some defensive responsibilities. 'When we haven't got the ball, John, make sure their right-back doesn't get past you,' said Graham. Defending did not actually occupy me much because of Watford's configuration. When both teams line up 4–4–2, the most common formation in England, the wide midfielders oppose each other. Watford, though, were 2–4–4 under Graham so I played against the opposition right-back and our left-back, Wilf Rostron, faced their wide midfielder. Graham's approach was very effective and adventurous. 'Push on, push on,' Graham kept shouting at us. If their right-back had possession, I pushed on to him and Wilf marked their midfielder or winger. Such harrying tactics so high up the field forced the opposition to hurry the ball forward, often in the air and bypassing midfield. Watford had big centre-backs, who gobbled up these punts upfield.

The moment Watford had possession, our targets were Ross and Luther, who worked brilliantly together. Graham's attacking plan was basic but difficult to combat. Either a cross came in or Ross flicked the ball on through the middle for Luther to chase. The moment the ball was flying through to Ross, I also sprinted in to pursue his flick-ons. Normally only the two attackers hunt for the ball. The winger stays wide in case the ball comes out again. I never did that at Watford. Our 2–4–4 formation meant we were pushed so far forward that Wilf collected any balls returning out wide. I was ordered to get in the box. Everything was so methodical with Graham. The individual had to sacrifice his own thoughts for the team. We did what Graham told us. The one flaw was that Watford could be caught too far advanced if Luther or Ross failed to win the header.

Graham's tactics brought Watford promotion from the Second Division in 1982. I will never forget the moment when we knew we were up. As the final whistle blew on our victory over Wrexham at Vicarage Road, fans flooded on to the pitch, lifted us up and the whole town threw itself into a massive party. Even now, I can clearly remember the feelings of joy, excitement and achievement. When that whistle sounded, all the players, supporters, staff and directors knew that unfashionable Watford were going to be playing at Liverpool and Manchester United next season. People just looked at each other in amazement at the thought or mention of Anfield and Old Trafford. The season had been an amazing one for me personally. My record of fourteen goals was beaten only by Ross, who managed fifteen, and Luther's twenty-two. We all had much to celebrate that night.

Probably the most emotional fan on promotion night was Elton John, Watford's chairman and one of the nicest men you could meet. When I arrived at Vicarage Road, I was in awe of this world-famous singer. But he was in awe of the players. Whenever Elton came into the dressing-room, he was like a little kid bubbling with excitement but also very humble and respectful. He adores Watford. The Elton John of popular legend, the superstar of a thousand tantrums, was never seen at Vicarage Road; we just saw a charming, polite man who wanted the best for the club he worshipped. Regardless of whatever Elton does in his professional and private life, his love of Watford will keep him grounded. He loved talking to the players. One day Elton told me with great pride that soon after starting out in the music business, he was voted 'Best Black Singer in the United States'. The Americans had never seen him, merely heard his records. When Elton went over to collect the award, the organisers said, 'Mr John, you are not black.'

Vicarage Road overflowed with characters. Watford's dressing-room played host to many strong personalities, professionals who ran out of the door shouting 'Come on, let's get stuck into them.' But it was Graham Taylor who galvanised and organised us. In a way, the identity of the players was irrelevant; everyone from regulars to understudies knew what was expected of them. They were great lads to be with. In goal was Steve Sherwood, who did not have a goalkeeper's typical personality. He was very softly spoken, quiet and gentle. Steve was a great goalkeeper but he suffered because people associated him with certain high-profile goals he conceded. Against Leicester City once, Andy Peake shot from a long way out and Steve didn't dive for it. Phil Neal put two penalties past him. If goalkeepers stand up for penalties, particularly in a shoot-out, they have a good chance of getting one. Unfortunately, Steve stood up for these two penalties and they went in. People gave him a hard time but Steve was still one of the best keepers I ever played with.

At left-back was Wilf Rostron, a quiet guy from Sunderland. Wilf arrived at Vicarage Road as a left-winger but Graham spotted another dimension to his game and turned him into an excellent left-back. Watford's other full-back was Pat Rice, the captain, a legend with Arsenal yet free of any airs or graces. When Pat joined, Graham told him, 'Just because you are coming to the end of your career doesn't mean you can have any days off training.' Graham need not have bothered. A man driven by doing what was right for the team, Pat fitted straight in. He was a phenomenally hard trainer, always up there at the front of the cross-country, always mucking in and never complaining. Old pros, particularly one with a double to his name, might have been tempted to take days off or condemn Graham's over-physical training as rubbish. Pat never did; he was the perfect professional and an example to all.

Between Pat and Wilf stood Ian Bolton and Steve Sims, who was eventually replaced by Steve Terry. Steve Sims was a funny guy, a great, big hulking centre-back who was as soft as a pussy-cat. When people saw Steve with his broken nose and his habit of kicking attackers, they never believed he was really gentle, shy even. Whenever we teased Steve on the bus, he pleaded, 'Don't, don't.' He was like a big baby; a lovely, popular guy. Ian Bolton, who partnered Steve, had a fantastic right foot. I have played at many levels, from Sunday League to World Cups and Ian's right foot was the best I have ever seen. He had been around the lower leagues and scored a lot of goals from free kicks. Ian hit superb balls down the channels for Luther and Ross to chase. He was made for Watford. In typical Taylor style, Ian came out of the dressing-room breathing fire, refusing to be worried by opponents' reputations and determined to impose Watford's game on them.

Watford's central midfield was the domain of Kenny Jackett and Les Taylor. Kenny was a local boy who rose through the ranks. Along with Steve Terry, Kenny was one of the first of Tom Walley's youth-team players to make the senior grade. A quiet man, Kenny had Watford in his blood. As a Welsh international highly regarded within the game, Kenny probably had opportunities to sign for bigger clubs but he stayed on because Watford were on the rise. He probably remained at Vicarage Road too long, until he could not move on to anywhere better. Les was a real Geordie, always cracking jokes and laughing. Les was one of those Watford players who had been around the lower leagues and relished life on the grander stage.

Out on the wings were myself and Nigel Callaghan. Nigel was a local boy, a curious character. I saw him recently DJing on *Greece Uncovered*, that Sky TV exposé of Brits abroad. Nigel was always DJing. Even when he was eighteen and starting out at Watford, Nigel would be off to Greece doing stints in nightclubs. He moved on to Derby County and Aston Villa but he often DJed on a Friday night because he loved it. This was never the best preparation for Saturday matches and his career suffered through his fixation with clubbing. Nigel possessed great ability but his attitude was all wrong. The world was at Nigel's feet but he trod on it. He could have represented England, become a great player. Graham always had to fight with him to make him concentrate on football. When I arrived at Watford, Nigel was the one player whom Graham regularly had at his house, trying to inject some sanity into his life. Graham really liked Nigel and wanted to get the best out of him.

'Right, Nigel, you've got to spend four days with me,' said Graham, 'to make sure you get some proper food and sleep.'

'Oh Boss, please, I don't want to sleep at your house,' Nigel moaned. But Graham insisted so Nigel bunked down in the Taylors' spare room. Graham's main concern was that Nigel was actually in bed the night before the game. When Graham became manager of Aston Villa he took Nigel with him. But Nigel was older then and he was not going to answer to the Boss any more and certainly not consider staying at his house. I felt sorry for Graham. He appreciated what great talent Nigel had and pulled his hair out trying to get Nigel to work at it. Graham was harder with Nigel than anyone else. He had to be tough simply to make him deliver.

Nigel and I supplied the crosses for Luther and Ross. Luther had been at Watford for some time, had experienced life in the Fourth Division and was used to fighting for everything he got. Stigmas clung to Luther as he grew up. People kept telling him how bad he was, that he didn't possess this trick or that skill and that his touch was not good enough. But Luther was a fighter and proved everyone wrong, becoming top scorer and earning a move to Italy. I was delighted when he went to AC Milan because he deserved it, but I will admit to jealousy, too. I wished it had been me climbing into an airplane, flying off to Italy and playing in all those great stadiums surrounded by world-class players.

Even at eighteen, I loved Italian football. Not many teenagers owned a satellite dish beaming in *Serie A* games, but I did. Watching such rich technical and tactical football really inspired me. Watford's style lay at the opposite end of the scale to Italian football. Never mind Watford to Liverpool, a jump I was to make in 1987, Watford to *Serie A* was an unimaginable leap. There was I, turning out for Watford, fitting into Graham Taylor's doctrine of directness and then slipping off home and gorging on European football, Italian or Spanish. The year was 1982 and I almost worshipped players like Roberto Bettega in the Juventus team. I loved Barcelona. Real Madrid particularly intoxicated me. I found their white kit irresistible. That white would have looked so good against my black skin. Throughout my career, I always wanted my team, Watford, Liverpool, Newcastle United or Charlton Athletic, to play in an all-white strip. I always tried to catch Leeds United on television in the seventies to savour that splendid all-white strip. Every time I bought a kit it was always all-white. Milan dressed in red and black but I still envied Luther. I never went to see him at the San Siro. I would have been too jealous and also he was not there long enough.

Ross Jenkins was the archetypal centre-forward – 6ft 4in, great in the air and good at making runs. His touch, awareness and line-leading experience made him a formidable presence. Ross would always score goals but more in the lower divisions than the top one. Many players are prolific outside the élite grade, such as Iain McCulloch at Notts County, a lad from Kilmarnock who scored 51 times in 215 league games from the wing. I aways wondered why he never had a shot at the big time. It was the same with Ross. Maybe Ross and Iain McCulloch found their level.

Driven by such determination throughout the side, Watford charged into the First Division. In that first season, 1982–83, opponents did not know what had hit them. These brash new boys dictated how established sides played. Teams were not confident enough to play the ball out from the back under the sort of pressure Watford subjected them to. Defenders would not risk dwelling on the ball or passing into midfield. They kicked it long which was manna to our defenders. Watford struggled only against those teams with the self-belief to build from the back, who could handle the pressure and bombardment. Liverpool exposed us. Nottingham Forest played the ball around and we lost 3–1 and 5–1 to them. Good teams could handle Watford.

I never questioned Taylor's long-ball style openly, although I did in private. During our promotion season, I craved to move infield and rip off my left-wing straitjacket. I never dared air my feelings to Graham or stray from the script during a game. Fortunately, Graham used me more through the middle when Ross Jenkins left in 1982, allowing me greater freedom to move around. Watford's obsession with speed and relentless forward momentum remained the same but the attacking was now spiced with variety. I was more mobile than Ross but not so powerful aerially, although I still challenged for the ball to pressurise opposing defenders. Watford desisted from belting so many high balls up for flick-ons but they did lift balls into the channels for Luther and me to chase. The pair of us thrived on running down these corridors to reach the ball. On collecting possession, Luther usually sped on. He was very direct and scored countless goals but Luther wasn't the type to create. I was. Having gained possession in the channel, I didn't just redirect it to the winger as Ross often did. My licence to be different, to play one-twos or other little moves, endowed Watford with an extra dimension that season. This splash of unpredictability within the long-ball framework provided the overriding reason why Watford flourished, finishing runners-up to Liverpool. The strike-force of Ross and Luther was methodical right up to the point of the ball entering the net. Luther's partnership with me carried more strands, more possibilities and we shared twenty-two goals when we were paired together for the final nineteen games of the 1982–83 season.

Yet Graham questioned my scoring rate. 'I'm not sure you get the goals that real goalscorers get,' he said to me. 'You know, the ones off the knee, the close-range stuff.' Fans and the so-called experts in the press often criticised my supposed lack of a poacher's touch; their opinions were rooted in the wider notion of 'John Barnes is too laid-back'. My goalscoring record destroys that argument. A tally of 65 league goals in 232 Watford starts hardly represents a bad return, particularly for someone predominantly used out wide. Even if my record proved I could score, I admit I was never an out-and-out goalscorer. The actual act of scoring did not mean that much to me. I would rather create something beautiful than have the ball bounce off my knee and bobble over the line. I preferred to be the player who beat three men and crossed the ball for it to go in off someone else's knee. Ian Rush, Alan Shearer and Gary Lineker were not interested in being involved in the build-up to a goal, only in being in at the death. Those three would be ecstatic if the ball went in off their knee because they were real goalscorers, who lived to see the ball in the net. I did not hurt inside when I came off the field not having scored. It never bothered me. Rushie, Alan and Gary suffered if they failed to score. Alan still does.

I remain proud of my scoring record and particularly the goals I managed in the 1982–83 season, the best year of my career. Even the vintage 1987–88 season at Liverpool could not match this year at Watford. Liverpool were expected to win the League and did in 1988. In 1982, I was young and Watford were the underdogs. Vicarage Road bubbled with the sort of spirit that since then has characterised Wimbledon. Our attitude was one of defiance towards the game's élite, of raising ourselves to play against the big boys, of rubbing their noses in it. My philosophy has changed a lot since then. I am no longer a fan of the underdog. If a group of players are the best, they should win. It irritates me when the media make such a huge fuss over Cup upsets, claiming that victory for the underdogs is a romantic event to be welcomed. In America, they cannot understand the logic of being on the underdogs' side. Wanting the little guy to win remains ingrained in the English mentality.

But at Watford, I shared the country's affection for underdogs. I loved being the unheralded, unfancied side who went to Highbury and won at the home of mighty Arsenal. We were surrounded by all these famous players, who all looked down on these scruffy visitors who earned so much less than them. Arsenal tried to belittle this newly promoted, unfashionable club and here we were showing them. It was marvellous. I loved facing Tottenham Hotspur. Spurs were famed for playing good football, for their pursuit of the Glory Game. They fielded Ossie Ardiles, a World Cup-winner. They had Glenn Hoddle, a wonderful ball-player. Watford were the total opposite of what Tottenham stood for. Spurs players came out of the tunnel and booted the ball up in the sky, taking the mickey out us, saying that was the only way Watford played. When the match kicked off, they called us 'donkeys'. So we used to love getting among them, sorting them out, trying to embarrass them. Most First Division clubs echoed Spurs' superior attitude towards us. Opposing players would jog past me and remark, 'Your football is crap. It's just kick and rush. How can you play this rubbish? Why don't you pass like proper teams?'

Watford were ridiculed by so many within football for much of that 1982–83 season. Wherever I went, I heard that 'Watford's bubble will burst soon'. Watford were still doing well at Christmas but the scepticism continued. 'Remember Crystal Palace, the team of the eighties,' opposing players hissed at us. 'Look what happened to them.' Watford ignored the doubters; if anything, the criticism simply strengthened our spirit and ambition. As we sat around in the dressing-room and discussed the comments made about our style, we felt it was us against the world. Whatever was said within football, the press loved Watford, as they now do Wimbledon, because it was easy to sell an underdog story to the English public. Watford may have been underdogs but on the last day of the season, we beat Liverpool. Defeat for Manchester United meant we finished second, which was a fabulous achievement for a small club as well as making a big difference financially to finishing third.

Midway through the season, Zico described me, rather flatteringly, as 'the future of English football'. The great Brazilian obviously based his judgement on one game when I shone. Zico remains a legend and his comment was a huge honour for someone like me who reveres Brazilian football and maestros like him. But I basked in such praise only briefly. I thought of the bigger picture. Zico had not seen many of my games. He did not know me. So I refused to be distracted by Zico's observation, however gratifying. On placing a foot for the first time on the professional ladder in 1981, I promised myself that I would be the judge of my form. Press and public are fickle in their opinions. Newspapers called me Watford's 'black pearl' one week, after a good game, and slaughtered me the next week. I never understood how I could metamorphose from the best player in the world to the worst in the space of a handful of days. If I listened to praise in the press, I would have to believe them when they said I was rubbish. So I just ignored them. The only people who mattered were my Watford team-mates and Graham Taylor. If they were happy, so was I.

Watford were a real family club. We were brothers-in-arms. Nowadays I try to separate my personal from my professional life, but not then. Watford were my club, my work, my life as well. My own family had headed back to Jamaica, I wasn't married, I didn't have any children. Everything revolved around Watford. I was being fulfilled personally, professionally and emotionally through Watford Football Club. A myth has developed that Luther helped me settle in at Vicarage Road and became my guide and mentor. As much as I liked Luther he was no more important to me than anyone else at Watford. I was given a good grounding by Tom Walley and Graham Taylor. If the football hadn't been so successful maybe I would have needed someone to turn to, but it was easy to settle into a team enjoying exciting times.

Watford were so friendly. In the summer, the team played cricket against local village sides. The standard was good. Having trained at Middlesex's indoor school in Finchley, my batting was pretty decent and I regularly rattled up 50s for Watford, although Graham questioned my ability when I ran him out once! The cricket provided an opportunity to have a laugh with the other players. We all enjoyed each other's company. My main mate at Watford was Steve Terry. I shared digs with him for nearly three years. We trained from ten until two and then went into town for lunch at the Wimpy. No one hassled us. Watford has never been the sort of place where fans come up and demand autographs. I would walk around town with Steve, do some shopping and then head home. At night I was often out until 4 a.m. Nightclubs have played a very large part in my life. Most footballers go to Stringfellows and the Hippodrome but I was never one for those sort of glitzy places. I was into black clubs where I could dance to soul music. I rarely drank, I was young and fit, so my football never suffered. Graham pushed us so hard in training that I never dreamed of easing up.

We had to keep proving ourselves. For our second season in the First Division, 1983–84, the critics opined that Watford would struggle now that all the other teams knew our tactics. We had caught everyone by surprise, but now teams were prepared for us. Graham, believing in his direct approach and wanting to revert to the old Ross Jenkins-type centre-forward, brought George Reilly in from Cambridge United. At 6ft 4in, he was Ross Jenkins Mark II. Graham also signed Mo Johnston to replace Luther, who had moved to Milan. Along with Ian Rush and John Aldridge, Mo was one of the greatest goalscorers I ever played with. Maurice was fantastic when he came to Watford; he trained hard and scored some tremendous goals. It says everything about Mo's fitness and natural striking talent that even in 1999 he was still playing, over in Kansas. Graham did his research well into Mo as a goalscorer but not as a person. Mo loved the nightlife and his Champagne Charlie lifestyle meant he didn't achieve all he could as a footballer.

When he arrived from Partick Thistle, Watford housed Mo and his girlfriend in a flat above the club shop at Vicarage Road. They were having problems and Mo ended up trying to avoid her, which was difficult as they lived together. After Saturday away matches, the

Watford team coach drove past the flat before dropping everyone off in the car park. Mo's girlfriend would peer out of the window looking for him and sometimes he would hide on the coach so she would think he had not returned with the team. His plan was to tell her that he had been doing some business in another part of the country, while he would really sneak from the coach and have a night out without her. She always caught him.

Mo's capacity for enjoying himself was prodigious. He could drink all night, not get a wink of sleep but still come in and train in the morning as diligently as the rest. When Mo first came to Watford, we all willingly went out with him because he was such a popular, friendly guy. After a couple of weeks, we were all giving him a wide berth whenever he was ready for a night out. We couldn't keep up with his drinking or match his all-night stamina. We were rescued by George Reilly, a mate of Mo's who had arrived shortly before. George was from Bellshill in Scotland and was a big drinker, too. But when even George was not up for a session, Mo started on the first-year pros. He just wanted company for his nights on the town. It was so funny seeing the first-year pros stagger in the next morning. That was Graham's main problem with Mo – the exhausting effect he had on others at Watford!

To accommodate and supply crosses for Mo and George, Graham's new strike-force, I returned to the left wing. Although Graham had his beloved big guy-little guy double act, Maurice was not as mobile as Luther, whose touch was better. Although it seemed a reversion to old Watford ways, things inevitably changed with new signings. Players who had been at Watford in the early 1980s had been Taylor boys, either bought in or home-grown and all moulded by Graham into a unit. After finishing second in the League, Graham started buying established footballers like Maurice, a superstar in Scotland chased by a lot of clubs. But it was a mistake to sign those who had their own idea of playing. The old Watford spirit did not exactly disintegrate – we were still good enough to finish ninth and tenth in the First Division – but the momentum had gone. Football changed; players became well-paid stars, vital to a manager's future, so they wielded more influence on playing style. The shift in power from dug-out to dressing-room commenced around this time.

Nowadays, players possess so much power. When I started at Watford in 1981 it was unimaginable for a potential recruit, at any club, to demand to know who else the manager would be signing. These days, footballers can say, 'I'm not signing unless you are going to sign world-class players.' In the past, the manager would have replied, 'Who I sign has nothing to do with you. The point is, do you want to come?' A manager cannot do that now. Managers must persuade players. They have lost much of their strength because players stand up to them. It is difficult for a manager earning less than his top-name players to wield complete control.

Although I felt the steam was going out of Watford, we still reached the third round of the Uefa Cup. Europe proved a good experience, exciting too, but we didn't have a particularly easy time. We successfully negotiated a way past the Germans of Kaiserslautern in the opening round. In the first leg of the second round we drew against Levski Spartak, a Bulgarian side, at Vicarage Road. Most people, including us, thought that was it, but in those days, English sides travelled far better than continental teams. European sides wanted to win 3–0 at home, otherwise they felt concerned about going away. English teams didn't mind getting home draws. They had the spirit to survive in awkward places. So we travelled to Sofia and won there. The third-round draw pitted us against Sparta Prague with the first leg at home. We lost at Vicarage Road but the mood in the dressing-room remained positive. 'We can do this again,' players were saying. 'We can go abroad and win.' But when we arrived in Prague, the temperature was –10°C and the pitch was rock solid. I wore gloves but still froze. All Sparta's players wore normal studs and seemed fine while we moved as if on an ice-rink. We tried pimples, all different types of soles but to no effect. Sparta were used to the conditions; by half-time, we were trailing and on our way out of Europe.

Watford still had enough momentum to reach the FA Cup final on 19 May 1984. I have played in a lot of Cup finals, on the losing more often than the winning side unfortunately, but that Watford Cup final was the best I've ever been involved in. It was wonderful. The whole build-up to the meeting with Everton was special. During my time at Liverpool, a Cup final was just another game for the club – we went down to London on the Thursday, trained on the Friday, got on a coach to Wembley on the Saturday. It was no big deal. We knew the procedure by heart. With Watford in 1984, we spent the whole week preparing for Wembley. By Monday, Graham had us in the hotel. Each day for the rest of the week something special was happening. There were newspaper interviews, there were television cameras and radio men were everywhere. The whole build-up was how it should be for a Cup final. It was a really special week, full of events, stunts for the media, training and focusing on the Saturday. Such an approach is less prevalent now. Players just wake up and go to Wembley. The sense of occasion, the whole euphoria surrounding the Cup final is non-existent nowadays.

Television cameras don't follow players around in the build-up as they did for us. We put on little skits and sing-songs for the cameras. We messed about whenever a TV crew were near. ITV even filmed me at the Eton Wall Game. This came about because I had been coaching the boys at Eton College. Eric Steele, who used to be a goalkeeper at Watford, coached there and was asked to bring another Watford player down. I volunteered and soon found myself working on the ball skills of one of William Gladstone's descendants. In the run-up to the Cup final, ITV asked Eton if they could film me playing the Wall Game. The Wall Game goes on for hours with a big scrum moving ten yards forward and ten yards back trying to get into a position to hit one of the two goals, a door in the wall or an old elm tree at the other end. It's crazy. I don't think a goal had been scored since Gladstone was at No. 10. I was never going to play the Game but ITV set up a shot of me kicking at the old elm tree. From eighty yards away, I was delighted to get even close to the tree. It was a bit of fun for the cameras.

Television crews came down to training every day. Our coach, Steve Harrison, is the funniest man in football and they loved him. Steve is now coach at Aston Villa and John Gregory worships him. Every manager does. Steve will never be short of work because people in football know he is very good at coaching and lightening the mood in a dressing-room. Steve's coaching skills are brilliant. He was a left-back so he takes the defence in training, working on positioning and footwork. Steve's enthusiasm is so infectious that players are bound to respond positively and learn. In the evening, when the Watford lads went out for a drink, Steve was always in the middle of it, leading the singing or cracking jokes. Steve's greatest gift is that he can make the switch in an instant from being one of the lads to being serious on the training field. Steve would never let anyone take the mickey out of him in training just because they had a great laugh together the night before. He had the balance right. Steve was ideal in a Wembley build-up with his ability to concentrate on the task in hand while breaking any tension with a few jokes.

The whole week was geared to having a fun day out on the Saturday. Graham let us enjoy it, which wasn't really him. The relaxed approach continued on the day. Michael Barrymore was with us. Freddie Starr was on the coach to the stadium. I was so excited all the way to Wembley. Wembley is such a special place. I love all that Twin Towers tradition – the White Horse, the spectacular goals of Ricky Villa and Norman Whiteside, the drama and the fans flocking up Wembley Way. For me, the FA Cup final is football's greatest occasion apart from the World Cup final. Liverpool's European Cup successes were more prestigious achievements but nothing beats the FA Cup as an occasion. There is no other country in the world which pays such respect to their Cup final. Cups in Italy and Spain mean nothing. Winning the championship is more important but, as for the day, nothing surpasses the FA Cup final.

Unfortunately, the build-up proved more enjoyable than the match. Watford were hampered by a lack of defenders. Steve Sims was injured and Wilf Rostron suspended after being dismissed in an earlier game. It was a terrible decision. He made an innocuous

Family affair: Me, aged five, with my mother and sisters, Gillian (left) and Tracy, at our house in Jamaica

Happy days: I loved life at Up Park Camp which proved a playground for the first years of my life

Another season, another trophy: Stowe Boys Club, here in 1977, could not stop winning. I'm in the front row, smiling after our latest cup

Parental approval: My father enjoyed visiting me at Watford, whose insistence on discipline he deeply admired (*Graham Burton*)

Boxing clever: At fifteen, I was shown the skills that had made my father Sandhurst's heavyweight champion

Sitting pretty: Suzy and I hanging out in October 1982. Suzy was the girl next door who became my beloved wife

Helping hand: I often visit children's wards, like this one at the Countess of Chester Hospital in September 1993 (*Liverpool Daily Post and Echo*)

Dressed to thrill: This fashion show fundraiser for Alder Hey Children's Hospital gave me the opportunity to take to the catwalk (*Liverpool Daily Post and Echo*)

Hand of God: Diego Maradona's act of larceny against Peter Shilton and England never affected my admiration for him as a footballer (*Bob Thomas/Popperfoto*)

All behind the skipper: Bryan Robson always inspired respect. I join Kerry Dixon, Glenn Hoddle, Dave Watson and Terry Fenwick behind the England captain (*Bob Thomas/ Popperfoto*)

Through the wind and the rain: Liverpool will always be in my thoughts, whichever club I am with (*Liverpool Daily Post and Echo*)

Looking up to the manager: I have always respected Kenny Dalglish, pictured here before Liverpool thrashed Watford, my old club, in 1987 (*Popperfoto*)

Glitter and Gazza: The PFA named me Player of the Year in 1988 while Paul Gascoigne won Young Player of the Year (*PA*)

Making a point: Graham Taylor, my mentor at Watford, signals to me and Gazza how he wants England's training to go (*PA*)

Perfect couple: My parents have always been a source of inspiration and support

Sisterly love: When Tracy married in April 1999 Gillian was her bridesmaid

To John Barnes, Compliments & Best Wishes. NMandela 18·10·95

Proud moment: I felt deeply honoured to meet Nelson Mandela, a serene, dignified and principled man, when Liverpool played in Johannesburg

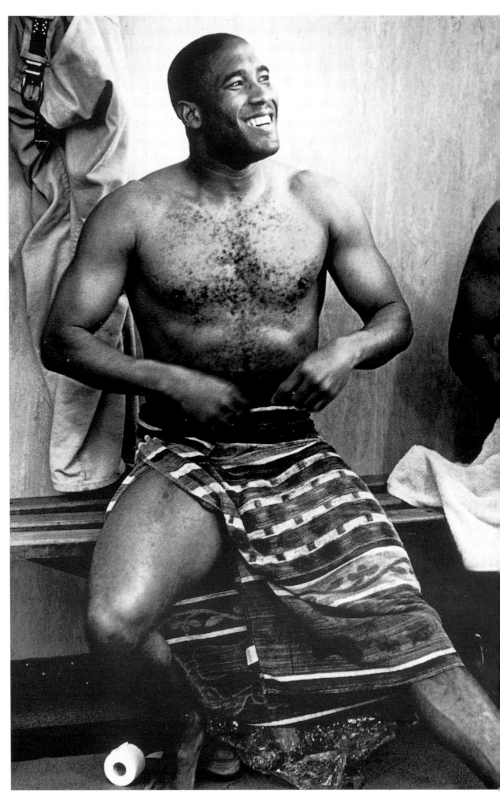

Fit and ready: I worked hard to stay in shape, weaning myself off fast food and running up the hills near my Wirral home (*Bob Thomas/Popperfoto*)

tackle, which was never a foul but the referee sent him off. Wilf is very placid and accepted the referee's decision, walking off without complaining even though he knew he was going to miss the final. I could not believe how philosophical he was. So Les Taylor was captain. When Les had a shot in the first minute, Watford began a very promising twenty-minute spell. We were the better team and our superiority brought a few chances. I had a go. Then Gary Stevens made a very good tackle as I was about to shoot from the edge of the box. Our spirits were high. We thought we would go on and win the game. Everton were not the most daunting of opponents; we had beaten them in our opening game in the First Division. Confidence filled us. When Graeme Sharp hit a shot on the turn which went in off the post, we looked at each other in disbelief. We faded fast after that, unable to rekindle our earlier momentum and spirit. Andy Gray scored a second for Everton and that was it.

Danny Blanchflower, writing in the *Sunday Express*, made some nice comments afterwards but all I felt was disappointment, particularly as Watford's supporters had been so wonderful, singing and waving their banners throughout. Watford have always had a good bunch of fans, really nice people. Those who enjoyed knocking Watford said the supporters were never really passionate about football, but they provided marvellous support for the 1984 final. They were loyal too; if anyone experienced a dodgy patch, the fans never really got on our backs.

The 1984 Cup final proved to be Watford's zenith. Everyone at Vicarage Road expected the rise to continue year after year but it couldn't because, the way we had been going, Watford would soon have become European champions. We reached the FA Cup semi-finals in 1987 but the portents were not good. Both our goalkeepers were injured and Gary Plumley, the son of our club secretary, Eddie, was summoned from a wine-bar to keep goal. Gary was playing non-league at the time and was delighted to help out. He let in three goals early on and it was a truly demoralising experience for all of us against Spurs. Glenn Hoddle ran past me, looked me in the eye and said, 'Keep going.' He could see how depressed I was by Watford being so utterly outclassed. In the dressing-room afterwards, we were all down except Gary Plumley, who was happy and lively. Gary's attitude initially irritated me because of the emphatic nature of the 4–1 defeat. But Gary was just so thrilled to have taken part in an FA Cup semi-final; the rest of us were lost in bitter reflection.

The ride at Watford turned out to be a rollercoaster; dips inevitably followed the peaks. But for me they were special years, and I'll always be grateful to Graham Taylor for turning me from a non-leaguer into an England international.

chapter five

that goal

Maracana Stadium, Rio, 10 June 1984, Brazil versus England. Everyone I meet, everyone I listen to or read commenting on my career assumes my dribble through Brazil's defence was the greatest thing that ever happened to me in football. They are all so wrong. I am too team-orientated to be seduced by the glory of an individual goal, however dramatic. I loved the goal, of course, but it created many problems for me, particularly in changing perceptions. After scoring a goal like that, I never lived up to England's expectations again.

Before Rio, I was not an established England international, although I had twice been recognised at Under-21 level. My debut came only a year before, on 28 May 1983, in a 0–0 draw against Northern Ireland in Belfast. I came on for Luther Blissett, an appropriate exchange given how I began at Watford. Some newspapers talked of another 'black pearl' being polished by Bobby Robson, England's manager. Increasing numbers of black players had arrived on the England scene, or on the fringes of it, good footballers like Viv Anderson, Cyrille Regis, Mark Chamberlain, Brian Stein and Ricky Hill. Bobby expressed a sentiment which I wished the rest of the nation would feel, when he said, 'If the eleven best players in the country were black, that would be my England team.'

That summer, Bobby took me on England's tour to Australia. I was stunned by how lovely the country is. I felt I could live there. The place has so many attractions – a laid-back lifestyle, natural beauty, a good climate and unpretentious people. Australia is similar to America in that everyone arrived in the country on the same level. People succeeded through their own perspiration and inspiration. No one was given a start, a helping hand. Australians' attitude is very American – they brim with get-up-and-go. They want to do something with their lives. Their ambition and adventure is embodied by Australian footballers. When Craig Johnston left Australia at fifteen, it was not like an English kid popping over to France. Craig wanted to make his way in the world and if that meant moving thousands of miles so be it; he did not give it a second thought.

It was a great trip. We joined in the centenary celebrations which were going on at the time and enjoyed overselves thoroughly. In those days, it was accepted for footballers to drink. Although I didn't drink much then, I went out with the other players. Drinking was considered a way of bonding for English teams.

We played three matches in Australia. I was on the left with West Brom's Derek Statham behind me. It was a rare outing for Derek. Kenny Sansom was the established left-back with over eighty caps to his credit, but he had not come on the trip. Bobby's team-talks usually included the instruction, 'Get the ball out to Kenny; Kenny get down the wing,' and I felt sorry for Derek in Australia because Bobby kept talking about, 'Kenny doing this' and 'Kenny doing that' even though Kenny was on the other side of the world.

In September 1983, England suffered that infamous 1–0 European Championship qualifying defeat by Denmark at Wembley. I was immediately dropped. Everyone expected England to win but just by looking at what Denmark achieved in 1984 and 1986, our critics should really have appreciated what a gifted team the Danes were. Players like Jesper Olsen were very talented individuals. People ignored this important fact and insisted the result was unacceptable; heads had to roll and mine was one of them. Knee-jerk reactions to England defeats were something I became wearily familiar with. Wingers are often the first to be discarded. When England failed to score, the critical spotlight burned on those assigned to supply the strikers. Apparently I failed to deliver enough service against Denmark so Bobby went for change.

I was brought back in from the cold to face Scotland at Hampden Park, following my performance in the 1984 FA Cup final. Bobby had used me as a substitute since the Denmark game. Now he gave me a chance to regain my place. Richard Gough lined up against me. I looked at this gangly, aggressive right-back with a South African accent and wondered who he was. England drew 1–1 which was a good result on Scottish soil and I performed well against Gough. Afterwards, he moved to centre-back where he proved a resounding success, most notably during one of the most productive periods in the history of Glasgow Rangers. Gough was not the only one to shift position after facing me. One of my first and best games for Watford came against Mark Wright, then a right-back for Southampton. Wrighty subsequently developed into an outstanding central defender for Derby County, Liverpool and England. I always wondered whether it was because I played against them early in their careers that they switched to centre-back!

The Scotland game was important for me because it pushed me back into the reckoning again. Although England subsequently lost 2–0 to the USSR, Bobby Robson still took me in his squad to South America, to play friendlies in Brazil, Uruguay and Chile. The trip was not particularly exciting, apart from the game against Brazil. On arriving in Rio, the photographers asked Mark Chamberlain and me to come down to the Copacabana Beach and juggle a ball. More volleyball than football is played on the beach but we were still surrounded by kids who could keep the ball up brilliantly. Mark and I donned England shirts and did some tricks for the cameras but it was a bit embarrassing because of those kids' skills.

When we reached the Maracana and saw the small crowd, the

grotty changing-rooms and the rutted pitch, we were really disappointed. Everyone raved about what a fabulous occasion it was but it felt very low-key in my estimation. The Maracana had 57,000 people in it, a relative handful by its proud standards. The lack of interest was understandable. The game was only a friendly. England were not particularly rated nor in the best of form, following one success in four. Brazil themselves were undergoing transition between the exceptional team of 1982 and the decent one of 1986. Leandro and Junior were on the field but not many other established dayers were ranged against us.

The Maracana is of similar size to Wembley. The only reason it once held 200,000 was because everyone stood up. But I could not even hear the Brazilian fans because they were so far away and there were so few of them. That took a lot of the pressure off England. It was less intimidating than we expected. My knowledge of the Maracana had been gleaned via tapes when it was always full of people and reverberating with noise. If there had been 200,000 Brazilians baying for English blood, we might have been nervous. But it was quiet and I felt no inhibitions stepping out on to the pitch. The modest-sized crowd failed to inspire Brazil, who were feeble against us. Despite the absence of atmosphere, the awful facilities and a below-strength Brazilian team, I was still treading the turf of the fabled Maracana, a name which always conjured up magic in my mind. Nothing could really ruin my feeling of excitement that this was the Maracana, the home of Brazilian football.

If I was going to score a special goal anywhere, the Maracana was the best place. Wembley would have been wonderful but still second to the Maracana as a setting. As I waited for kick-off, I looked around at the famous, if dilapidated ground and thought Pele scored his one thousandth goal here, he played on the same pitch I was now standing on. The match may have been only a friendly but it was against Brazil, in Rio, in Pele's backyard, in a place where England had never won. Never mind the decay, the Maracana has history and the mystique of great names and days gone by.

Real determination flooded through me. This might be my only chance at the Maracana. The moment had to be siezed. So a minute before half-time, I picked up possession and began running at Brazil's defence. For all the superlatives heaped upon that run, I can honestly say that if I had seen someone to pass to I would have done. On drifting inside from my normal left-wing station, my instinct had always been to pass first. Only in situations where no one was available would I carry on dribbling. Having slipped round the first Brazilian, I looked up to see if an England team-mate was nearby. There wasn't, so I kept going. A pattern developed – look around, no support, keep going, beat another Brazilian, look around, no support, keep going, beat another Brazilian. I was not sure where I was until I found myself in front of goal facing the keeper. That was how the goal unfolded.

If the game had been a World Cup tie, a Brazilian would have tackled me properly. When I swerved past Leandro, he didn't even make an attempt to challenge me. I can imagine Leandro thinking, 'Somebody will tackle him because we've got enough defenders between this guy and goal.' Leandro's colleagues took the same approach until eventually Junior was the last defender. His attempt to stop me failed because I had built up too much momentum. But I should never have got to Junior. Being a fan and student of Brazilian football, I know I would have been dispossessed or brought down if the international had been competitive.

I have always been a dribbler. At Watford, Graham Taylor drummed into me, 'Take them on, take them on, take them on.' I have gone on runs similar to the one at the Maracana but always out on the left wing with the sole aim of delivering a cross. Rio was different. At the time, it was impossible to absorb what I had done. If there had been five minutes before half-time, I could have reflected on the goal. But the moment the ball crossed the line, the referee blew for half-time. We headed towards the dressing-room and the goal was swiftly forgotten amidst Bobby's talk. Some of the England players whispered 'great goal' but the praise was lost in the exhortations of 'come on' and 'we've got to keep it going'. We did and won 2–0.

Goalscorers find it difficult to describe their goals until they have seen them on television. I felt fine about the goal. I knew it had been pretty good, that I had tricked my way around a few Brazilians and scored at the Maracana, the spiritual home of flair football. But the goal seemed ten times better on television. Sitting down and watching it, I appreciated its special nature. It almost shocked me how good it was. The dribble was far more difficult than it appeared at the time. Weaving through a defence and scoring was so different from something as method-based as a free-kick goal. At dead-ball situations, I would look at the ball, then the wall, taking time to assess the angle. As I addressed the still ball, I knew what I was going to do; in my mind's eye, the ball was arcing over the wall and into the top corner. I could envisage it without even doing it. But when I was dribbling, there was no time to analyse, no time to plan reactions to defenders' challenges. It was so fluid, so unpredictable. Dribbles have always been celebrations of instinct.

The television broadcast had a slight problem. First-half satellite feed time lasted exactly forty-five minutes and the goal arrived in injury time at the end of the opening period. The feed was up by the time I scored. The commentator said, 'We've seen this amazing goal but you can't see it back home just yet.' Television showed the goal at the beginning of the second half when the feed re-opened.

I didn't appreciate what an impact my slalom dribble was having. Apparently, one Rio paper described it as 'the greatest goal ever seen at the Maracana'. I don't speak Portuguese so local headlines meant nothing to me. England flew out of Rio the next day and, although a few Brazilians made comments at the airport, I didn't understand them. Maybe if England hadn't left town so soon I might have been feted. But then I would probably have stayed in Brazil and played football on the Copacabana for the rest of my life!

Reaction was actually mixed in Rio. It must be remembered that Brazil's fans were unhappy with their national team at the time. If I had danced past members of Brazil's 1982 or 1986 team, perhaps a bigger fuss would have been made. But in 1984, Brazil had a scratch side. Socrates and Zico were not on the field so some Brazilians downplayed the goal's significance. 'So what?' they said. 'It's only against a second-rate team.' Other Brazilians were far more enthusiastic. I have since been told how much the goal was discussed in Brazil. Brazilians appreciate a good goal, whatever the strength of the defence attempting to prevent it. The goal was special, the type not expected from someone wearing an England strip.

Some still mention it, although I find many Brazilians have short memories. I clearly remember Nelinho's goal which so deceived Dino Zoff when Brazil beat Italy in the World Cup third-place play-off match in 1978, but I have spoken to Brazilians who cannot recall it. Maybe it is because Brazilian teams score so many flamboyant goals. English people always remember. Any supporter aged over ten in 1984 will be able to paint a mental picture of my Maracana goal even though it is not often shown on television. People were ecstatic about it back home. I was not immediately aware of the commotion because England continued to Montevideo, where we lost to Uruguay, and then Santiago for a 0–0 draw with Chile. If we had flown straight home from Rio, we would have returned to even more headlines in the newspapers.

Events in the Maracana didn't change me, but they did change people's attitude towards me. The English public thought John Barnes is obviously the greatest player in the world, we have a superstar on our hands. They expected me to repeat that dribble again and again and again. When I didn't, I was criticised. I heard reproachful words – 'If John Barnes could score that goal in Brazil, why doesn't he do it every time for England?' My whole England career was judged on one spectacular goal. When I passed, fans wondered why I wasn't dribbling. If I didn't score, fans wondered why. After Rio, I tried too hard for England. Because of the Maracana and the heightened expectancy, I attempted to do what people wanted me to do, to go on mazy dribbles. If two defenders shadowed me, the right thing to do was pass because we had a free man elsewhere. I kept losing the ball because I was trying to take them on. I didn't do that for long. I soon realised pandering to public expectation was unprofessional. But when I gained possession and played it simple, I still got stick. I could hear

England fans moaning, 'Why isn't John Barnes taking on defenders like he did against Brazil?'

Having gone through that, I tell young players one thing, 'If you are having a bad time and fans are on at you, pass to a team-mate. It will give you confidence to know that you haven't made a mistake. Then when you feel confident again, take someone on.' My England managers never moaned like the fans about me not taking people on. They recognised I was being sensible and professional.

Although the goal created crazy expectation levels and all manner of problems, I wouldn't have had it any other way. I would rather I scored that goal in Brazil and subsequently be censured for not doing it every week than never have experienced my Maracana moment. My passion for Brazilian football means that goal remains so special to me. I loved playing in the Maracana against Brazil, facing Leandro and Junior. If I do not achieve anything else in my life, at least I have the memory of Rio.

While the press and public got carried away, the reaction from my fellow professionals was more rational. Footballers appreciated the goal's quality while acknowledging I would have been tackled in a competitive game. Professionals perceived it as a preventable goal and said how surprised they would be if I scored one like that again. To my face, they said, 'Great goal, great skill, great pace, great body-swerve, great finish.' But in private I knew my fellow footballers were adding, 'John Barnes at the Maracana was the goal that should never have happened.' I agree with that view. Dribbling through a whole defence should never happen. I would have been deeply disappointed if that had been my Celtic defence opening up like that. Any British manager would have been apoplectic. When George Best dribbled and swerved his way through the Benfica defence during Manchester United's European Cup quarter-final game in Lisbon in 1966, it was fantastic, a fabulous expression of one man's talents, but a defender should have got a proper challenge in. It may sound unromantic, but not many goals are scored without a defender making a mistake.

However, following the Maracana goal, I found that opponents' perceptions of me had changed. I played for a long-ball club side yet here I was scoring a goal that contrasted with everything Watford embodied. No matter how much an opponent might think that I shouldn't have been allowed to score a goal like that, it was still in the back of his mind that I could repeat it. When the next season started, I found defenders doubling up on me, trying to stifle me. I had to come to terms with that. Suddenly being shadowed by two markers meant I was even more likely to pass. Yet people still wondered why I wasn't taking defenders on. Fans would be happy if the opposition put four men on me and I took three of them on but lost the ball to the fourth. 'Well done,' they would say. 'You are having a go.' That attitude was absolute rubbish and goes to show how little people actually know about football. The situation angered me. Football is a wonderful sport because everyone, from chairmen to directors to fans, holds opinions. But who is right? One thing is for sure: professional footballers should be left to do their own job.

Back at Vicarage Road, I still took people on, still spirited the ball past full-backs. It helped me that Graham Taylor was so committed to attack. Watford's fans were brilliant, very forgiving. I couldn't do anything wrong in their eyes. Watford wasn't a problem; England was. After the Maracana, I had something to live up to with England. Watford rose from a lower division so expectations were more reasonable. It was much easier playing for Watford than for England.

The fact that Watford had reached a plateau had yet to be a concern. So I never thought about using my Maracana fame to engineer a move to Italy, like Mark Hateley did to AC Milan. Mark scored the other goal in Rio from my cross and his aerial strength impressed Milan. I loved Italian football but, despite my pangs of envy when Luther Blissett went, I realised that I would be better off maturing at Watford. I told myself that I would head to Italy in a few years' time, to Juventus or another of the big teams. Maybe if I had pushed on the strength of that Maracana goal and the ensuing excitement, I could have gone to *Serie A* then, but I was still only twenty. I had my career before me, although it became more intense and scrutinised after the Maracana.

Everyone believes Rio was my greatest achievement as a footballer. It wasn't. As a professional, the only triumph that matters is the collective one. Football is a team sport. Winning the League or FA Cup is more important than any personal glory, like scoring the goal in Brazil. From an individual point of view, becoming Player of the Year and twice Footballer of the Year were very special achievements. But I look at success in football as a question of what the team has accomplished, not from a personal perspective. That's the way I was brought up, the way I train, the way I am with my family. There's no point in one member of the family being happy if the family itself isn't happy. I look at the bigger picture.

Whenever I take a broader perspective on football, one name always jumps to the forefront of my mind – Kevin Richardson. How many people know of Kevin Richardson? He won the championship with two different clubs, Everton and Arsenal, and achieved as much as almost anyone in domestic football. As an individual, people might not appreciate what Kevin did, but anyone with any under-standing of team sports will acknowledge his importance. He worked so hard for the team. The team ethos is everything in football. No one can achieve anything without team-mates. Watford and Liverpool, the two main clubs of my career, both had collectivity as their abiding ethos. I have always felt that way, but Rio confirmed it. The goal has to be seen in the context of the team's performance and eventual result. Rio became a millstone around my neck but I wouldn't wish it away. The memory is too precious.

nationalism

I am fortunate my England career is now complete so I don't have to sound patriotic any more. Nationalism causes so many problems. I hate it. I first encountered the worst strain of nationalism, unadulterated racism, on that 1984 tour to South America. After Rio and Montevideo, England set off for Santiago and the final match of the tour against Chile. Sitting at the back of our scheduled fight were four National Front sympathisers, occasionally shouting abuse down the aisle in the direction of England's three black players – myself, Viv Anderson and Mark Chamberlain. They kept saying, 'England won only 1–0 because a nigger's goal doesn't count.' I leaned back in my seat and thought to myself, 'Well, I crossed the ball for Mark Hateley's goal, so does that not count either?' Viv Anderson, Mark Chamberlain and I just ignored the four of them. They never came up and said anything directly to us. They probably thought we would give them a good kicking. I suppose it might have been different if Ian Wright had been on the plane, or Paul Ince.

These NF guys did approach England's white players. 'How can you mix with blacks?' they said. The players were very uncomfortable. White footballers always are when confronted by racism like that, but what could they do, short of violence? The NF guys also heckled Ted Croker, the Football Association secretary, saying, 'You fucking wanker, you prefer Sambos to us.' Somebody said something to the NF four but it was not that confrontational. When the plane landed at Santiago, the four NF guys joined some others already there and unfurled a banner for the TV cameras. It read: 'NF – Send Them Back'.

They were all National Front stooges using England's high profile to make a statement. The four sad men on the flight actually didn't cause much trouble. They waved their Union Jacks and National Front banners. When they boarded the plane in Montevideo, people took pictures of these English fans with their big flags. They shouted more racist comments during the game in Santiago. Unintelligent and unemployed, there was no way they could have afforded the £750 each the tour cost. They were funded by the National Front. It would have been difficult for the FA to stop a booking like that, not knowing these four particular individuals were being underwritten by the NF. When they started shouting abuse, the FA could still do little. They couldn't kick them off the tour. The NF quartet had tickets on scheduled flights, official match tickets and hotels paid in advance. It was not an England charter plane, so the FA were powerless.

People muttered how disgraceful it was but nothing more. Neil MacFarlane, the Minister for Sport, spluttered something about holding an inquiry but nothing ever happened. It was all token gestures. What could be done? These people were racists. The views of hardened National Front members were not going to be changed by a bunch of worthies conducting an inquiry. Such racists were not going to embrace tolerance at the first sight of hastily erected signs within grounds saying 'please don't make racist chants or wave offensive banners'.

The England team is traditionally the magnet for rampant nationalism but the authorities are hardly going to order the team's disbanding. I loathe the fact that the England team embody and foster nationalism. I feel both Jamaican and English. I've lived in England longer than I spent in Kingston but my roots are all Jamaican. I feel more Jamaican than English because I'm black. A lot of black people born in England feel more Jamaican than English because they are not accepted in the land of their birth on account of their colour, but they are not approved of in Jamaica because they speak with a funny accent. I am accepted in Jamaica because I was raised there and my father is respected across the island.

Extreme nationalism provokes a non-acceptance of people because they come from somewhere else. According to that tenet, I should not be accepted in England or even now in Scotland. But I am just an individual trying to make a life for myself in a different country. Why should extremists stop me? Why should nationalists like those National Front morons on the flight to Santiago try to inhibit my career? I believe we should join Europe and just make the whole continent one country. I crave freedom of travel so we can go where we want, do what we want, so long as it's legal, and work wherever we want. Life is hard enough without being restrained by boundaries or rejected simply for being born in a different country. Nationalism is such a curse on the world. It causes so many wars, so many problems. Boundaries and greed for land have caused the slaughter of countless millions.

None of my England team-mates ever questioned patriotism as I did. Overtly patriotic players would talk about how much they wanted to play in Italy or Spain. Now the Premiership has metamorphosed into the 'in' place, the same players are probably happy to stay at home. I didn't mind them talking about patriotism in terms of wanting to win matches, to be proud of playing for England. But when we sat around talking on England trips, I stirred up arguments by saying, 'It's impossible to be prouder of being English than French. England as a country is not better than France. England's sense of superiority is irrational.' I don't know how that went down with Terry Butcher or Stuart Pearce.

Nationalism is an evil part of English society. Being a Commonwealth citizen enabled me to chose whom I wanted to represent at football, England, Scotland, Northern Ireland or Wales. England selected me before the others. Maybe if Scotland had asked me before England I would have represented Scotland. I would have tried as hard for Scotland as England. Being a footballer, I would do my best for whomever I played. Was I more patriotic for England than I would have been for Scotland? No. To keep everyone happy throughout my international career, I always said that my only choice was England because England is where I settled, but that wasn't true.

Look at John Aldridge representing the Republic of Ireland. He sweats commitment. Although Aldo is English, a real Scouser, he could not have strived any more determinedly for England than he did for Ireland. It is not a problem for Ireland because if a player works hard in the green shirt, the Irish love him no matter where he comes from. The English are too introspective and nationalistic. What about Andy Townsend for Ireland or Vinnie Jones for Wales? They gave everything although they weren't born in those countries. If a professional footballer is offered an opportunity, he will try his hardest. How patriotic for Wales could Vinnie Jones be? Not that patriotic because he is not from Wales, but what Vinnie did do was give one hundred per cent for whomever he represented. When I played for England, I could never declare that nationalism is loathsome and illogical. I couldn't say that if I played for France, I would try just as hard, which I would. I tried hard for England out of professional pride not patriotism – because I never felt any.

touched by the hand of god

A zteca Stadium, Mexico City, 22 June 1986, World Cup quarter-final, Argentina versus England. When footballers are confined to dug-outs, they are expected to watch their own team, live every move and feel every fluctuation in their colleagues' fortunes. Substitutes are expected to scream exhortations to those out on the field. But as I sat there in the Azteca, I found it difficult to follow my England friends. I was spellbound by a spinning-top of stealth and skill called Diego Maradona. I could not take my eyes off the Argentinian, a man who revealed both the devilish and angelic in his game in four second-half minutes.

Of course, I wanted England to win. When we had the ball, when Peter Beardsley or Gary Lineker ran forward, I hoped fervently that England would score. But when possession passed to Argentina, who invariably gave it to Maradona, I sat there intoxicated by his ability, his movement, the fact that his thought patterns were one step ahead of everyone else on the field. Maradona embodied something special and I was transfixed by the sight of greatness in motion.

I had yet to feature at the Mexico World Cup, being on the bench during the defeat by Portugal and the revival against Morocco, Poland and Paraguay, which carried England to a massively hyped quarter-final. England had not met Argentina since the Falklands conflict and the build-up was predictably rabid. I just focused on the football and, with the match under way, waited for the moments when the ball danced to Maradona's tune. Argentina's captain was in a class of his own in the 1980s, a formidable achievement given the reality of footballing life in an age of cynicism, bad fouls, man-to-man marking and defensive tactics. Maradona's impact, his constant expressions of creativity and the thrillingly unexpected, was extraordinary.

That decade suffered a period, like now, when athletes predominated and players with more stamina than skill sought to stifle those with a touch of magic in their souls. But no one could stop Maradona. He was so gifted. Argentina's greatest footballer claimed his was a God-given talent. He was certainly faster than everyone else, more technically gifted, even physically stronger. In vision alone, Maradona operated on a different plane from the others. When Maradona lost the ball, he never strived hard to recover it but, in possession, the feats he performed were unbelievable. I can do the odd trick but Maradona's repertoire was sensational. Opposing managers would deploy two men to mark him and he would be powerful enough, inventive enough and aware enough to pass the ball out of trouble or dribble through the two of them. Defences resembled rows of statues with Maradona the zephyr blowing through them. I had never seen a player like him in the flesh before. Of those I have analysed on tape, only Pele, Johan Cruyff and George Best occupy Maradona's stratosphere. Of course, comparisons between generations can be misleading. Pele's era was different from Maradona's. Watching tapes of the Brazilian in the mid-1960s, I felt he could sit on the ball and no one would come near him. If fast-forwarded through time, Pele would still be the best in the world, but the gap between him and the rest would not be as great. Scoring a thousand goals would be impossible for a start.

As I sat on the Azteca bench, my mind concentrated on the mesmerising present, on the sight of Maradona running at England. Six minutes after half-time, Maradona and Jorge Valdano lost the ball which Steve Hodge looped back to Peter Shilton. That was when Maradona made his leap into the annals of infamy. We saw the hand-ball straightaway on the bench. Everyone jumped up and shouted 'HAND-BALL'. We could not believe the Tunisian referee, Ali Bennaceur, allowed such a blatant offence to stand. The way Shilton and Terry Fenwick reacted showed it was a hand-ball. Even now, more than a decade on, I still cannot comprehend how the officials missed Maradona's cheating. The linesman was right there but still failed to flag.

That act of larceny did not diminish my professional admiration for Maradona. I never respected him for his personal life, with his drugs and other problems, but I appreciated him as a footballer. His hand of God did not affect that reverence at all. Maradona cheated for his team. The obsession with fair play tends to grip those who watch rather than play. If Gary Lineker had committed a similar offence and tipped the ball over Neri Pumpido, Argentina's keeper, I would not have told Bennaceur. England would have accepted the good fortune, smiled and gone through to the semi-finals. English players pull the same tricks. In St Etienne during France '98, Michael Owen went down far too quickly against Argentina. It was never a penalty. Paul Scholes tried to win a spot-kick as well. If Scholes had conned the referee into giving that penalty and England had progressed, we could not complain about Maradona. I don't know whether I would dive or cheat like that. Impulses dominate such situations. I have never cheated although I have bent the rules in terms of penalty decisions; there were times when I could have stayed on my feet but chose to go down, but there was always contact first. I have never blatantly dived when no one was near me, as happens a lot. Maradona, Owen, Scholes, myself – it is just a question of degree.

During my playing career, I did resort to subterfuge to succeed. I tripped opponents if they got past me. I pulled the shirts of full-backs or pushed them off-balance to steal a yard. I deliberately hand-balled but no one scored from it. These were not incidents that decided games. My hand-balls occurred in midfield, which makes them pretty nondescript and unimportant. The offences were spotted by the referee and punished with a free kick. Maradona's offence was not spotted by the referee and resulted in a goal. People would not have called for his head if he had hand-balled in midfield. The ultimate significance may be different but it's the same offence, cheating by use of a hand-ball.

Argentina were a nasty team. They always have been. Daniel Passarella, who objected to Maradona's bad behaviour during the 1982 World Cup, instilled some discipline when he coached them for France '98 but generally Argentinian sides have been dirty. Who can forget their spiteful captain, Antonio Rattin, in 1966? Argentina have always been aggressive and unsportsmanlike, fouling and spitting. Every Argentinian side I have faced have niggled away, committed off-the-ball offences and questioned every decision. Many South American teams are like that. Before England played Paraguay in the second round of Mexico '86, the Paraguayans made lots of noises about just going to enjoy the occasion at the Azteca. They kept saying they were so happy to have reached the knockout stage of the World Cup. But the Paraguayans were disgraceful during the game, particularly in the second half. One incident which revolved around the Syrian referee, Jamal Al Sharif, ended up with one of the Paraguayans kicking him on the back of his leg. When he turned around to see who it was, he was kicked by someone else in the back. Latin Americans react like that. Uruguay have always been dirty. Brazil never really stooped to the brutal, apart from in 1974 when Johan Neeskens was taken out terribly by Mario Marinho and Luis Pereira. The team Argentina sent to Mexico were not the dirtiest in Latin American history but they still had kickers and cheats. Julio Olarticoechea was a master at shirt-pulling.

I was desperate to join the fray, to share the same space as Maradona. I wanted to experience this extraordinary footballer at close hand, to see for myself the darkness and light in his play. I still managed to stay relaxed on the bench. I always did, even when my team were losing. Whenever I went on, I changed immediately. Those fans who glance at the bench and think subs do not care simply don't understand. When the sub crosses that line, it's a completely different situation. Any footballer will acknowledge it is very hard to be intense on the bench. Even the most emotional, volatile characters find it difficult to look fervent when their involvement is restricted to the dug-out. Look at Temuri Ketsbaia at Newcastle United. When Temuri gets on the pitch, he becomes very aggressive and seriously het up. On the bench, Temuri is a picture of calm and restraint. Benches can be very relaxing places. The Azteca bench was too short so we lounged on the grass. What made it even more relaxing was Bobby Robson couldn't see us. All of us subs had our boots on but were just lying around, chatting. It felt like a picnic.

Disgust and disbelief spiced the subs' conversation for four minutes after Maradona's hand of God goal. But then the villain of the piece scored that fabulous second goal. 'What a great goal,' I said to the other subs and they all agreed. I knew Maradona's goal would probably send England home from the World Cup but it was so fantastic I felt like applauding. No one could have stopped that goal. It was a World Cup quarter-final, a game of desperate importance, players were trying to halt Maradona but they couldn't. Maradona got the ball and Terry Butcher came across. He went inside Terry and past Peter Reid and Gary Stevens. I thought one of them was going to catch him, but despite having to control the ball as he ran, Maradona actually accelerated away from them. He ran at Terry Fenwick, who would have brought Maradona down if he had not already been booked. Peter Shilton came out. The ball was on Maradona's right side and he should really have used his right foot to strike it but he preferred his left, just as Terry Butcher was about to make his tackle.

Terry's challenge reminds me so much of Ray Houghton's on Michael Thomas when Michael scored the goal that won Arsenal the League at Anfield in 1989. Ray was racing back and was just about to tackle Thomas when he toed it past Bruce Grobbelaar. I don't think Michael knew Ray was closing in. It was the same with Maradona. I'm sure he didn't realise Terry was so close as he went past Peter Shilton. On the bench, we could see Terry chasing him. We were shouting 'go on Terry, go on' because he was eating up the ground and just about to tackle him, but Terry didn't make it. It was both exhilarating and distressing to watch. England's subs were never going to applaud Maradona but everyone turned to each other and praised the goal. 'What could we do?' was the feeling. Maradona's goal was that good, the best of the tournament and one of the greatest in the history of football.

It was generally accepted that the legendary Argentinian was a rare talent. Had that goal been scored by one of my peers, someone whom I felt was on my level, envy might have entered my thoughts. But I didn't see Maradona as one of my peers. He was special, a level above me. I was happy when Maradona shone because it reinforced my belief that he was from a different planet. Argentina had some other great players, such as Jorge Valdano and Jorge Burruchaga, but Maradona's magnetic presence inevitably distracted from their important contributions. To be on the field with Maradona was the main thing for me, not to be on the field with Argentina.

With sixteen minutes remaining and England trailing 2–0, I got my chance. Bobby had already sent on Chris Waddle for Peter Reid. Then he decided to go for width on the left as well. Trevor Steven came off and I ran on with Bobby's words ringing in my brain – 'Just get crosses in.' It was good management by Bobby; in pressurised situations like that, simple instructions are the best. My job was to speed or slip past Ricardo Giusti, Argentina's right-back, and deliver the ball to near-post or far. A myth exists that wingers aim for team-mates when we actually target areas. After beating Giusti, I never aimed for Gary Lineker across the Azteca pitch; I just targeted the far-post and Gary happened to be there. When he scored, we thought we would go on to equalise. Maybe Argentina would have prevailed in extra time but at that point England were in the ascendancy. Three minutes from time, I eluded Giusti again and whipped in another cross. Again Gary connected but, agonisingly, could not put it into the net. That was as close as England got. At the end, I wanted Maradona's shirt but there was a bit of a queue. When the final whistle goes, players traditionally exchange shirts with their nearest opponent. I think Steve Hodge man-marked Maradona for the last five minutes just to get his shirt.

In the dressing-room afterwards, every England player felt deflated except me. Disappointment coloured my thoughts but there was also delight that I had experienced World Cup action, becoming England's one hundredth player in the finals. Depression, however brief, might have set in if Bobby had not sent me on. I would have hated to go through my whole career without savouring the precious experience of a World Cup. I looked around the dressing-room and saw all these drained people. Inside, I thrilled to the fact that I had just shared a World Cup pitch with Diego Maradona. Afterwards, people reflected on what might have happened if I had started, rather than being limited to the final sixteen minutes, which, with England 2–0 down, effectively represented an attempted salvage job. I never thought about what might have been. I could have begun the game, fallen over the ball in the first minute, lost confidence and disappeared. Similarly, if David Beckham had stayed on the pitch against Argentina in St Etienne in France, England would not necessarily have won. All that can be said is that I played well for the sixteen minutes. And I had my close-up of Maradona.

Some time later, I watched Maradona guest in Ossie Ardiles' testimonial at Tottenham. Chris Waddle was on Maradona's side and the pair were doing party-tricks. I would have loved to have been on the pitch. Testimonials are occasions when flair players can be showmen and it doesn't really matter. No nutty defender is going to kick them. Maradona appreciated Chris very much in Ossie's game. Chris was juggling the ball and Maradona said afterwards that it was a great honour to play with Chris, and how good he was. Maybe if I had played, I would have tripped over the ball but I would have loved to have been involved in another match with Diego Maradona.

moving on up: joining liverpool

After treading the same soil as Diego Maradona in Mexico, I returned to homely Vicarage Road for a final season of direct football. Watford were a wonderful club, full of honest characters, but I had outgrown them. It was time to move on, to start winning trophies with a heavyweight club. Liverpool, the leading team of the era, first made overtures in February 1987 but I knew I was going to stay at Watford until the end of the season when my contract expired. I wanted to keep my options open. If I committed myself to Liverpool in February, Juventus or Real Madrid might have come along and that would have been desperately frustrating. Holding on represented a gamble because of the threat of injury or Liverpool's interest cooling. But, having decided to leave Watford, it was important to see what was around. My actions were misinterpreted up on Merseyside. They felt I was snubbing Liverpool. They thought I craved the intervention of a London club like Arsenal or prayed a continental club would come in offering immense glamour and money. A game of brinkmanship began.

On 3 March, I rejected the new contract offered by Watford who promptly placed me on the transfer list. Graham Taylor notified all the First Division clubs and personally telephoned Liverpool, Tottenham Hotspur and Manchester United. The point of no return was reached. Staying at Watford was never an issue. I was in danger of under-achieving. All the transfer talk affected my performances. From March until the end of the season, I scarcely put in a decent display. At times, I yearned to tell Watford's fans how sorry I was to be disappointing them after all their love and support. However guilty I felt, I had to escape from Vicarage Road which had become a cul de sac. After the promotion, the high league positions, the FA Cup final and the last sixteen of the Uefa Cup, life at Watford became stale. Even Graham Taylor was planning to depart, although I had no indication of that. Maybe Graham realised Watford had run its course. He went to Aston Villa that summer. Without Graham, the organisation and spirit would never have been the same. It was time to leave the brotherhood.

Watford's long-ball football had lost its sense of surprise. A flair player like myself never warmed to it anyway. I held my own ideas on how the game should be played and they were far removed from Graham Taylor's. Watford's tactics were right for them but not for me. The football was too direct, too one-dimensional. Back at home, I sat on my sofa, savouring the sight of *Serie A* on satellite, all that smooth passing, possession and good touches. Italian football dripped with intelligence. 'This is the way to play,' I told myself. 'If only I could get in a team playing that type of football.' Watford's approach seemed increasingly archaic and alien.

A real commotion was stirred up by my agent, Atholl Still, actively trying to sell me while I remained contracted to Watford. To interest a leading Italian club, I had to promote myself properly. If it had been any middle-ranking *Serie A* side or Liverpool, I would have chosen Liverpool, but my heart was set on AC Milan or Juventus and it was Atholl's task to talk to the Italians. I was Atholl's first football client; representing opera singers was more in his line, having been one himself. Fluent in Italian, Atholl spent much of his year in Milan, Rome, Genoa and Turin. He knew Mantovani, Sampdoria's owner, but I was thinking higher than them; Sampdoria are one of those clubs who prosper only occasionally.

Graham Taylor was upset by Atholl's approaches, but that was pointless. Agents were already part of football, although it's far worse now. His priority, of course, was Watford Football Club not John Barnes. He might have been angered by Atholl's upfront style but Atholl operated the way he thought best. A video compilation of playing highlights from my Watford and England career was one marketing tool. I was lambasted for selling myself on a tape but videos were as common on the Continent then as they are in England and Scotland now. *Serie A* coaches who hadn't seen me play could at least make an initial assessment from the tape. Wherever Atholl travelled in Italy, clubs requested a video. Stacked on a shelf in a Juventus office were Liverpool videos of Ian Rush, who was already high profile. Having watched him live or on television, Juventus knew all about Ian Rush yet they still wanted to have him captured on video. So why shouldn't I be? Watford remained a small club and no matter how good I was, Italian clubs did not know much about me. It was different with Luther Blissett and AC Milan because they could judge him on his goal record. The problem with videos, and a flaw I am wary of now that I seek signings for Celtic, is that anyone can look good in highlights.

I hoped my video would tempt Juventus or Milan. My heart was set on an Italian club of their stature. *Serie A* was the most exciting league on the planet. All the world's premier footballers were drawn there, as if magnetised. Even now, *Serie A* remains Europe's élite league because the leading players still choose it ahead of an improving Premier League. The Italian lifestyle was not the attraction. I was driven only by a desire to play a part in the greatest footballing show on earth; and ten years in England felt enough.

Italian football would have suited me as it would any flair player. Given my technical skills, I would be more appreciated in Italy than England. Day-to-day involvement with so many great footballers would inevitably help me to improve. Italy improved Luther Blissett and Ian Rush. Both strikers loved balls to run on to but these were rare in Italy where they tend to pass to feet. Luther and Ian were not considered great successes in *Serie A* but they returned with important parts of their game strengthened. Having balls played in to them all the time improved their first touch and awareness. Italian football would have made Paul Gascoigne a better player but he was held back by injuries. Ball-players flourish in *Serie A*.

As I pondered *Serie A* versus Football League, I spoke to Luther about his Italian experience. He struggled, but I didn't allow his problems to influence my judgement. Even if Luther had spoken only positively about Italy, it wouldn't have affected my desire to go out there. I listen to opinions but always make up my own mind. I'm naturally positive. If six players went to Italy from England and of them only Liam Brady enjoyed himself, I would be inspired by Liam's example not others' failure. I could have handled Italy. I have the right temperament. During my time at Anfield, when young Liverpool players mulled over interest from Italy, I asked them, 'You are a local boy, you have never been away from home, you can't speak Italian, do you really want to leave?' They would think about that. Intelligent, ambitious footballers such as David Platt coped comfortably with a move to Italy, but others could not. I could have survived and flourished there.

Verona's interest soon became apparent. Atholl was often in Verona because of the opera connection, and he spoke to the club. They had a vacancy for an overseas player because Preben Elkjaer was leaving. Although Verona were not a big club, they had been champions, but it didn't work out with them. The situation was complicated by the fact that Watford would make more money by selling me to an English club. If I had gone to Italy, the transfer fee would have been set at ten times my Watford salary, which was £30,000 a year in 1987. The fee would have been well within the Uefa maximum of £450,000 but Watford sought far more than that.

France seemed a possible destination. Monaco attracted me for the Mediterranean lifestyle and their way of playing. If I had gone to Monaco, I would have looked on the transfer as a stepping-stone towards Italy. The network in Europe is well-established. On the Continent, coaches from different countries move around, like the Czechs working in Italy. They have a general knowledge of players throughout Europe. A player may be transferred from a small club like Nancy to AC Milan, the equivalent of leaving Stockport County for Bayern Munich. It just wouldn't happen here. Such moves occur in Europe because of the network. Switching from Monaco to Juventus would have been easier than moving from Watford to Juventus or even from Manchester United to Juventus. When I watch continental matches on Eurosport, I wonder where clubs get these unknown players from but Italy's top clubs are aware of all the promising players in Europe, not just those at the famous clubs. English football remains far too insular. Even the overseas players at Premier League clubs tend to be those who have played for big *Serie A* clubs, those we have heard of, although there are exceptions such as Horacio Carbonari at Derby County. At Arsenal, Arsène Wenger knows the Continent's smaller clubs and lesser-known names. Few people had heard of Nicolas Anelka, Emmanuel Petit or Patrick Vieira when Arsenal signed them. Wenger was part of the European network.

Arsenal were actually interested in me in 1987. Highbury's manager, George Graham, thought about it. Tottenham Hotspur were apparently keen as well. London's lure would have been considerable if Arsenal had pushed. I had never been north of Birmingham before, apart from on a coach travelling to matches. The thought of moving to a new city frightened me. But as the season wore on, it looked increasingly like my destination was to be Manchester United or Liverpool. Alex Ferguson was very eager to sign me but he had just bought Jesper Olsen, a left-winger. I'm not sure I would have gone to Old Trafford anyway. Things weren't going particularly well for Ferguson. United in the 1980s presented a far less attractive proposition than the United of the 1990s. Liverpool seemed the best bet.

Deep down, I knew I needed to escape the capital. Londoners

are so blinkered. Insularity claimed me for a time. The north-south divide may be imaginary but, believe me, moving to Liverpool seemed like voyaging to the Outer Hebrides. Quitting London forced me to appreciate that life exists north of Birmingham. Breaking out from London's narrow-mindedness has given me more humility, the greatest quality a man can have. I remember a kid from Runcorn enrolled at our school in Marylebone. Everyone took the mickey out of him – 'Here's the thick northerner', 'where's your cloth cap?' I was never as cruel to him as some but I did become aware of my southern attitude. 'I'm from London,' I told myself, 'so I'm better than people from up north. Never mind Manchester United and Liverpool having good football teams, haven't they all got funny accents? And do they have running water and electricity?' Such bias coloured my outlook until I was exposed to life in a northern town. My London friends, Lofty, Tony, Anthony and Lenny, love coming up to Liverpool, which they prefer to London. 'It's so much friendlier,' they say. Northerners are generally more open than southerners. I hate the attitude of Londoners to northerners. 'It must be a nightmare living up there,' is the normal comment I get from people who live in the capital. Such partiality would have remained in me if I had stayed south. London will never again be my base. It's lovely to visit, and I enjoyed my time at Charlton Athletic, but I will end up in the north-west, as close to Liverpool as possible.

Anfield beckoned in June 1987. After Graham left for Villa, Dave Bassett was appointed Watford manager. I went over to Dave's house to discuss the situation.

'Is there any point trying to dissuade you from leaving?' Dave asked.

'No,' I replied. 'I'm definitely going.' Our meeting was pretty short. Graham's exit and Dave's arrival were never going to affect my decision to seek pastures new.

The new season was still some way distant so I never felt there was any rush. Then Liverpool indicated they might not sign me. I told them I wanted more time but they set a deadline of 8 June. On 3 June, the *Liverpool Echo* printed a quote from me saying, 'If I cannot go abroad, I would prefer to stay in London with a club like Arsenal or Spurs and I simply cannot believe they are not interested in signing me.' Liverpool were understandably upset – I was livid. I never said anything like that. Those sentiments are far too boastful to belong to me. Newspapers overflowed with talk of me going to Arsenal but that was all it was – talk. Apart from Liverpool, my only other interest lay in Italy, although I do not know what would have happened if Arsenal had come in strong. Emlyn Hughes, the former Liverpool captain, lambasted me in the press, asking who did I think I was to snub Liverpool. Hughes insisted that Liverpool should not sign me anyway because I was not good enough to play for them. By saying that, Hughes was actually attacking the club's judgement, but then Emlyn always could be relied on to give the newspapers a good quote. I was still disappointed in him.

All I was doing was keeping my options open. I signed for Liverpool in early June, not two weeks before the season starts as happens normally. I spoke to Kenny Dalglish, Liverpool's manager, and Peter Robinson, then secretary, and said, 'I'll come up.' We met at the M6 Sandbach services near Crewe on 9 June and I followed the Liverpool contingent up to Anfield to sign for £900,000.

Deceived by their newspapers, Liverpool people thought I did not want to come to Anfield and that I was using the club they love to engineer a move to Italy or Arsenal. Kenny realised that and said to me, 'Let's nail this concern immediately.' At the press conference, Kenny said, 'We can assure the public that John wasn't using Liverpool as a makeweight in any other negotiations.' Kenny made the whole transfer sound very amicable, as though there had never been a problem between the two sides. Kenny knows the value of team spirit and he understands how it can be affected by the attitude of the fans. That is why he is very guarded in what he says publicly about players. Kenny does not want to upset a player and, equally importantly, he would hate fans to berate someone because the manager has just said he was crap. My respect for a manager would ebb if I was booed following remarks he made about me. Kenny kept everyone together, the board, the fans and the players.

Although Dalglish really impressed me, I signed for Liverpool, not for Kenny Dalglish. Everton had just won the championship but Liverpool were the biggest club in England. Why should a footballer sign for a manager, however much he respected him, when the manager could leave? Liverpool were the ones who paid me, not Kenny. My loyalty lay with them, not the manager. The Dalglish legend carried less weight with me than it did with others who signed for Liverpool. I grew up admiring Graham Taylor, so I never believed greatness as a player was a pre-requisite for greatness as a manager. Graham was not a good footballer. Even taking into account that he was forty, Graham was by far the worst at five-a-sides at Watford. When I watched a forty-year-old Kenny Dalglish in five-a-sides, it was obvious he had been an outstanding player. But Graham was fantastic as a manager. Many people think chairmen should appoint former famous players as managers in order to entice current players to sign, but I don't agree. Kenny was a fabulous manager but it was coincidental that he had also been a fabulous footballer.

At the press conference, I was also honest and upfront. 'When it became obvious I wasn't going to Europe there was only one club in England for me,' I told the media, 'and that was Liverpool.' My yearning for Italy was so well-documented that I could hardly duck the issue. Liverpool fans would have laughed at me if I blithely insisted Juventus and AC Milan were never in my prayers. Just to end any local tension over the saga of my signing, I talked to as many Liverpool fans as possible. Four days after the press conference, I came out of Anfield to find hundreds of supporters queuing for season-tickets. Here was the ideal opportunity for a good chat, to clear the air and bury any festering grievances.

'I have always admired Liverpool,' I told them. 'When we used to come here with Watford, we always felt a real thrill at playing at Anfield. Hearing the Kop was always special, even though they were behind the other team.' Liverpool put me up in a city-centre hotel, the Moat House, a centre for the local community. I quickly got to know lots of people. One night, an Evertonian had a go at me in the bar. 'You'll never last here,' he said. I walked over, introduced myself and we ended up getting on fine. After the extended negotiations, it was important to break down the barriers with the people of Liverpool, red or blue.

Signing for Liverpool proved an emotional, exciting period. Vicarage Road was a very comforting, secure environment. People say I was the greatest player in Watford's history but Graham Taylor gave me the stage. The finality of leaving got to me. I wished I could have said goodbye properly, although I did pop back pre-season. While naturally sad, I also felt the thrill of anticipation. Liverpool stood for everything Watford didn't. The Liverpools of this world had inspired me because Watford were the underdogs. We used to love trying to put one over Liverpool. I think that's why Liverpool pursued me because I always played well against them, often scoring. Kenny recalled one game when I beat Alan Hansen to score. After that match, Kenny said to Alan, 'We'll sign that John Barnes.' On one occasion, I man-marked John Wark but often I played centre-forward against Liverpool. Ian Rush was leaving for Juventus and I was completely convinced Kenny bought me to partner John Aldridge upfront.

'Kenny,' I asked shortly after signing, 'where will I be playing?' Without a second's pause, Kenny replied, 'Left wing.' Kenny knew that Peter Beardsley, a clever, skilful support striker, would soon be joining. I had thought my left-wing days were over.

Many pundits and punters questioned whether I was suited to Liverpool's style. In the true English tradition of pigeonholing, people laboured under the misconception that I was a precocious, left-footed winger obsessed only with dribbling and crossing whereas Liverpool's hallmark was passing and moving. Spurs full-back, Chris Hughton, insisted I would not be consistent enough for Liverpool. Hughton unfairly judged me on my final season for an increasingly erratic Watford, which masked my overall consistency at Vicarage Road. My record at Watford was not one of a dribbling dilettante. I became the only player in Watford's history to reach double figures for goals every season for six years, predominantly from a left-wing position.

Still this belief persisted that John Barnes and Liverpool was a marriage doomed to failure. Sceptics insisted that Watford were poles apart tactically and philosophically from Liverpool. At Anfield, the game revolved around passing and patience whereas at Watford, it had been hurry, hurry, chase, chase, cross, cross. As I travelled to training at Melwood for the first time, I wondered if I was going to fit in. But Liverpool were evolving under Kenny, a strong-minded manager imposing his own playing patterns after Bob Paisley and Joe Fagan. Kenny recruited Peter Beardsley who, technically speaking, was not from the Liverpool mould. Peter played off the front man, in a similar way to Kenny himself, but was far more of a dribbler than Kenny, more flamboyant.

As training started, I kept expecting some kind of initiation into the mystique of Liverpool playing. Liverpool's secret training methods were part of football's folklore; no one knew what they were but everyone was convinced they existed. Me too; I waited for the blindfold, for the silver goblet to be pressed against my lips and for the order to drink blood to confirm my ordination into the Anfield brotherhood. There was no ceremony, no intrigue. Liverpool's way involved five-a-sides, messing around, going out and getting drunk. 'What the hell is this?' I thought. 'How can they be so relaxed compared with Watford?' But Liverpool trained properly and I took to it from the first day. I looked around Melwood, at the other players and saw what training entailed. 'This is where I belong,' I told myself.

Liverpool practised small-sided games every day and it was high-intensity stuff. We used to do a very light warm-up, jog around the field a couple of times to loosen the limbs, do a few stretches, put the cones down for goals and then go into five-a-side or eight-a-side. We played twenty minutes of that, had a few sprints and more small-sided practice.

'That was interesting, what are we going to do tomorrow?' I asked the other players after my first day.

'Same again,' they chorused and headed for home.

So I went back to the Moat House, returned the next day and

went through exactly the same routine of gentle warm-up and five-a-sides. It was the same every day, every single day. There was no tactical work, none whatsoever. All the strategic stuff was done within the small-sided games. Liverpool believed that everything we faced in five-a-sides would be encountered again on match day. That was why the five-a-sides were so competitive. No one ever cheated. No one ever attempted a one-two without being prepared to make the run. No one ever thought this was only training and they were not going to track back. At some clubs, players often do not try in training. If someone went past them, it was not the end of the world. That never happened at Melwood. Every player treated five-a-sides as if they were Cup finals on a small pitch. Liverpool's training characterised Liverpool's play – uncomplicated but devastatingly effective.

Practising on smaller pitches, Liverpool were always going to play a short-passing game. We only trained with small goals so there was little long-range shooting. We passed the ball until we got close enough to score. The philosophy centred on passing, making angles and one-touch football. Echoes of my Jamaican scrimmage days abounded. After training, the players would occasionally practise crossing and shooting, primarily so John Aldridge could hone his finishing. If there was any secret to Liverpool's success it lay in the fact that the fixation with five-a-sides gave us an extra edge on match days. Bigger pitches and goals made us feel we had more room. Our build-up play didn't need to be quite so precise to get the ball to the box or out wide where someone would put in a cross to Aldridge, whom we knew would score.

Liverpool's training was more effective than anyone else's. Some training grounds resemble motorways with so many cones dotted across them. Players run around performing lots of different exercises and functions, but when do such situations occur in a match? Coaches are praised for coming up with new ideas, but at Liverpool, the most successful club of that era, training was a celebration of simplicity.

In the late 1980s, Liverpool and, to a lesser extent, Norwich City were the closest England had to a continental team. As an attacker, Liverpool's approach was marvellous because my team-mates passed to me, even if someone was in close attendance. English teams are often nervous about doing that. At Liverpool, each player exuded confidence in the sureness of his own touch and happily received the ball under pressure. Small-sided games sharpened the touch. Liverpool made me a more complete player. On Watford's stage, I was a method actor – get the ball, run for the line and cross, and repeat. I rarely received the ball in a deep position because I hardly ever dropped back there. With Liverpool, I could be standing deep and someone would pass the ball and I would have to deal with it. Lumping the ball forward was forbidden. Possession was to be cherished. So I anticipated the incoming ball and prepared myself positionally earlier and better. Liverpool's doctrine would help any ball-player. I began to pass more than dribble.

Everything was simple at Liverpool. Some re-development work has changed Melwood slightly but it remains pretty basic. It doesn't bear comparison with some of the sumptuous Italian training grounds like Inter Milan's Appiano Gentile. When I arrived, it even lacked dressing-rooms so we used to change at Anfield and were taken on by coach. It surprised me how rudimentary it was. That was typical Liverpool; all they were worried about was the football. Coming from Watford, which was so organised with a really close community relationship with the fans, it all seemed so different. Anfield's code was essentially: 'Run on the pitch and win.' Success was all that mattered. When Liverpool won the League, the players received their medals together with a note of when to report for pre-season training and another venture. The moment a trophy was lifted, it became history, to be forgotten about. Liverpool always expected to win but they never allowed anyone to dwell on it. Complacency was anathema at Anfield. Every season started with a clean slate and that kept players as keen to win as ever. It encapsulated Liverpool's ethos that one of the poorest pitches at Melwood, where the manager and coaches used to conduct their occasional messing-about matches against the kids, was called Wembley. That was Liverpool's aim – the pursuit of excellence.

'am i black
or something?'

Racist abuse stained my life even before I moved to Merseyside. Walking home from school, in one of the better areas of London, kids shouted 'black bastard' at me. The situation in the East End was far worse. At Watford, opposing fans from countless clubs but particularly Millwall, West Ham and Chelsea, showered me with spit and abuse. Banana after banana came flying from the terrace throngs towards me; hundreds of them. Of the away grounds, Upton Park was the worst. If I tried to make a joke about the bananas, the West Ham fans intensified their abuse. On the field, so many white players called me 'black bastard' that I developed an immunity to it. Racism never hurt me. Never. Insults and dirty kicks were the only way opponents felt they could intimidate me. I never reacted. The moment I examined why they vilified me as a 'black bastard', I realised the abuser was either ignorant or trying to wind me up, both very good reasons for ignoring them. I thought about my father and knew he would never react; most intelligent people wouldn't.

Encountering such racism actually gave me a sense of superiority. These foul-mouthed yobs were obviously thick and lacked any inkling of what they were talking about. When Watford visited Upton Park, West Ham fans cheered their black player, Bobby Barnes, while tossing bananas at me. Find the logic there! Racists are inherently sad people so it is best to overlook them. If I was racially abused by someone I respected intellectually, that would pain me.

My philosophy is to treat racists with the contempt they deserve, to ignore them or laugh about the situation. Neither of these approaches endear me to the black community, who still call me an Uncle Tom. 'John, you hide behind a joke too easily,' they chide me. But pandering to the black community by lashing out or labelling opponents racist is simply not me. Revenge does not feature in my psyche, even if an opponent racially taunted me. The black community loves how Ian Wright reacts, the way he flings out a fist or mouths off. That's fine for Ian Wright but not for me. I'm different.

Even with my experiences in London, Merseyside still represented a shock. I did not know any black people in Liverpool. I did not know any black people who had even been to Liverpool, except one. Howard Gayle had been Liverpool's only black footballer before me so I phoned him. We chatted about life on Merseyside but Howard's experience was inevitably tainted by him not being particularly successful at Anfield. So fans heckled him.

When I arrived at Anfield, racist slogans were daubed on the stadium walls: 'NF', 'White Power', 'No Wogs Allowed', 'There's No Black In The Union Jack' and 'Liverpool Are White'. I expected it. Evil exists in football as in life generally. I received letters from sad old men apoplectic that blacks should represent Liverpool. 'Liverpool are all-white,' wrote one guy, echoing a general theme. 'You are crap, go back to Africa and swing from the trees.' The letters did not bother me; blacks hear sentiments like that all the time. The writers' comments were such nonsense, their spelling and grammar so atrocious, their ignorance so palpable that I passed the letters around after training. All the players laughed on reading them just imagining the type of pathetic people who had written them.

Many of the letters came from outside the Liverpool area, which hardened my conviction that it was just the usual racists seeking to stir up trouble. Redhill, Surrey was one of the postmarks. I learned subsequently that these were only a small percentage of the racist letters written about me. Liverpool received many more. The club were more concerned about my attitude towards the letters than I was. Liverpool held back most of them and did not tell me about them, worrying I would be upset.

From written to verbal taunts, graffiti to bananas, racism was something I had to deal with on my own. I never mentioned it to the club. What were Liverpool going to do about it? An official statement, declaring 'Racism is wrong; please stop', would have represented a token gesture. Liverpool made some effort but campaigning clubs elicit only the sceptical in me. Black players were racially abused at Anfield before so why were Liverpool reacting now? It was common knowledge that teams with black players encountered racism in England. Liverpool and Everton didn't have many black players. My high-profile move and presence made both clubs decide to clean up their act. The reaction of Anfield and Goodison to the abuse I received may have made people aware of the racism endemic on Merseyside but I cannot believe it changed anything. Campaigns to stamp out racism were simply exercises in political correctness. It achieves nothing to erect notices warning that, 'If there is any racist chanting, you can be ejected from the ground'. Racists may have to stay silent for ninety minutes, but they remain racist. Such signs could worsen matters by driving it underground. Just because the public suddenly do not hear racist remarks does not mean racism has been eradicated. Society is too racist for the intolerance to disappear simply through a few pamphlets pleading with fans to stop calling John Barnes a nigger. Before racism can be tackled in football, rugby or cricket it has to be addressed in society.

Kenny Dalglish spoke out against the racists. 'At Liverpool, we are not concerned with race, creed or the colour of a person's skin,' he said, although I never discussed the situation with him. For me, the solution was simple – deliver on the pitch to make the fans love me. The Kop would have slaughtered me with racial abuse if I had faltered on the field. I knew that. Imagine a black player at a high-profile club like Liverpool playing badly. What a target I would have been. The Kop treated out-of-form white players cruelly so they would have crucified a struggling black. A bad aura already clung to me because Liverpool fans believed I only came because Arsenal did not step in. Had I played badly, it would have been hell for me. Pure hell.

A black man who supported Everton, which a lot of black guys do, once made a really poignant comment to me. He was out of work and living on the streets when I bumped into him.

'I'm an Everton supporter,' he said.

'Do you go to Goodison?' I asked.

'I will go to Everton only when they sign an ordinary black player,' he replied. His observation was so true. If Everton or Liverpool buy an ordinary white player, it's no big deal. But for a black player to go to Goodison or Anfield, traditionally racist venues, he has to be special.

My assimilation into Anfield was eased by the Kop being closed for the first three games of the season due to a sewage problem. If my Liverpool debut had taken place at Anfield, I would have been booed and that could have affected me. But by the time I ran out in front of the Kop for the first time, it was all smiles. I was playing well away from home, Anfield's anticipation levels had risen fast and all of a sudden I was a hero, the fans' new darling. I was fairly circumspect about all the adulation, about all the cries of 'we love you, we love you'. Liverpool's fans did not love John Barnes, the person. They worshipped John Barnes, the No. 10 who plays for Liverpool. The same supporters would have abused me if I had failed to settle in so spectacularly. Anfield's first sight of me came against Oxford United. We won 2–0, I scored and the fans became hysterical. My opening six months at Anfield were probably my best at Liverpool. This was just as well given that I arrived under a cloud and I was black.

On my first day at Melwood, I sat down with a group of players who had been at Liverpool for ages. The tea-lady came over and gave cups to all of them except me. 'What?' I said. 'Am I black or something?' Everyone laughed. As a player, I said it all the time. If we were having keep-ball in training, and no one passed to me, I shouted, 'What? Am I black or something?' It's just a fun thing to say but they all passed to me really quickly! When people asked what my nickname was, I replied, 'Digger. That's Digger with a D.' I make tongue-in-cheek comments just to gauge people's reactions. Dressing-rooms are rife with humour and many of the jokes are racist. Newcastle United's players used to say about Shay Given that 'he's Irish, he's thick'. When I inquired 'am I black or something?' it was because I wanted people to understand I am comfortable with it. If other players wanted to make racist jokes, I was fine about that. Banning Bernard Manning would be daft; some of his jokes are very amusing. I know blacks who find Bernard Manning funny. They would never admit as much in public but they watch Bernard Manning at home. And why not? Eddie Murphy and Richard Pryor get away with the type of jokes about whites that white comedians would never be allowed to tell about blacks.

Racism should be laughed at. In my first season at Liverpool, I attended the team's Christmas fancy-dress party as a Ku Klux Klansman. I originally intended going as a banana but I could not find a banana suit anywhere on Merseyside. My KKK impersonation angered many blacks. 'It's no laughing matter,' they shouted at me. 'Look what the KKK did to black people.' I replied, 'The Ku Klux Klan should be laughed at.' My family found the thought of me dressing up as a Klansman terribly funny. Black people's senstivities confused me. How many people go to fancy-dress parties as Adolf Hitler? Loads. Do the Jews burst into tears? Do they say 'how disgraceful'? No. If a Jewish footballer went to Liverpool's Christmas party as Adolf Hitler, it would be taken as a joke. It saddens me that some people lack an appreciation of humour and history. Initially, the Ku Klux Klan were heroes, even being looked upon as knights; burning blacks came later.

My first experience of mass racism occurred on 28 October 1987 when Everton visited Anfield in the Littlewoods Cup. Everton fans spat at me, threw bananas and chanted 'Niggerpool, Niggerpool, Niggerpool' and 'Everton are white'. Evertonians apologised afterwards but the abuse never concerned me. Even if the whole crowd, including Liverpool supporters, had made monkey noises it would not have affected me in the slightest. Fans are fickle; if I had been playing for Everton, and doing well, their fans would not have been throwing bananas and spitting at me. Liverpool's would.

Four days later, Everton and Liverpool were thrown together on league duty again at Anfield. Philip Carter, the Everton and Football League chairman, appealed for restraint from his fans, calling their behaviour towards me 'deplorable'. Carter described his fans as 'scum' but they were scum before that derby match. Everyone but me made a big deal about the situation. I was completely phlegmatic about it because I have great self-belief. These were ignorant people so why should I get upset? I wasn't really interested in the debate going on, in what Carter said. Maybe if the abuse materialised on the pitch, if it had been Gary Stevens heckling me, it would have been different. Carter's campaign made no impact. Everton's fans abused me relentlessly again. Many wore badges that read 'Everton Are White – Defend The Race'. They pelted me with bananas again. 'The local fruit and veg shops must be doing well,' I told the press afterwards. My stance was to belittle the whole situation. The racists wanted me to make a fuss, to show hurt. I refused.

My wife, Suzy, was present at Anfield with our first son Jamie and she was incensed. Jamie, who was only four, kept turning round to the Everton fans who were booing me. 'Stop it, stop it,' Jamie shouted at them. Jamie and Suzy were really upset. I explained how small-minded my abusers were and how important it was to ignore them. The situation was probably harder on Suzy. She doesn't understand racism because she has never had to deal with it. Suzy's white so she doesn't come into contact with it. She very rarely goes to games and when we are out together, I am never racially abused. I am 'John Barnes, the Famous Footballer' and everybody loves me so I don't often encounter racism outside grounds. If I walk down the street in the most racist area, people will say, 'Oh, there's John Barnes.' When I've walked by, they probably add, 'black bastard.' They tolerate me for what I am, not who I am.

I never talk to Suzy about the racism blacks are subjected to. Being black, I have to think about it deeply; Suzy, being white, does not. So we skim over the subject. In the players' lounge after a match at Liverpool, Suzy would say, 'It's terrible how people shout those things at you.' I would nod my head and reply, 'Yeah, it was terrible, they are idiots. Now, let's go and get something to eat.' After all the campaigning in Liverpool, Suzy probably believes racism has gone away. But the taunts will happen at Hartlepool, Huddersfield or other grounds. I talk to my four children about it because they are half-black and they will encounter intolerance in life.

The bananas kept coming. On 21 February, I backheeled a banana off the pitch in the second half of our FA Cup fifth-round tie at Everton, a game televised live to seven million people. Philip Carter had again appealed for good behaviour from the Everton fans to little avail. However, when Liverpool and Everton met for the fourth and final time that season, in the League on 20 March at Goodison, there was little racism. Maybe people were embarrassed by the sight of so many bananas during the televised game in February; maybe they became bored; maybe my refusal to respond stopped them trying. It was certainly nothing to do with any campaigning by the clubs. It saddened me that it took so ridiculously long for the people of Merseyside to recognise such a shameful situation. Because of those televised games, the public became aware of the racism running through English football and society, but nothing was done to change the situation. The Everton fans who had desisted from throwing bananas were still racists who wanted to throw bananas. If they had an opportunity to give a black man a job, they would still turn him down because of his colour. Society remains racist.

The English have always perceived me as a black footballer rather than a footballer. White people still say, 'John Barnes is all right, he appears intelligent on television, but what about that dreadlocked layabout who works down the corner shop? I don't trust him.

Whites' attitude towards me may have changed since I became successful, but not towards black people generally. Only when everyone can accept the lowest-of-the-low black person will the situation have improved. It's easy to love John Barnes, but people must love the black guy without the fame, money or special skill. 'I'm not racist,' white footballers say to me. 'I've got lots of black friends.' Fine. But they still worry about the black guy who passes them on the street with his hood up. White team-mates came with me to black nightclubs and they felt fine because they were with me, Les Ferdinand or Ian Wright.

'It's the other blacks in here who worry me,' they said.

'You know that club I went to with you? I replied. 'They were all white people in there. Should I have felt uncomfortable?'

'No, of course not,' they countered.

'But why?'

'Because they were all right, weren't they?' they replied. White footballers mix irrationality with a touch of racism.

Occasionally Liverpool players called an opponent a 'black bastard'. I would pull them up on it.

'Oh, John,' they said, 'we don't really mean it, it's just something we say. You shouldn't get upset. Black people call us white bastards but we don't get upset.'

'Why not? If a black person is insulted, why aren't you if he calls you a white bastard?'

Their attitude was that because there is nothing wrong with being white, how could they be insulted by having it brought to their attention that they are white? My logic was irrefutable but I wouldn't push the argument too much. Dressing-rooms are not the best place for heavy debates.

Kenny Dalglish was once doing some tactical work with us on a magnetic board covered in little figures at Melwood. All the figures were red except for one black one. 'This one is you, Digger,' Kenny said pointing at the black one. Kenny was being tongue-in-cheek but many people are racists. Racism exists at Anfield, Old Trafford and everywhere because racism permeates English life. Players and managers have their beliefs formed in society, not in football. Players will not call me 'black bastard' to my face but it does not stop them being racist. The press are similar. Some of the comments written about me, calling me 'Black Pearl' or describing how 'Sambo samba'd down the wing', reveal racist propensities. When a reporter says a black player had a bad game, his readers do not think the journalist is being racist because he criticises white players as well. But some reporters make conscious criticism of black players.

Towards the end of that 1987–88 season, Liverpool went to Norwich City without me. I was injured. As the Norwich players ran out at Carrow Road, Liverpool fans booed Ruel Fox. When I heard about it I was hardly surprised. Football fans are like that. Black players are used to it. I rarely discuss racism with other black people in football. Everytime I meet Les Ferdinand or Ian Wright it's at some nightclub where there's a fund-raising event going on. We swap chit-chat but the music is always too loud to enjoy a proper conversation. Each of us knows the reality of being a black person in a white country.

When the report into the Stephen Lawrence murder was published in 1999, I was playing for Charlton Athletic. Every day as I drove through Eltham to Charlton's training ground I passed the spot where Stephen was killed. Even after all that time, flowers were still being placed on the spot. People used to say to me, 'Be careful when you go out around here.' But what happened to Stephen Lawrence could have happened anywhere in London. Eltham isn't much worse than anywhere else.

Overt or covert, racism is rife in England. If a black woman requests flesh-coloured tights in a department store, she will be given those for a white woman. The *Daily Mirror* conducted some tests to find the most beautiful people in the world. The paper's conclusion? Leonardo Di Caprio and Catherine Deneuve. Such embodiments of whiteness represent what the *Mirror* thinks its readers want to look like. But what about the billion Chinese? Or hundreds of millions of blacks? Or Indians? It's so narrow-minded and stereotypical. What does black stand for? Darkness. The contrast is white, Snow White. It's such rubbish.

Racism is part of black people's everyday existence in a white country. At bus-stops, blacks are looked at suspiciously. In restaurants, the attitude of whites towards blacks reveals the intolerance. Almost one hundred per cent of white people harbour subconscious racism within them. It's just a question of degree. 'If you had a daughter,' I asked white team-mates, 'would it make any difference to you whatsoever if she married a black man or a white man? Both are good men, with the same professions and equal love for your daughter.' Not many would honestly choose the black man. 'You would be quite happy having John Barnes living next door,' I would tell them, 'but you would be deeply unhappy if it was some unknown from Toxteth.' Whites prefer to live next to whites which reflects their racist tendencies. Many blacks find this silent racism the worst to deal with, to think that invisible barriers are being erected around them. At least you know what you are up against if the racism is visible or audible, like being the target of verbal abuse, bananas or spit.

Films encapsulate the problem. *Frankie and Johnny* depicts the ordinary lives of two people. Michelle Pfeiffer plays Frankie, a shy waitress, while Johnny is a short-order cook acted by Al Pacino. No film-maker in Britain or Hollywood would ever cast black actors in those roles, which is crazy because so many blacks work as short-order cooks and live in poverty. A black *Frankie and Johnny* would not fit white stereotypes or even black people's view of themselves. Films about ordinary black people do not exist. Black films are invariably like *New Jack City*, detailing the lives of drug dealers, spiced with killing and swearing. Infuriatingly, black people make these films, so reinforcing the myth of black lives. Black directors want to make money-spinners and the quickest, safest route to a box-office bonanza is if their film features Wesley Snipes shooting people. Spike Lee has improved matters by using blacks almost exclusively on his films but he also perpetuates the myth through the stereotypical story-lines. If a film was made with a background of my existence in Jamaica, it would depict a nice middle-class family whose relatives are all doctors and lawyers. Cinema-goers would take one look and say, 'That's not black people's lives. Where's the singing, dancing and shooting?' Rap music also typecasts blacks with lyrics about killing white policemen and other acts of violence.

This stereotyping frightens me. Black role models in England are predominantly sporting. People admire Linford Christie because he runs fast, Lennox Lewis because he boxes hard and Ian Wright and me because we play football well. The concept of black sporting role models is anathema to me. Being an athlete, boxer or footballer will not change perceptions of black people for the simple reason that the common consensus is that blacks are supposed to be good at sport. Only by following the professions will we alter public perceptions, but where are the black doctors and lawyers? Unfortunately, most black kids attend schools where they will never receive the education for that. But blacks must start to believe they can join the professional classes rather than thinking, 'I know I can become a doctor or lawyer but this white society won't let me.' Such suspicion stops them trying. Whites will never welcome blacks with open arms; blacks must seize the initiative. Football's experience should be an encouragement. When I started, black footballers were relatively rare but not now. Currently, a tremendous stigma surrounds Asians in English football but in twenty years' time there will be as many Indian, Pakistani and Bangladeshi footballers as black ones. But for the first few, it will be difficult.

Before I addressed the Oxford Union, I told the organisers I wanted to say something meaningful, to interact with the students and discuss real issues. I entered the great hall at this famous seat of learning, where some of the nation's most perceptive minds were gathered, and the interaction began. The first question was, 'When you scored that goal in Brazil, what was it like?' I was astounded. I struggled to contain my frustration and irritation as the questions continued in similar vein. I wanted to discuss meatier subjects than football. I do have views beyond sport. It was so depressing. I drove away from the Oxford Union wondering how I could destroy this typecasting. Television gives me a possible avenue but my current involvement extends only to delivering studio sound-bites on football matches. Besides I want to try management first. Hosting a non-sports programme would be ideal one day, although I would avoid light entertainment. I love Ian Wright's chat-show; that format suits Wrighty's bubbly character. It wouldn't do for me, although people would accept it, I'm sure, because I'm black, I can dance, I've got rhythm and I can talk like a real Jamaican. But I have had enough stereotyping.

When Liverpool went to South Africa in 1995, just as the handover to the ANC was going ahead, Granada TV asked me to do a documentary on my experiences there. We were going to play some exhibition matches, do a bit of coaching and relax. The Granada producer, an exuberant guy called Rob McCaffrey, now with Sky Sports, kept pushing.

'You can't relax', he said, 'we've got to go and see people for the documentary.'

'Rob, leave me alone,' I replied, trying to grab a few minutes by the hotel pool. But he insisted and eventually I relented.

I'm glad Rob badgered me. We had a fascinating time. We went to see F.W. De Klerk, whom I interviewed for ten minutes. It was all very formal, a real contrast to my meeting with Nelson Mandela. I first talked to Mandela, admittedly very briefly, when he came into the dressing-room before one of Liverpool's games in Johannesburg. Rob heard about it.

'You have to interview him,' he said. 'Let's get a message through to him and see whether he will do it.'

Mandela sent a message back saying to come over to his house. So Rob, two white South African cameramen and I climbed into Rob's hire-car and headed off to the white suburb of Johannesburg where Mandela lived. We had the address but no directions so we drove around for a few minutes. We saw a black guy by the side of the road and one of the South African cameramen leant out of the window to ask the way.

'Excuse me, do you know where Nelson Mandela lives?'

'No, I don't know,' the black guy said nervously, scuttling off. We drove very slowly alongside him and attempted to ask again. Suddenly, he looked in the back of the car and saw me. He stopped walking and tapped on the window.

'John Barnes? You play for Liverpool?' he asked.

'Yes,' I replied.

'You want Nelson Mandela? Turn second right down there, first left and it's the house three hundred yards along on the left.'

I could understand his earlier reticence. If white guys asked where Nelson Mandela lived, you said you didn't know. Even though South Africa's political landscape was changing, old habits died hard.

We pulled up outside Mandela's house and the man himself let us in. He made coffee and we did the interview. We talked only briefly about football. I don't know if Mandela is a football fan. He is a people fan. When you have been on Robben Island for twenty odd years, you get out of touch with football. I think Mandela is more into boxing. Of his many qualities that became apparent during the two hours I spent with him, the most shining was his humility. When Mandela reflected on the ANC movement, he was so self-effacing, talking of his sadness that greater men than him had not survived the struggle against apartheid. I have never been in awe of anyone. I love Pele but I cannot understand why anyone would want to collect his autograph. Pele is flesh and blood like the rest of us. But I was in awe of Mandela because of his unbelievable humility. The whole visit proved an eye-opening experience for me and made a great programme.

I really enjoyed doing that documentary. It would be fascinating to host a general discussion programme one day. I would debate everything from unemployment to footballers being overpaid when nurses deserve more. The show would challenge racist attitudes. I want to change black people's ideas and to do that they have to understand they are wrong as well as whites. No black person on television would dare say that. They just stress that the white man committed unspeakable crimes against blacks. I would address the issue far more objectively. I am not the type to seek kudos with the black fraternity by saying, 'Look at the racism directed at me, the bananas and abuse, let's fight against the white man.' That's rubbish.

Black people tell me, 'I'm proud to be black.' Well, I'm proud of myself and I happen to be black. What pride can there be in simply emerging from my mother's womb and being black? I derive my pride from my achievements and the successes of black people. When I ask, 'Why are you proud to be black?' they call me 'Uncle Tom'. 'It's up to whites to change their attitude because we are not in the wrong,' I hear them say. But who is suffering? We are. Whites are not going to change. They have the best deal in life.

People, black and white, need re-educating. Whites do not understand their racism evolved from slavery, which itself was not about prejudice but economics. The cheapest form of labour was black. Slavery stemmed from greed not enmity. The result, though, was that blacks became second-class citizens. Blacks also need to take another look at slavery. They need to appreciate that their forefathers were sold into slavery by their own kind. Most blacks believe all slaves were caught by whites, but ninety-five per cent of them were sold by their own people. West Africa's coastline was dotted with black kingdoms where the English, Portuguese and Spanish traders could not land without permission. They had to offer guns and money to buy the slaves. When I hear the misguided mantra that 'we hate whites because they enslaved us', I have to respond. 'White people didn't enslave you,' I tell them. 'Your own people enslaved you. If you hate the people who sold you into slavery, you have to hate your own black people.' Blacks do not want to listen to that.

Improved education and integration are the only serious means of overcoming racism. It is too late for a forty-year-old racist to change, but his son might. It is too late for a forty-year-old black man who hates whites because he thinks they enslaved his forefathers, but it's not too late for his son. At school, my sons learn about other communities, about Indians, Muslims, Hindus and Jews, about their culture and history. History must be seen from different perspectives; received wisdom is often false. I grew up indoctrinated by television about cowboys and Indians. I loved the stories of ten brave cowboys defying two thousand redskin savages. If I had known the real history of how the cowboys had persecuted the Indians, my views would have changed. Historians are now acknowledging that the English and Americans protected many Nazis after the Second World War because they feared Communism spreading across Europe.

It seems to me that lessons encouraging toleration should become part of the national curriculum. If one child of racist parents emerges from the school system saying they may not accept blacks but will tolerate them, it will have been worthwhile. We need to teach tolerance towards all ethnic minorities. Intolerance stems from ignorance. I tell my sons, 'Don't go on about the boy at school who wears cloth wrapped around his head. You should try to understand why he wears a turban.' They must learn. Music can help us become more multi-cultural and tolerant. White teenagers are into black culture. The music of George Michael and All Saints is essentially black. Integration is vital. Most blacks on Merseyside generally live in Toxteth because they face racial abuse outside it. So they stay in Toxteth and the vicious circle continues. Life will be tough for the first black people who decide to leave Toxteth, but someone has to break the chain.

England should take its lead from America, which is far more advanced in terms of integration. Black businessmen, doctors and lawyers proliferate. American culture is money-based so people can get on, become established and accepted, although America is as racist as England, if not more. England's class structure accentuates a suspicion of those who rise above a modest background; ambitious blacks encounter a wall of intolerance.

I draw massive inspiration from Martin Luther King and his non-violent protests in the United States. If Martin Luther King had raised a fist, he would never have achieved anything. Whites would have said, 'We told you so. Black people are just violent anyway, look at them.' Martin Luther King's intelligent approach ensured black people were seen to be non-violent. Malcolm X's more militant stance did some good but it was Martin Luther King who encouraged America on the path towards integration. Gandhi was the same in the 1940s with his non-violent protests. Change can be achieved only through such sane, unprovocative means.

chapter ten

dna

D espite encountering bananas and verbal abuse on Merseyside, Liverpool proved to be the perfect club for me. Great sides such as Liverpool in the seventies and eighties possessed what I call a DNA, an instantly recognisable shape that was unique to them. From my first day at Melwood, I appreciated Liverpool's special DNA. I quickly gathered that I would be dribbling less but seeing more of the ball. Anfield's emphasis was on passing the ball and keeping moves simple. Players fitted into the Liverpool way while giving it an added dimension. Before I arrived, Liverpool's DNA was formed by Sammy Lee and Ray Kennedy flanking Jimmy Case and Graeme Souness. Sammy and Ray were passers, wide midfielders rather than wingers. Rather than playing as a centre-forward in a wide position, Ray, formerly an attacker with Arsenal, changed to fit in with Liverpool's DNA. Although I was more of a winger than Ray, I played the wide position the Liverpool way, the running and passing way.

If I had joined Manchester United instead of Liverpool, I would have operated more as an out-and-out winger to dovetail with their DNA structure. Alex Ferguson has developed a very strong and obvious DNA at Old Trafford built on a back four, with David

Beckham and Ryan Giggs on the wings, Roy Keane and Nicky Butt or Paul Scholes in the middle, with a split attack of one up and one off, like Andy Cole and Eric Cantona or, more recently, Cole and Dwight Yorke. Whatever happens, whether Jesper Blomqvist replaces Giggs or Wes Brown steps in for Gary Neville, United's DNA remains constant.

Dominating world football have been those teams with the strongest DNAs – Brazil in 1970, Germany and Holland in 1974 and Argentina in 1978, 1986 and 1990 when they reached the World Cup final with Diego Maradona not at his best. Argentina's Italia '90 side lacked the flair of the World Cup-winners from four years earlier. They progressed because they had a structure. Italy made the Pasadena World Cup final in 1994 with a team which, for them, were relatively ordinary. Italy were not technically sensational but they had a structure. Each Italian understood the job expected of him and the importance of keeping the team's shape. Although Italy failed to overcome Brazil in California, simply getting there was an achievement.

In England, some club sides have structures which allow them to punch above their weight. I admire teams like Leicester City, Wimbledon and Derby County, who will never win the Premiership. For one of them to finish eighth, as Derby did in 1998–99, rates better than Newcastle United trailing in thirteenth or Liverpool coming seventh. Liverpool, who once had the most formidable DNA in English club football, do not currently have a structure so I respect them less than Leicester, Wimbledon and Derby. Wimbledon possess a very strong DNA, built around commitment and aggression. Opponents feel they have to fight against Wimbledon, to earn the right to play and beat them. That's a mistake. Teams are never going to outfight Wimbledon. It's derogatory for a manager to say, 'We must stoop to Wimbledon's level.' Teams should stick to their own DNA. Unfortunately, most teams don't have one. They react to situations rather than set the tone through their own style as Liverpool did and Manchester United do now.

When I was at Anfield, Liverpool's coaching staff told me that football is not as simple as I thought, that it's not like chess where one person goes here and the other there. We are all human and people make mistakes. I understand that, but it's important to develop a structure. To continue the chess allusion, managers should be like chess grand masters in having a plan. Imagine Anatoly Karpov and Gary Kasparov playing chess against each other and the crowd shouting 'go on, go on' in exhortation. Neither Karpov nor Kasparov is going to play any quicker. Each works to a plan. Those chess players who don't have plans might respond to the fans' urgings and move a piece rashly. Football is the same.

Footballers are easily bored when being taught, but if being bored means you may win the championship, how hard is that? Players must understand a manager's philosophy. The hard work, the constant repetition on the training ground paid off for Ferguson at United. Drilling the back four was the foundation of Arsenal's success under George Graham. The forwards went off and fooled around while George took the defence who soon become bored to death because they were playing against no one, just shadow-playing. 'Move across here, move across there, do this, do that,' George would shout. Arsenal's defenders might have complained privately but look at them now. Arsenal's DNA is in their blood.

Over the years, Ajax have possessed the strongest DNA, a 3–4–3 system which they play, home and away, whether they are 3–0 down or 3–0 up. Ajax have struggled recently but when they fielded footballers like Patrick Kluivert and Clarence Seedorf, their DNA was particularly powerful. The players were young yet they performed like men because they understood the team pattern. Sadly, I see a lot of footballers who have still to be taught about team structure, aged twenty-eight or twenty-nine.

Ajax's European Cup-winners of 1995 were special because their players were completely in tune with the team's DNA. From a young age, they had been prepared to fit into the team structure. Total football's ethos still holds sway, with Ajax's footballers expected to play in different positions. Kluivert, one of the best centre-forwards in the world, could slot in at right-back. If, for some reason, Kluivert did that during a game, a team-mate knew to move into the vacated centre-forward's area, so Ajax's shape stayed the same. At Liverpool, if Alan Hansen went forward and I played a pass to him and he carried on, I dropped back into his centre-half position. When Stevie Nicol belted upfield, I covered the left-back position. I spent quite a few Liverpool games standing in at centre-back or left-back for three or four minutes. As we normally had possession, I was rarely threatened. My job was to ensure the shape was kept.

Pattern of play is vital; the team must be the star. A classic example of the problem was David Ginola at Tottenham before George Graham arrived in 1998. Ginola was being named man of the match most weeks but Spurs were lurching close to relegation. George organised everyone, got Ginola to play for the team and results improved. A similar situation developed when Kevin Keegan brought Tino Asprilla to Newcastle United in February 1996. Tino delivered amazing individual performances, often scoring, but Newcastle began drawing and losing and eventually surrendered their twelve-point Premiership lead to Manchester United. Newcastle faded because the star of the team became Tino, not the team itself. Tino was not to blame. Tino was just being Tino, playing the game his exotic way. Keegan probably thought Tino would give Newcastle an extra dimension, which I felt they did not need then. Keegan failed to realise that Newcastle were good enough to win the Premiership with the players they had. He clearly felt the grass was greener on the other side, bought Tino and the momentum disappeared. Any stars in my team will not be allowed to operate for themselves only to the detriment of the team. Although I appreciate individuals like Tino and Ginola for their skill, they do not do enough for the team unless pushed. My main priority is to incorporate flair players into a framework. One of the most talented footballers England has ever seen, Paul Gascoigne, can be a good team player if coached and coaxed properly. If a manager gave Gazza his head and said 'do what you want', any structure would crumble. Gifted players still require guiding.

Although I did not admire his chosen style, all of my principles are derived from Graham Taylor's. Graham operated a 4–2–4 system, almost 2–4–4 at times, and everything he did was methodical and organised. My preferred method contrasts with Graham's but the principle of organising, in possession or seeking the ball, remains the same. Graham spent hours, days, weeks and months drilling us on where we should be when the other team had the ball. I lost count of how many practice games we played against imaginary opposition. Graham threw a ball into play and each Watford player immediately assumed his well-rehearsed position. Graham could move the ball five yards away and each player re-adjusted. When Watford held possession, Graham gave the ball to the right-back and shouted, 'What are you going to do?' The right-back would reply, 'I'm going to play it into the channels, Luther Blissett is going to come short, Ross Jenkins is going to run down the channel.'

In Britain, most managers' training sessions involve crossing, shooting or the cross-over run. The manager will work with the full-back and the two centre-forwards, which means the other eight players are just standing around, picking their noses, feeling completely uninvolved. But they will be needed on match-day if the cross-over run is closed down. The best managers work on each player's function or possible contribution to every move. Such practice is monotonous but breeds winners. I was watching a profile on Youri Djorkaeff and the cameras filmed him at Inter Milan's training ground, Appiano Gentile. Inter have a room set aside for studying videos and working on tactics with sketchboards. It looked familiar. Watford adopted the same approach under Graham Taylor. Developing DNA requires three hours' concentration in front of videos and training books; then the manager's plan would be understood. At most British clubs, if players sit down in the meeting room to watch videos or tactics they fall asleep within ten minutes. Most managers relent and pack them off to play five-a-side. I would keep players there for five hours until they appreciated what was necessary.

The very best players, such as Marc Overmars, can switch DNAs.

When Overmars received possession at Ajax, the opposition's full-back and wide-midfielder invariably marked him. Overmars knew what to do. He was brought up to realise if he was being doubled up on, Ajax must have a free man. The free man is always on the other side of the pitch so Overmars passed the ball inside quickly, even going back to Edwin Van Der Sar in goal. Ajax would then whip it out to Finidi George. On joining Arsenal, Overmars again found himself doubled up on. Again he passed the ball inside. But the English reaction was different from the Dutch. Far from praising his team-minded intelligence, critics accused Overmars of not dribbling any more. Because he is so talented, Overmars adjusted and started taking two men on, a move that Ajax coaches would never have encouraged for fear of losing possession. That's why Georgi Kinkladze suffered such a hard time in Holland. Ajax would not stand for Kinkladze dribbling around as he did at Manchester City.

Ajax's admirable DNA ensured possession was retained and attacks directed to where the opposition were undermanned. Teams who utilise their spare man best invariably prevail. Such tactics are particularly pertinent in English football because most teams are one-dimensional. It fills me with dismay to see teams playing a back four when the opposition have only one upfront. In Europe, where man-for-man marking is common, defenders are happy to push into midfield when faced with only only one centre-forward. This intelligent approach reduces the opponents' numerical advantage in midfield. But an English full-back or centre-half stays rooted in his domain, even if an opponent is miles away.

As a footballing breed, the English never treat possession with the reverence it deserves. Possession is almost a dirty word. Liverpool are the best in England at keeping possession, but send them into Europe, against a team like Celta Vigo or real top-quality continental opposition, and Liverpool look ordinary. European teams cherish the ball while the English play pass-the-parcel with it. Fans are mainly to blame. Players can hear the screams from the terraces: 'take a risk', 'take the player on' and 'attack quicker'. Supporters do not worry about gambling with possession because opponents soon return the ball anyway in England. Fans hate seeing English teams being methodical. Gung-ho rules for supporters. Managers must be brave enough to change that thinking, to make fans appreciate that a more cerebral, continental style can work. Fans follow any style of football if it brings success. Introducing a touch of chess to the high-speed Premiership could only be done by a strong manager. His attempts would be crucified initially. He would need to explain his philosophy to fans, using media interviews to outline the team's structure and pattern, rather than slipping into the usual managerial-speak of, 'We had a good game, scored a great goal and the referee was rubbish, blah, blah, blah.'

However strong-willed and respected, no manager will ever change the pace of the game in England which is stuck in the fast-lane. Manchester United have adapted best, bridging England and the Continent. Ferguson's United DNA involves keeping possession at a good pace. A myth has developed that possession does not win matches. That is nonsense. A cursory glance at most games confirms that the team which sees the ball most tends to win. Wimbledon are an exception because time in possession matters less to them. Whilst at Wimbledon, Joe Kinnear defended his long-ball game by arguing that for every twenty goals he saw on *Match of the Day*, fifteen were scored via long balls. Yet situations allowing a long ball to be played only arise because of the possession football played beforehand. Teams wait for the moment, drag opponents out of position before pressing the launch button. Long balls must be used intelligently. Glenn Hoddle was fantastic at it. But a predictable barrage of long balls will just encourage opposing centre-halves to stand on the edge of their box and head the danger away.

Football should learn from other sports' tactical enlightenment. People perceive me to be a footballing creature of instinct but I dis-like off-the-cuff football. We should be moving in well-established patterns like in handball, basketball and rugby league where they defend in particular ways and pass the ball quickly in set plays. Teams have well-developed DNAs in these sports. In football, if a right-back is closed down, his team-mates should spring into set positions as they do in handball. If a handballer is closed down, he and his team-mates swiftly transfer play to the other flank where the spare man waits. The quicker they react, the more time the receiving player has to cross or shoot.

Handball goalkeepers should not stand a chance against shots because the distance is too short. So they make themselves as big as possible by spread-eagling themselves, stretching out their hands and feet in star-jumps. Peter Schmeichel was an outstanding handball keeper back in Denmark and he bought the tricks of that trade into football. Schmeichel's star-jump is a classic handball move. Jan Molby played handball in Denmark, too, and when Peter went to Manchester United, Jan said, 'Just watch Schmeichel keep goal in the handball style. Just watch his star-jump.' Schmeichel's star-jump has proved amazingly effective in one-on-one situations. When I ran at a keeper, I always hoped he would commit himself early and dive at my feet, so I could dink the ball over him. When Schmeichel does his star-jump, he blocks out so much of the target. People suggested that I should slip the ball through his legs but I never had the time to think and there was often a United defender sliding in.

Basketball also provides lessons for football. When the five players defend the basket, they do not mind if an opponent shoots from long range. The shooter would have to be very accurate or risk losing possession. Basketballers are programmed not to permit the drive to the basket through the middle, a play Michael Jordan excels at. Basketball teams defend a narrow area, forcing the opposition out wide where the danger of conceding a basket diminishes. Football teams should follow suit. Watching Euro '96, I noticed how Portugal and Germany seemed unperturbed about allowing opponents the wide areas to work in. In Europe, they are not used to big centre-forwards latching on to a steady stream of crosses as in England. Europeans focus more on defending the narrow corridor around the box, moving rapidly against any player coming through the middle.

The best route to goal is straight down the middle. If a team cannot travel down that avenue, they should go as close to the middle as possible. Most teams assume the opposition will defend heavily against that possibility so they head wide to whip crosses in. Steve McManaman is special because he can penetrate through the middle. The English are so obsessed with stopping the threat from the wings that they push defenders and midfielders out wide. That opens up the middle for clever, skilful players like McManaman, Eric Cantona and Patrik Berger, who relish these inside positions and go on to score great goals. At Arsenal, Marc Overmars has not created so many goals from going down the wing and crossing but from kniving through the middle. Overmars realised English teams are so afraid of crosses that they throw players outside, giving him space to exploit. English teams do not expect runs like those from Overmars.

When rugby league sides move the ball along the line quickly, opponents will not open up and allow any space. If a pacy winger goes round the end there is little a team can do, but what really angers rugby league coaches is if an opponent goes through the middle. Their whole defence is geared to defending narrow. When I watch rugby league on the television, I am always struck by how rarely I see one person in the middle making the tackle; it is always two or three because they defend narrow.

A spell in front of the video machine, analysing other team sports, could significantly enhance footballing DNAs. So could a tape of Liverpool in the 1987–88 season.

chapter eleven

the team of all the talents: liverpool '87–88

Just before my move to Anfield, I stumbled across Stevie, an eight-year-old who typifield Liverpool for me. I was up at Anfield, playing one of my last games for Watford amidst a whirlwind of speculation that I would be heading north permanently. As I made my way to the Watford coach afterwards, a crowd of Liverpool fans surrounded me, seeking autographs and asking, 'What's happening, Barnesie, are you coming?' Amongst the crowd was Stevie, whose mate was looking for him.

'Stevie, Stevie,' came the shout. Stevie ignored him. 'Stevie, Stevie,' came the shout again.

'What is it?' replied Stevie exasperatedly.

'Where are you?'

'I'm standing beside John Barnes getting a stiffy!' Stevie shouted back. I just looked at Stevie and burst out laughing. It was so different from Watford, where you tend not to get eight-year-olds out at night on the street. Stevie was a real Scouser, the type you see standing outside Anfield flicking V signs at visiting players.

Stevie's humour was very upfront. Liverpudlians' temperament is very Latin, similar to the Geordies. People from Newcastle and

Liverpool are so far removed from the traditionally reserved Briton. Merseysiders and Tynesiders are very passionate and volatile. These traits find echoes in their football and the way they lead their lives. Londoners are so different. When I travel on the Tube and see some kids messing around, it amazes me that no one says a word. Londoners just hide behind their newspapers, hoping the commotion will go away. Liverpool friends of mine go down to London, talk to strangers on the Underground and wonder why they get blank stares. In Liverpool, people come up and talk to them and it's no big deal.

Every Scouser believes he is a natural comedian. Merseysiders are always taking the mickey, particularly out of me. When I couldn't get into the Newcastle side in early 1999, I was down in Liverpool one day walking through town.

'Hey, Barnesie,' said this guy sitting outside a pub, 'give us a rap.'

'My rapping days are over,' I replied.

'Your football days are over as well,' came the retort. It was so cutting. I wanted to hit back with something clever but I didn't know what to say. Scousers are very sharp and witty and always keen to get one up on you. Rule number one in life: never have an argument with a Scouser.

Liverpool Football Club was no different from Liverpool the city. Humour reigned in Liverpool's dressing-room, the home of a thousand wind-ups. When I arrived, it teemed with characters including Alan Hansen, Ian Rush and Ronnie Whelan. As in any working environment, be it an office or factory, some people hold more status than others. You know your place. The good thing about Liverpool is that when we went on the pitch, there was no ego, no one with a higher status. Pecking orders exist at all clubs but a lot of teams carry that on to the pitch, which causes problems. Stratas are perpetuated in the media. Some players consider themselves to be the club's top player and no one can take the mickey out of them. Status at Liverpool was not necessarily talent-related. Stevie Nicol won Footballer of the Year, was Liverpool's best player most years but remained the butt of everyone's jokes, including reserves

Signing up for life: Although Suzy and I are chalk and cheese, what we have together is very special and unique

Feeding time: My four children mean everything to me. Here I am feeding Jordan

An angel at my table: Jasmin, the youngest, is adored by everyone

Spice girls: Jemma and Jasmin love dressing up and dancing around the house, but always look neat and smart in their school uniforms

My boys: Jamie, the eldest, is blessed with a range of abilities and wants to become a psychologist; and Jordan, here in my Liverpool shirt, is the joker, always telling stories and singing songs

On a roll: Elton John helped drive Watford into the forefront of the public attention. In 1981, I was still in the background (*Colorsport*)

The king of defenders: Alan Hansen's retirement was one of the main causes behind Liverpool's slump in the 1990s (*Colorsport*)

Striking poses: Luther Blissett was a great friend and we formed a powerful attack for Watford (*Popperfoto*)

That Goal: My dribble against Brazil at the Maracana in 1984 changed people's perceptions of me, creating huge expectations (*Popperfoto*)

'Just get crosses in': Against Argentina at the 1986 World Cup, Bobby Robson's instruction to me was simple and effective although the game ended in disappointment (*Colorsport*)

The new wave: Mark Chamberlain and I try the surf at the Copacabana Beach in Rio in 1984 (*Popperfoto*)

The English wave: David Seaman, Chris Waddle, myself and Gazza get into the swing of Italia '90 (*Colorsport*)

From jeers to cheers: My free kick goal against Holland in 1993 delighted fans at Wembley, who had spat vitriol at me the match before when England played San Marino (*Colorsport*)

Marked man: I was often targeted for special treatment, such as persistent fouling, as in this international versus Albania (*Colorsport*)

Words of wisdom: Terry Venables, who coached me at England level, was always worth listening to (*Colorsport*)

Palace appointment: Suzy and I were so proud when I was named MBE in 1998, for services to football (*Charles Green*)

and apprentices. Stevie took it well because he knew he was the whipping boy at Anfield. The stories about what Alan Hansen, Kenny Dalglish and Graeme Souness did to Stevie are legendary. Kenny once primed a hotel receptionist to send Stevie a message that a man who owed him money would meet him at Burtonwood Services. Stevie waited there most of the afternoon. It took almost a week for Alan, Kenny and Graeme to stop laughing.

If any of the players made mistakes in what we said, or ricks as we called them, Kenny and Alan ripped us to pieces. Even when I was saying something serious, like if I had given a goal away and got my words jumbled up explaining it, Kenny would slaughter the rick. I used to have arguments with Kenny which sounded like World War Three kicking off. What mattered, for me, was the substance of the words not the words themselves. But if I mixed up words or mispronounced them, Kenny leapt on that, laughing his head off, completely forgetting the importance of the debate. I naturally speak very quickly except when I am with Kenny and Alan. With those two in listening distance, I always slow down my speech to ensure no ricks creep in. Yet if Kenny does it himself, he becomes defensive and denies utterly he has made the mistake. 'I never said that,' he would insist despite all of us knowing he had.

Kenny and Alan are great friends, partners in golf and humour. They made Ian Rush the butt of their jokes every now and then, particularly if he was seen doing interviews, which he wasn't very good at. When Ian Rush flew into Turin to join Juventus, an Italian TV crew asked him whether he had a message for Juve's fans. Rushie looked into the camera, drew a deep beetle and said, 'Welcome.' That ranked alongside some of Stevie Nicol's daft comments, but because it was Rushie, who had a higher status than Stevie, his mistakes were not seized on as much. When I first walked into the dressing-room, I was my normal self, lively and chatty, so I wasn't wound up that often; nor was I the type to take the mickey out of people. The serial wind-up men were Hansen, Ronnie Whelan and Jan Molby, who turned into a real Scouser. Jan's like Philippe Albert, who became a real Geordie while at Newcastle United. Some foreign players can assume the culture and accent of whichever city they inhabit. Jan is very clever; cutting as well.

Their humour never hurt deeply because Jan, Alan and Ronnie knew who they could wind up and how far they could go. I still felt they treated Stevie a bit harshly. Coming back from a Scotland trip once, the lads got the car to stop and explained to Stevie that because of the snow the windscreen-wipers weren't working. Stevie dutifully got out and they drove off without him. When Stevie had had a drink, he told stories against himself. Before becoming a professional footballer, he was an apprentice brickie up in Scotland. One day the foreman called him over.

'Go and clean the water out from the spirit level,' the foreman demanded, 'it's dirty.'

'OK,' said Stevie and tried to do as he was told. That's Stevie. He takes everything in good heart, so people carried on doing it. If they had performed similar stunts on me I would have boiled over. Sometimes the lads went too far.

Liverpool's dressing-room knew me as Digger. Every Barnes in football is called Digger. Bobby Barnes at West Ham was Digger. So was the left-back at Ipswich, David Barnes. I remember playing at Portman Road once and Terry Butcher shouting, 'Digger, Digger.' I looked up and he was trying to get David's attention. I am so used to Digger now that I find it strange when people address me as John. One day, I was talking to Peter Beardsley and a friend of his, and Peter kept referring to Digger. Peter's friend said, 'Who's Digger?' People in football just assume everyone else knows the nicknames. Nicknames were part of Anfield life.

The club was full of characters, people as different as Ray Houghton and Peter Beardsley. Ray was Scottish but played his heart out for Ireland. Ray's a lovely guy but he and his brothers used to love a scrap. Peter Beardsley never really became involved in Liverpool's dressing-room humour. He was into his family and football. I roomed with Peter and we got on really well, still do. I was fascinated by him because he is a model professional and a model person. He always tries to do the right thing. He doesn't drink but when the lads went out drinking, Peter drove us around. He tried to fit in but when all the banter and mud-slinging started, Peter shrank from it.

It was the dressing-room full of characters that helped make Liverpool so special. All that talk about teams going to Anfield a goal down was right. Each time I visited with Watford, I thought how difficult it was to play there and how great it would be to be part of the Liverpool team playing at home. I stood there in my Watford strip, looking around Anfield and thinking how unfair it all was. Watford would be 3–0 down, being jeered by the Kop and I could not wait for the agony to end. I was so excited when I signed. I thought now I am playing for Liverpool, it's going to be easy; and from the first day, it was easy. It almost seemed as if the opposition expected to lose at Anfield. Visitors' spirits fell so quickly; one goal down and teams accepted their fate. Anfield exuded a sense of inevitability that Liverpool would win. Sadly, Anfield is a fortress no longer.

My first season at Liverpool was my most enjoyable there. Kenny was re-building and all his recruits gelled immediately. Kenny was hardly signing superstars from great clubs – Peter Beardsley was brought in from Newcastle United, who were not big then; I was from Watford; John Aldridge, who was in his first full season, and Ray Houghton, who arrived later that season, were both from Oxford United – but we clicked from day one. It felt like we had been together forever. When a manager assembles a side, he assumes it will take time to blend. Not with Liverpool in 1987–88. We were flying from the start, winning ten of our first eleven league games and drawing the other. Defeat was not tasted until 20 March.

The season opened, on 15 August with a 2–1 win at Highbury. Peter and I created the first for John Aldridge, and Stevie Nicol scored with a header after one of my free kicks had not been properly cleared. We thrashed Coventry City 4–1 and then drew 1–1 at West Ham before making our Anfield debuts against Oxford United. A collapsed sewer under the Kop meant Anfield had to wait until 12 September to see the new team. We did not disappoint fans whose anticipation had been heightened to feverish proportions. Aldo got the first and I hit the second from a free kick which sent the Kop into paroxysms of delight. We were irresistible, playing with fluency and imagination, creating chances at will. Every time Bruce Grobbelaar gathered the ball, he threw it out and we were off, weaving our way into the final third. The accuracy of our passing and each player's confident touch ensured we rarely gave away possession. So each time we got the ball, we expected to make a chance for John Aldridge or whoever was in the box. The opposition must have been terrified.

All eyes were on Liverpool's three new boys. John kept scoring, eleven in the first nine games, but Aldo was purely a finisher, rarely becoming involved in the breathtaking build-up play. Peter contributed to the team cause, without being particularly outstanding himself during the first part of the season. My style of play guaranteed I attracted most attention. Liverpool teams of the past never had my type of flair player; their tone was set by Kennedy, Case and McDermott. Buzzing around Ray Kennedy, Graeme Souness and Sammy Lee, Liverpool were almost machine-like. They just passed until they scored. Then Liverpool had Rushie, an exceptional finisher but not flamboyant, never the type to go round beating players with pure skill. Kenny sparkled with intelligence, vision, one-touch football and goals, but Kenny would never light up Anfield with his dribbling. Apart from possibly Steve Heighway, Liverpool had never unleashed a player like me who could dribble past opponents. Even when Liverpool won their European Cups, they never played that way. So although I fitted into their passing DNA, my dribbling skills gave Liverpool an extra dimension, as a skilful Peter Beardsley did. Fans kept approaching me in the street and saying: 'We love you.' I appreciated the compliments but naivety has never featured in my make-up. I knew Liverpool fans would have slaughtered me if I wasn't delivering.

Staying at the Moat House Hotel, right in the centre of Liverpool, I was often seen walking around town, heading to shops, nightclubs or restaurants, particularly in Chinatown. As a person in the public eye, it was important I reacted sensibly to the interest. Famous people who skulk around with hunched shoulders, hood up and sunglasses are liable to attract attention; people bother them more. I was different. Approached by fans in the street, I smiled, inquired how they were and kept walking. Being relaxed and polite is important to me. Being well-known should not change your life. I go out, I go shopping, I go round Marks and Spencers and push the trolley. I never wear dark glasses. The more often people see me, the more they leave me alone. When I walked down Church Street in Liverpool to go shopping the first time, many fans stopped me. The second day, the interruptions were less frequent. Soon it was, 'Oh, there's Barnesie again.' That's why people accepted me on Merseyside.

If I go down to London, I travel on the Underground. If I'm on Oxford Street, I'll jump on a bus to go to Hyde Park. People come over and ask, 'What is a famous footballer like you doing on a bus?' I tell them it's the easiest way to go along Oxford Street, which it is. I'm a normal person from a middle-class Jamaican family who does not like the idea of being cocooned from the real world. Most footballers hate going out because they cannot handle ordinary people coming up and talking to them. I was more concerned about being able to face myself in the mirror every day. It's not a conscious effort now. I really just wanted to be like everyone else.

At Watford my sponsored car was a Renault 25, a big family car. On moving to Liverpool, I got a 2.8 fuel injection Capri which was fun for a year. I really enjoyed driving around Liverpool, which is a vibrant city. The nightlife is fantastic. Liverpool's own music does not appeal to me. I'm not into the Beatles. But one of my best friends, Charlie C, is a local DJ so I tell him what I want to hear anyway! Charlie, forty-three going on sixteen, must be the most famous person in Liverpool. When I stroll down the street with him, more people know him than me. Charlie has been DJing on the club scene in Liverpool since he was eighteen. All the young people recognise him and so do their parents. Through Charlie, I became great mates with Albie Cherry and Joe Speare, an actor who has appeared in *Coronation Street*.

The players were always out on the town. People were bound to be friendly because the team were in such thrilling form. We never saw many Everton players enjoying a night out; they knew they would get too much stick because Everton were not playing well. All players loved going out, though. It was part of the nation's football culture. English football has become more restrained in its drinking habits these days, more in line with Italy and Spain. It was over the top and over the limit in the mid-eighties to early-nineties. The alcoholism admitted by Tony Adams and Paul Merson is symptomatic of what has happened in football. The sport has sobered up. Twenty years ago, the drinking of Adams and Merson would not have been recognised as a problem. Footballers going out to the pub were the norm. Thinking has changed.

During my time at Newcastle, players who had been there when Kevin Keegan was manager said that all of them went out together at least once a week; no one missed out. Newcastle's players said how good it was for team spirit. The Liverpool way was for all the lads to go out in groups and have a good drink. The main group comprised those who lived in Southport including Gary Gillespie, Barry Venison, Steve McMahon, Ronnie Whelan, Alan Hansen and Kenny. I was in town so I didn't often go out on benders with the Southport crew. When I moved to the Wirral, I would see Ian Rush, Jan Molby, Bruce Grobbelaar and Stevie Nicol, who all had homes there. But I'm not into pub culture. I often preferred to go clubbing with my own core of close friends.

On pre-season tours and other foreign trips, all the players socialised together. We went out, played pool and got drunk. Ronnie Moran and Roy Evans insisted we enjoyed ourselves. They often accompanied us, although Kenny, as manager, was occasionally reticent about coming out for a drink. When we toured Scandinavia, Liverpool ordered four taxis at a time to go to the same bar or club. Little groups did not break away on their own. We'd all go together. The return to the hotel was fragmented but we all went out together, organising pool and darts competitions. That is the way most clubs were at that time. Socialising got the team spirit going. People could have a good drink because football was not the goldfish bowl it has become. Stories would never get in the paper if an incident occurred. Nowadays a player cannot sip a glass of wine in public without it becoming front-page news. If the media had been as intense in those days, Liverpool players would have been on the front pages every morning. Most footballers can relate stories of being picked on in a pub by some jealous, half-cut punter, and a fracas ensuing.

Liverpool players were no different from any other group of young men going out. Altercations and disagreements arose but nobody ever got hospitalised. We certainly never disgraced Liverpool despite the quantities of alcohol consumed. Some of the club's heavier drinkers would still be intoxicated when they arrived at Melwood in the morning. The other players could smell the alcohol on them but the drinkers trained as hard and professionally as the rest. Terry McDermott was famous for both his lifestyle and for leading the running the next day. Stevie Nicol could drink for Scotland and he was always at the front. Whenever the fitness assessors checked the players, Stevie Nicol was among the fittest every time. What Liverpool refused to accept was one of their employees not being able to perform on the pitch. If a player let the side down, Liverpool would show their tough streak. I found the whole ethos different from Watford, where Graham Taylor would never have tolerated the consistent binges embarked on by Liverpool players.

I have never drunk beer, although I seemed to be surrounded by it. The beer culture used to be massive in football. Players trained hard to sweat the lager and bitter out of their system. Bryan Robson and Peter Reid enjoyed a drink but they could never be accused of lacking dedication. I know few players who trained harder than those two. Bryan and Peter reflected life in England where pubs form a cornerstone of national life. If I hit the town on a Saturday night, most of the people I see are drinking beer. On the Continent, they tend to sip wine, but beer dominates England. A degree of temperance has only recently arrived because footballers need to be fitter, faster and stronger just to survive at the highest level. The squad system has also changed attitudes. Once upon a time, a team virtually picked itself with maybe one or two others coming in to cover for suspensions or injuries. Players now know that if they are late for training or below-par because of a session the night before, five internationals are clamouring for a chance to climb off the bench, and the drinker might not get his place back.

When I was at Liverpool, managers generally saw the players' night out as a bonding experience which would make the team better able to cope with awkward situations on matchday. During my latter years at Anfield, drinking became increasingly condemned by society and particularly newspapers. Press and fans expected us to behave like dedicated athletes leading almost monk-like existences. Hundreds of millions of pounds flowed into football and supporters began to say, 'He's going out getting drunk and he's got to play tomorrow and I'm paying his wages; that's wrong.' That attitude confused me. When players earned smaller salaries, no one bothered that they were out getting drunk. Money should not be an issue. Whether a player makes £2,000 or £20,000 a week, he has a duty to perform.

Heavy drinkers or teetotal, Liverpool's players kept delivering on the pitch that season. Around late autumn, we had four games on the spin when we scored four in each, against Newcastle United, Derby County, Portsmouth and Queens Park Rangers. It was a golden period. Everything I tried worked; every trick or dribble, feint or pass produced something. After the Derby match, Bobby Robson, the then England manager, likened me to George Best. Our performance against QPR was astonishing. The memory of that match burns more vividly in my mind than any other I played for Liverpool. Rangers were league leaders and the game was shown on *Match of the Day*. Television was particularly excited because Ian Rush was back at Anfield, watching from the stand with his wife. Since his departure for Juventus, there had been endless talk about how Liverpool would fare without Rush's goals. As the cameras rolled, we proved against QPR that we could spread the goals around the side. Craig Johnston struck at the far-post,

Aldo converted a penalty and I came into my own, scoring twice in front of the Kop. Football does not come much better.

For my first goal, I played a one-two with Aldridge and was about to curl the ball along the ground as David Seaman, QPR's keeper, rushed out. But Paul Parker came sliding in, so I had to lift the ball which took off and sped into the top corner. It looked great; right-footed as well. I scored a lot of goals against Seaman in his QPR days. 'It always looks like you don't have any back-lift,' David said to me, 'which makes it difficult to tell when the shot is coming.' My second goal began in the centre circle. Although I usually started on the left, I often moved inside at Liverpool. Warren Neill was supposed to be marking me but I had drifted away from the flank so he left me. I was too deep for the centre-halves to step out and pick me up. Besides, Rangers had possession. Kevin Brock tried to dribble past me and I just stuck a foot out and nicked the ball. Terry Fenwick rushed in to repair the damage so I pushed the ball to the left of him. Whenever would-be tacklers came sliding in, I tried to toe the ball past them, ride the challenge and regain balance and the ball on the other side. After I pushed the ball past Fenwick, I landed and brought the ball back with my left foot in one movement. It was difficult to see why I didn't fall over or how I changed direction. Ryan Giggs is probably the best at it now, sprinting at defenders and then switching tack.

As I passed Fenwick, Peter Beardsley made a run outside him. Alan McDonald, who was tracking Peter's run, moved across. As I saw McDonald coming, I checked back inside him, tricked Gavin Maguire and glided through on goal. I meant to side-foot the ball and this time it stayed low and flew past David. Liverpool's official handbook described it as 'one of the most memorable goals Anfield had seen in years'. I scored a good goal at Arsenal, where I dribbled past four players, but that second against QPR was the most unforgettable. More importantly, Liverpool were top of the table for the first time that season (although we had always had games in hand over the others). I chatted to Rushie in the players' lounge afterwards. He was hugely impressed by the performance, by the range of the team's attacking options. So was the country. We had played well up to then but that display against QPR really announced to the nation that Liverpool were the team of the year.

When I reached the dressing-room afterwards, the players and coaching staff were already focusing on the next game. That was the Liverpool way: team before self. I was very happy personally but the win itself, the collection of maximum points, was of paramount importance. Collectivity ruled at Anfield. It was a special team. Stevie Nicol and I were adventurous down the left. Down the right, Liverpool were steadier but less flamboyant. Ray Houghton, when he arrived, was not a dribbler while Barry Venison was the personification of reliability. Although not as eye-catching or prolific as Stevie and me, those two on the right were as important to the team. Stevie and I needed them; they needed us. We moved around but ensured every position was always filled so no space could be exploited. While the public and press remained obsessed with goalscorers and flair players, I knew that everyone at Liverpool contributed the same.

Individually and jointly, Liverpool's players were strong. Kenny built a talented team and a team of talents. Anfield always bought the right type of player. The manager and coaches discussed whether a potential signing would fit into the team and what his temperament was like. Although the players went out drinking, they were generally very level-headed. There were not any really wild, temperamental types. Bruce Grobbelaar was a one-off and he could get away with being different because he was a goalkeeper. If Bruce played now, he would be the best keeper around. Bruce is very comfortable on the ball, a vital quality given recent changes to the back-pass rule. Not being able to pick the ball up when it is rolled back would not bother Bruce; he loved time on the ball. In the Melwood five-a-sides, Bruce played outfield. When we picked sides, Bruce was never the last one chosen because he was a competent footballer. But it always amazed me that Bruce rarely did any specialised goalkeeping practice. Once a week, perhaps once every ten days, someone shouted 'let's do some shooting practice for Bruce' and we pinged shots in at him, not for long though. Bruce was the most natural goalkeeper in the country. The saves he made were unbelievable. Bruce's critics used to say he dropped crosses but he caught most of them. Because of his quality, people made a real fuss about the few he fumbled.

Bruce was no different off the field – exotic and always taking risks. If he had turned up at Melwood in a helicopter, no one would have batted an eyelid. As we sat in the dressing-room or on the bus, Bruce regaled us with amazing stories of his upbringing in Rhodesia, not necessarily about the war but of diving in rivers and wrestling crocodiles and meeting the most extraordinary individuals. Once when he was there he met Clint Eastwood and they went off and got drunk together. Bruce's life is like that. We used to think him a lunatic.

Stevie Nicol was Liverpool's joker in the pack at left-back. On the other flank was Barry Venison, a strong character who captained Sunderland at a very young age. Barry was underrated until he went to Newcastle and played in front of Kevin Keegan's back four. Kevin understood Barry's value. So did the dressing-room at Liverpool, but the fans never really took to him because he was not as eye-catching as Stevie down the left. Barry wasn't quick. He didn't raid forward to get crosses in but he was versatile. If Kenny had asked him to play in any position he could have done it.

Alan Hansen played then as he performs now on television – very clinical in his reading of the game and very smooth. Alan was the best defender I ever played with. Critics claimed he didn't tackle but he always dispossessed opponents. His speed, positioning and rapid appreciation of how an opposing attack was developing were so good that he didn't have to make a thundering tackle that sent divots and opponents flying in different directions. Alan just ghosted in and intercepted the ball. He started off all our attacks. I never fathomed why Alan was capped only twenty-six times for Scotland; if he had been Italian, he would have won a hundred.

Liverpool's downfall commenced when Alan Hansen retired. It

has never been Liverpool's style to boot the ball upfield. They needed someone who could bring it out of defence and Alan was the best in the world at that. He collected the ball off Bruce, even if someone was marking him, beat that player or played a one-two and then glided into midfield. Alan suffered a problem with his knees that prevented him from kicking the ball further than thirty yards. That was one of the reasons why he always dribbled from the back. He had a phenomenal appreciation of when and where to pass, whether into space or to feet, even to which foot. If one of us had the ball and was in trouble, Alan was always available. He made Liverpool play. When Bruce got the ball and rolled it to Alan, we knew he would set something up. When he left, Liverpool didn't have anyone to do it.

Alan's natural replacement was Gary Gillespie, whom I felt was very underrated. On the ball, Gary was as good a footballer as Alan and would be the first choice at five-a-sides. He was not as commanding defensively as Alan, although at 6ft 3in he won his fair share in the air. He was unlucky with injuries which undermined his attempts to establish himself. Gary lived in Southport and was always out with Barry.

Jan Molby featured in central midfield. Jan was the best long passer I have ever seen. If his fitness and weight had been better, Jan would have been a Liverpool regular for many years. Nigel Spackman was also in there. Nigel was a hard-working player who never got the credit for his ability on the ball. Central midfield was mainly filled by Ronnie Whelan and Steve McMahon, who were like brothers. They roomed together, they both lived in Southport, they went out together. Their families were very close. Such companionship helped their partnership on the pitch. Ronnie and Steve were Liverpool's engine-room. Steve was a fantastic footballer driven by an unbelievable tenacity and will to win. Even in training, Steve had to win at all costs. Second best was never good enough for Steve.

Ronnie never received the plaudits he deserved. He regained possession so efficiently but he was from that Hansen mould of intercepting rather than tackling. Watching opponents and reading their intentions was Ronnie's forte. As the pass was executed, Ronnie nipped in to nick it. He was neither quick nor particularly skilful but his awareness, one-touch football and defending were outstanding. Ronnie embodied Liverpool's desire for selflessness in their players. He was the ultimate team player, using only a few touches before giving the ball to the dribblers or passers. When people debate the great individuals in world football, the name of Ronnie Whelan never comes to their lips. But in terms of contribution to the team, Ronnie was exceptional.

Liverpool initially struggled to find Ronnie's best position. When they had Jimmy Case and two central-midfield players, they used to play him out wide, on the left, although they knew he was never going to dribble past opponents; he was such a good player they had to get him on the pitch somehow. When he was moved to central midfield, he took to it seamlessly. Ronnie was the linchpin of that team, the brains of the midfield. He stood in front of the back four, which allowed McMahon, such a dynamic midfielder, to charge forward. My first goal in that famous game against QPR was set up by Ronnie. Rangers held possession outside their box and were trying to trigger a counter-attack. Ronnie pretended to go one way and then threw his weight in the other direction to gain the ball. As he intercepted it, two Rangers players went in, but he was very cute; he just toed it towards me and tried to jump out of the way, but he was still clattered. Ronnie was as hard as nails and would compete for any loose ball. He rarely got hurt. He used to give as good as he got and, because he looked innocent, he was not often punished by referees. If you asked footballers then who could really look after themselves they would name Ronnie Whelan. Liverpool, though, never needed to fight. We passed opponents into submission, so very rarely did a game deteriorate into a battle. If it did, we wouldn't necessarily win because it wasn't Liverpool's game. It is so important that a team's philosophy shines through, that players do not stray from the DNA. Ronnie helped us impose our beliefs.

Before Ray Houghton settled in, Craig Johnston played on the right of midfield. Craig was a Liverpool favourite – fast and dynamic, always working hard, always running up and down, crossing and shooting. No one would have known from his wholehearted commitment that being a footballer had never been Craig's sole dream. We thought of Craig as a mad inventor; he was a genius, very artistic and always coming up with ideas, such as the Predator boot. He was a hundred per cent Aussie. I loved going over to his house. Once I walked in, sat down and he offered me coffee. When I said yes, he shot off to the kitchen on his skateboard. A man with a zest for life, Craig was always doing crazy things like swimming with sharks. I once asked what he was doing in the holidays. 'Trekking in Kathmandu,' he replied. Craig retired from football at twenty-seven because there were so many other things he wanted to do.

Craig was more of an out-and-out winger than Ray, who made most impact when he came off the line. Although he proudly represented Ireland, Ray was the product of a real cocktail of influences. Born in Glasgow, he was a mad Jock with a touch of Cockney in him through being brought up in London who acquired some Scouse vernacular from hanging around with John Aldridge's mates. Ray and Aldo were two of the few who lived right in the heart of Liverpool. Ray almost became a Scouser.

Aldo was the archetypal Scouser, always laughing and taking the mickey out of people. I was so pleased he made it with Liverpool because he had been around the lower leagues with Newport County, and it looked as if the big time might pass him by. Aldo was probably under pressure when he came to Anfield because this was his big chance, playing for the team he loved in his home town. His style was perfect for us. Aldo didn't necessarily get involved in the build-up play. All John was required to do was put the ball in the back of the net which he did from all angles. Aldo was not a natural footballer but he was a natural finisher. Precise, clinical, nerveless, in the right place at the right time – all the predator's clichés apply to John Aldridge. John's success was at odds with his obvious assets. Not tall, he scored a lot of goals with his head. Not quick, he reached so many through-balls because of his intelligence and determination. Normally when such balls are driven over defences, it is the fastest forwards who thrive, lightning men like Michael Owen, Gary Lineker or Ian Rush. John would go through on timing. When we played five-a-side, which Aldo was not brilliant at, Steve McMahon always used to shout at him, 'Hey, Aldo, have you brought your diving boots?!' Bruce Grobbelaar would be picked before John. But Aldo was the best finisher I ever played with, although I never shared a field with Rushie in his heyday.

Much of John's success was down to the support work of Peter Beardsley, who operated in the deeper-lying striker's role which Kenny filled so famously for so long. Peter was more mobile than Kenny, although not as good with his back to goal. Kenny could have a marker breathing down his neck, kicking his ankles and calves, and still control the ball and lay it off. Liverpool fans assumed Peter's style would echo Kenny's. He came in, took Kenny's shirt but Kenny's way was never Peter's. Supporters expected Peter to get on the end of John Aldridge's flicks but Peter has never done that. The Kop's desire for Peter to play more like an out-and-out front man mystified me. Peter worked as a midfield player who joined the attack. Dwight Yorke has been compared to Peter but Dwight could stay upfront because he is strong and good with his back to goal. Peter's game was dropping off and picking up possession. He was fantastic at that. Peter was so important for Liverpool that I never comprehended why anyone wanted anything else from him. I was particularly appreciative of Peter because he always aimed to pass first time to me, which gave me a chance to use my pace. Peter is the player I most enjoyed playing with in my career; he is one of the main reasons why I achieved so much at Anfield. There are those who say he did not do enough for himself but selflessness is Peter's chief trait. He worked more for the team than himself. Rushie was the same.

I get on really well with Peter. When I picked up my kids from school in Newcastle, I often saw Peter. We took our kids to the same café in Jesmond. A lot of people have a funny attitude towards Peter, who does not mix naturally with the lads. Peter is different from most players. Clubs employ staff to carry the skips of kit; players never get involved in that. Peter does. He will go and collect the balls after training. Such acts have been greeted with snide remarks that Peter is being a goody-goody and sucking up to the manager. Those who criticise simply do not appreciate that is just the way he is. Peter would bring the balls in to help an apprentice or the manager. It is sad that his eagerness to help has earned him, in some quarters, the reputation of being a creep. But managers at Liverpool carry the skip. Roy Evans used to help clear up the dressing-room. For all the sarcastic jibes, I know Peter's true character.

Peter took time to win over the Kop. He began impressing them by scoring against Everton in November. Personally, I hated derby games, which are made for players like Peter Reid, who love to get stuck in. Such neighbourly spats are rarely good games. I knew they were great occasions for the fans because of the sense of anticipation that built up for weeks in advance; also because of the atmosphere over the ninety minutes and the result's significance for those with blue or red in their veins. But I preferred to perform in attractive shows not passion plays. Derbies make footballers nervous. No matter how composed we were as a team, whenever Liverpool played Everton, we all got fired up and played with our hearts rather than our heads. It is a cardinal sin in football to play the occasion or the fans. It was a mistake Liverpool kept making come derby day. Why should we have changed because it was Everton facing us? After all, we were Liverpool, the best. Everton should have adapted to us but that never happened; we just met in the middle, toe-to-toe, eyeball to eyeball and went for each other. Not pretty.

I tell young players, even if in the reserves, to play the game, never the occasion. A lot of players believe in football's myths and crumble in front of 100,000 fans or away from home. It is pointless for players to feel intimidated by Old Trafford. The fans' roar cannot beat them. I told myself that when I moved into management, I would make it clear to my players that derbies are just another game, that we should stick to our DNA. No derby is healthy.

Look at Rangers–Celtic or River Plate–Boca Juniors; never mind the Laws, feel the frenzy. Fortunately, Merseyside derbies appear to have lost some of their physicality. The heat has been lowered by the turnover of players and the influx of foreigners, who do not understand the match's immense local importance. Derbies are for the fans' benefit and the players are out there for the fans. We knew that by the reaction of fans we encountered in the street when derbies were due. 'It's Everton next week,' they would shout, 'come on, come on, come on.' Their fervour was inescapable. But for new signings or players who did not speak the language, the match was just another fixture, except with less travelling. For the players, derbies became less an episode of 'Neighbours at War'. Imagine the days of Graeme Souness when he knew all about Everton and was pumped up for every meeting. The opening whistle had the same effect as the first shot in a battle. Current derbies are not as frenetic or fierce as in my day, which was never as impassioned or physical as in Souness's day. I'm pleased the pace slowed and the passion ebbed.

Three weeks after Everton's visit, Watford came to Anfield on 24 November and I put one past Tony Coton in our 4–0 win. Tony and I had become really good friends during our time at Vicarage Road. We lived near each other and used to go out on the town together. Tony was a fantastic goalkeeper and could have gone on to represent England. Capped at B level, Tony made the senior squad once or twice but never won a full cap. At Anfield, I sliced one past him from thirty yards.

In February, I returned to Vicarage Road. There was no sense of homesickness. Watford seemed a lifetime ago. Anfield was home. I felt like I had been playing for Liverpool for ever. Watford's fans gave me a good reception. They were not just thanking me for the memories. They felt proud a Watford player was flourishing at Liverpool; they basked in the reflected glory. Here was proof that Watford could play despite all the criticism about long balls. When Luther Blissett went to AC Milan we all felt good. Luther was one of us and he was now a superstar playing for the biggest club in the world. Watford's supporters have always been decent people. I was delighted by their response, particularly as we thumped their team 4–1.

Liverpool's first defeat of an epic season did not arrive until 20 March at Goodison of all places. We had just equalled the record of a twenty-nine-game unbeaten start to a season set by the great Leeds United side of 1973–74. Everton were the worst opposition given the circumstances. They, more than anyone, even more than Leeds, would have hated us to break the record. Everton's commitment was unbelievable, almost scary in its intensity. They ran their hearts out in a poor game settled by a scrappy goal from Wayne Clarke. We were disappointed not to surpass Leeds' tremendous achievement but it was a relief that we could concentrate on playing. In the dressing-room afterwards, the players were saying, 'We can forget about trying to break records, let's just focus on winning the League.' We were still fourteen points clear with two games in hand.

April brought a three-match League and Cup mini-series with Nottingham Forest. In the opening encounter, a First Division game, we lost 2–1 at the City Ground with Steve Chettle doing well against me at right-back. A week later we met Forest in the semi-final of the Cup. I woke up that morning to discover a newspaper article with unflattering quotes about me attributed to Chettle. 'I'll have Barnes on toast' ran the headline. Chettle had probably been set up for the quotes; I know full well how underhand newspaper reporters can be. But I cannot remember ever being as fired up for a game. It was certainly the first and only time that comments in a newspaper motivated me to play even better, to push my talent and fitness to the limit to win a game. Chettle was young but my reaction was not one of indignation because of that. I just feel it is important always to show humility. I wasn't hurt but I was insulted. From the first minute, I was determined to express my anger by running Chettle ragged. I didn't harbour a desire to humiliate him, as actually transpired, simply to make a point. We won 2–1 and my contest with Chettle held the key. He brought me down for Aldo's penalty and was beaten by my run and cross for Aldo's fabulous volleyed second. The next day, the papers were saying it was the 'Barnes on toast' headline that stirred me up to play as well as I did. How true that was. I wish I had been that motivated more often!

Four days later, we faced Forest again. Our 5–0 victory was the most complete and best Liverpool performance I have ever played in, even better than the 4–0 defeat of QPR because Brian Clough's Forest were a far superior side. Following their Cup exit, Forest sought revenge. The two teams were rivals at the time anyway, not as intense as Liverpool–Everton but still niggly. So they were really up for it when they arrived at Anfield. Forest came at us and we responded with football that was absolute perfection. Tom Finney said it was the greatest he had ever seen. I still watch the video. Everything just fell into place – the runs, the passing, the finishing. Forest tried their hardest but the game was like shadow-play in training when teams practise goalscoring moves without opponents. Forest looked haunted by the end.

As if being involved in those games was not enough, in between the second and third matches I was named the Professional Footballers' Association's Player of the Year. The award was the personal highlight of my career. No matter what the newspapers write about me, and it was also a great honour twice to receive the Football Writers' Association's Footballer of the Year trophy, there is no greater accolade than being feted by fellow footballers. If I bump into a player from Barnet or York, Brighton or Cardiff, it means so much to me if they say 'you are a good player'. Football writers have never played the game so even if I looked good, how did they know whether I was good? But a compliment from a professional is so uplifting. To look at, the PFA trophy is bloody horrible. It resembles one of those cups that kids get – huge and tasteless. The Football Writers' one, shaped as a golden man, is far classier. I keep the two Football Writers' awards on show with the hideous PFA one hidden away, even though I treasure it more. Trophies have always fascinated me. The Jules Rimet trophy is the most stylish, glittering proof that small is beautiful. Ice hockey's Stanley Cup is massive. Dennis Wise could get lost in it.

Liverpool swept the board at the PFA awards that year. Steve McMahon finished runner-up in the individual section with Peter Beardsley third. Liverpool also had five players in the PFA Team of the Year. We all went down to the PFA party and, surprisingly, were placed on a table so out of the way it was virtually in the kitchen. Alan Hansen gave Gordon Taylor, the chief executive of the PFA, a really hard time about it, winding him up mercilessly.

'We've got most of the players in the PFA team,' Alan ranted. 'We've got first, second and third in the individual award and you stick us out here. It's an absolute disgrace.' Slightly embarrassed, Gordon told the waiter to send a bottle of champagne over to mollify us. We decided one wasn't enough. 'Bring us some more champagne,' Alan kept ordering the waiter. 'Don't worry, Gordon Taylor and the PFA will pay.' We got through twenty bottles of Bollinger. But then Liverpool players always could drink.

A few days later, on 23 April, we secured the championship with four games to spare. It was actually an anti-climax. We wanted to seal the League in a blaze of glory with goals galore but it came with a 1–0 victory over Tottenham Hotspur. It did not seem special. So many of Liverpool's players had won the League before, in 1986, and some before that as well. Even though it was my first title, I felt like a Liverpool player who had been there for ages, who had won trophies before so this did not feel unique or even particularly intoxicating. We went on a lap of honour, trotted back to the dressing-room and that was that. No one made a big deal out of our success. Liverpool never revelled in the present; they always said 'look ahead to next year'.

My time at Anfield taught me to forget how well we had played against Nottingham Forest and at QPR. I like that attitude because it keeps players grounded. Manchester United have developed that attitude under Alex Ferguson. I remember seeing United's players in the lounge at Wembley after they completed the double in 1996.

They were not celebrating. They were probably already focusing on next season. Liverpool were once like that.

The double was never discussed as we headed towards the FA Cup final against Wimbledon. In keeping with Wembley tradition, Liverpool released a Cup final song. Not in keeping with Wembley tradition, this was actually a good song. It was called 'The Anfield Rap' and Craig Johnston wrote it. We had an hilarious time recording it. All the players dressed up as rappers weighed down by gold chains – it helped that most of us were drunk. Craig wrote a special line for me to rap which went: 'When I do my thing, the crowd go bananas.' The words were wonderfully tongue in cheek; it was a slight dig at Everton's banana-throwers. Craig's original line had been: 'When I do my thing, all the crowd throw bananas.' But we changed it.

Apart from 'The Anfield Rap', the week leading up to Wembley was like any other. Where Watford had been seized by Cup fever in 1984, at Liverpool it was just business as usual; no television cameras, no fuss, no big deal. We understood the country's fascination with the match-up, the significance of Liverpool against Wimbledon, princes versus paupers, passing against long ball, flair against force. Everyone hyped up the contrasts, saying it was a mismatch. Not us. A mutual respect existed between the teams. Liverpool have never criticised Wimbledon. Many so-called experts thundered that Wimbledon's style was ugly and bad in comparison with Liverpool's. Our approaches were different but that did not make Wimbledon's wrong; it was right for them. Wimbledon's whole hoodoo reputation stems from the press saying opponents cannot get the ball down and pass against the master hustlers of South London. But Wimbledon are such expert battlers it is pointless turning the game into a battle. There were times after the Cup final when we played Wimbledon off the park because we concentrated on what we were good at, not what they were good at.

A myth has developed about the Cup final that we lost our nerve after Wimbledon's players verbally abused us in the tunnel.

Wimbledon always shout in the tunnel. They were not screaming at us but at each other to pump themselves up for the match. Wimbledon probably thought their noise would intimidate us but we certainly weren't scared. Being punched or shot is intimidating; mere words aren't. It irritated me after the game when Wimbledon's players kept declaring 'we knew we were going to win'. Anyone can say that with hindsight. Wimbledon's shouting before the match was unimportant, unoriginal and bore no influence on the game.

It was a scrappy match, although there were not many bone-crunching tackles. Steve McMahon and Vinnie Jones went head to head and there was definitely an edge between them but not between anyone else. Wimbledon were never a dirty team; they were hard and competitive but they got stuck with an unflattering image of being footballing yobs. Critics accused them of employing a hard man in Vinnie Jones. So what? Liverpool fielded enforcers in Steve McMahon and Ronnie Whelan who were as tough as they come. Every club has a raw or rugged player, capable of sorting out opponents. But it frustrates me that too many teams are influenced by the supposedly nasty nature of an opponent. As much as Vinnie's hard-man reputation may have contributed to his dismissals when he was innocent, it also helped him. Opponents were afraid to play against him.

While Vinnie and Steve locked horns, I was up against Clive Goodyear, yet another case of a centre-half used at right-back against me. Dennis Wise played right midfield and worked very hard in doubling back. Wimbledon ganged up on me but, like the rest of the Liverpool team, I failed to perform to my optimum. My crosses were rare but then I scarcely received the ball. Wimbledon's goal, the only one of the final, was particularly disappointing as it should have been avoided. Wimbledon are big and physical and we expected them to pose a danger at set-pieces. That is their forte. Dennis put over a great ball and Lawrie Sanchez, a six-footer, headed in.

I would not have minded if we had outplayed Wimbledon, hit the post five times and lost to a set-piece goal. I could have coped with that. But we were poor and should have done something about the way we played. We had a chance of equalising when Aldridge stepped up to take a penalty. I thought he would score but I must admit to a niggling doubt because Dave Beasant had made a name for himself for saving penalties. John had never missed one so I just wondered whether today was the day. When Beasant saved, it hardly surprised me. I knew then that it was not going to be Liverpool's day. Sanchez's goal proved decisive.

Wimbledon celebrated victory differently from the way Liverpool would have done. As their name indicated, the 'Crazy Gang' were a wild bunch of guys. They actually could not believe they had won. They jumped up and down shouting their heads off but not in a boastful way, more in disbelief and delight. What I refuse to accept is this nonsense that Wimbledon's win was one of the biggest upsets in FA Cup history. Wimbledon finished seventh that season, and have regularly featured in the top ten of the top division, so why shouldn't they beat Liverpool? The fact that the odds were so stacked against them was a testament to how good the bookies thought Liverpool were. A real Cup final upset is a team like Southampton beating Manchester United in 1976. Some critics suggested our defeat was good for football because it allowed an unfashionable team their day in the sun. I hate this celebration of the underdog. Good teams like Liverpool will always have off-days. Teams just hope such dips occur in the League when they are twenty points clear and not in a one-off event like an FA Cup final.

There was no sense of shock in Liverpool's dressing-room as some people suggested. From sixty-five minutes on we sensed that we were not going to create any real chances, that we were not going to win, so there was no sudden hammer-blow falling on us at the final whistle. Disappointment prevailed but when we returned to the hotel, we started looking forward to the next season. I was confident. I thought this Liverpool team were going to be together for the next five years and each season we would compete for the double, which we were really.

We realised we had let ourselves down at Wembley but what

was there to say? There was no point ranting and raving and arguing. It was not dissimilar to when we won. Ronnie Moran walked into the dressing-room and announced 'Pre-season starts 16 July'.

flair and flexibility

C oming from Jamaica, I am blessed with rhythm. My innate
balance and agility meant I could jump over all the tackles flying
my way at Watford and Liverpool. Footballers from Caribbean and
other warm climates are far suppler than the English, who are noto-
riously stiff. Brazilians' warm-up routines are limb-twisting. Even
the Saudi Arabians boast more rhythm than northern Europeans; I
will never forget Saeed Owairan scoring that wonderful goal against
Belgium in the 1994 World Cup. Owairan weaved through tackle
after tackle as the Europeans tried to kick him. It's too cold in
northern Europe to possess the sort of physical flexibility Owairan
has and I once had. I've been in Britain so long that I have stiffened
up. In my younger days, when my sinews were more elastic, I glided
through tackles. The only British player who matches the agility of
the Caribbeans and Latin Americans is Ryan Giggs. His suppleness
stems from the fact that he is half-black. There is nothing wrong
with Peter Beardsley physically but he cannot touch his toes. Peter's
hamstrings are the world's worst. Alan Hansen could not stretch at
all. Their muscles are too rigid.

The contrast between Europeans and footballers from hotter
climes is perfectly captured on my favourite video – Brazil's 5–2

vanquishing of Sweden in the 1958 World Cup final. The Swedes fielded some great technical players, really famous footballers in Nils Liedholm and Gunner Gren, but they looked as if they should be playing cricket, not football. They were not athletic, quick, agile nor strong. Sweden were simply very methodical. They passed and ran. Brazil hailed from another dimension; they looked like modern-day footballers. Where the Swedes were slow and stiff, Brazil's clever football flowed through Didi, Vava, Garrincha and Pele, each one a lithe, dexterous and skilful sportsman. Pele personified Brazil; his agility and ability to reach an aerial ball were astonishing for someone scarcely 5ft 9in. And he moved like the wind between the wooden Europeans in the Rasunda Stadium.

Pele possessed exceptional balance. Balance is not simply the art of riding a tackle. Balance is retaining your footing at the other end. Tino Asprilla has marvellous balance. I played with the Colombian at Newcastle and saw how he was repeatedly kicked. I kept thinking Tino would go to ground, so winning a free kick or a penalty, but he usually stayed upright. David Ginola is different. One of the exceptions to the European rule, the Frenchman has balance aplenty. When Ginola rides a tackle, he could come down fine on the other side but he often falls to earth seeking free kicks or penalties. It is frustrating to observe because Ginola could keep his balance, even against rugged tackling.

If a really hard tackle came in, I took evasive action. I knew when bad challenges were imminent. It's animal instinct. In the jungle, animals sense when a lion prowls nearby. Humans have similar intuition on the football field. I never suffered a bad injury from a tackle; solely pulled muscles. I anticipated and reacted quicker than most players.

I faced all the hard men of my generation. I remember playing against Jimmy Case at Southampton and he went in hard on everyone. I never experienced any problems with Vinnie Jones or David Batty. My career began in the eighties when the era of ugly challenges, of getting stuck in early to intimidate opponents, was drawing to a welcome close. Creative footballers are far more protected now. On the shelf at home sits a tape of a seventies game involving Norman Hunter at Leeds United. I was shocked by the incidents that the referee ignored as well as those he punished. There was one match in which Hunter was sent off. Niggle ruled for the rest of the game, players being kicked after the ball had gone amidst much general scuffling, punching and fighting. In the modern age of Sky TV's all-seeing eye, such matches would have become the lead item on the evening news with all manner of inquests. It seems violence and intimidation were normal then.

Fortunately for me and my shins, Mark Dennis played on the left for Southampton so it was Nigel Callaghan at Watford and Ray Houghton at Liverpool who were treated to the infamous Dennis hammering. As a general rule, right-backs tend to be saner than left-backs so I was less exposed to football's rough-house fraternity. The start of my career also coincided with the emergence of attacking full-backs such as Viv Anderson, who were not necessarily great defenders or you-shall-not-pass kickers. Viv was the right-back I most admired; he attacked all the time, in keeping with Nottingham Forest's approach. I was forever chasing him and if I ever gained possession I was usually deep in my own half and consequently less threatening to the opposition. The menace was going out of full-backs, particularly with wingers like Wilf Rostron at Watford being converted into defenders. The real cloggers lurked in central midfield and central defence.

Some flair players are tempted to retaliate, to seek some sly, off-the-ball revenge for the battering they receive. I have never deliberately gone in to hurt an opponent. I cannot tackle anyway. My caution count ran to only two in eighteen years, one at Watford and the other at Liverpool. The first yellow card was for fouling Tristam Benjamin of Notts County although he was not hurt by the challenge. Benjamin had kicked me all match. Eventually, frustration got the better of me and I flicked out a foot as he ran past. It was hardly the greatest crime and Benjamin deserved it given what he had been inflicting on my ankles. My only other yellow card would have brought dismissal in the current climate. Liverpool were at Loftus Road. Alan Hansen had just passed to me and I began working the ball through midfield. As was his tendency, Alan ran on upfield to give Liverpool an extra option. Alan floated forward but the return pass never came, leaving him out of position and Rangers in possession. Justin Channing, QPR's right-back, had the ball and went running through on Bruce Grobbelaar. As Channing crossed the halfway line into the area vacated by Alan, I grabbed his shirt, pulled him back and was duly booked. Nowadays that is a red-card offence, although I would have argued that Channing was so far from goal that the threat was minimal.

I have never had a problem with referees. Most refereeing mistakes are fairly innocuous. Occasionally, a controversial penalty incident erupts but a referee never made a team pass badly or miss a goal. I determined that when I became a manager, I would never moan about referees. I hate it when a manager rants at the ref, often blaming him for his own team's shortcomings. Referees do the hardest job in the world and no one is going to like them. Referees are human and, like the rest of us, they make mistakes but they deserve our support and sympathy, especially now because FIFA, football's world governing body, no longer allow them to use common sense in their decision-making. Refereeing standards have worsened but not because of the referee. The eagle-eyed, clipboard-wielding assessor in the stand makes it impossible for the referee to apply the spirit of the law. He must officiate by the letter of the law or risk the wrath of the assessor and the authorities. He may even be humiliatingly dropped from the referees' panel. The pressure is really on the referee. If a tackler comes in from an angle, the referee may know that it is not a sending-off offence but the law states that tackles from behind are punishable by dismissal. That pressurises the referee, who knows his career may be adversely affected if he doesn't reach for the red. He would doubtless prefer a short-term skewering by manager and media to demotion. Referees were fine in the 1980s when they could use their own discretion. Now that is no longer allowed, which is madness because every foul, incident and tackle is different. Sometimes a player slips as he makes a tackle and knocks over the man in possession. A dismissal for that is ridiculous.

Referees have more importance in cup-ties than league games. One error can stop a team on the road to Wembley or Hampden. If Liverpool were denied a penalty in the League, we knew we could make up the points during the rest of the season. (Although it had nothing to do with refereeing, Middlesbrough had three points deducted in 1996–97 for not turning up at Blackburn Rovers. Middlesbrough said it was this punishment that ensured their relegation but they still had time to catch up. I had no sympathy for Boro. It wasn't as if the points were subtracted on the final day. League football always offers another chance.)

Referees would be greatly helped by the presence of a fourth official checking replays on a monitor. Reviewing an incident need take only twenty seconds. Cricket uses it successfully with run-outs. In football, arguments over penalties can last a couple of minutes so the referee would actually speed the game up by having recourse to technology. Knowing there is a so-called spy in the stand, footballers would refrain from disputing the incident with the referee. The extra eye is perfect for crucial decisions like penalties and the ball crossing the line. Charlton Athletic were very unlucky when Mark Bright's effort against Newcastle United during the 1998–99 season was not given. Cameras showed the ball entered the goal.

There would have to be limits – free kicks on the edge of the box are not worth examining, for instance – otherwise the camera would be called upon for too many incidents. So much goes on off the ball, most of it innocuous, that every player would scream for a video replay. If Sky, ITV or *Match of the Day* wanted to make a meal out of an elbowing afterwards then fine, the player may be banned. But referees would have to be selective in how they use the camera during the match. Players would also dispute throw-in decisions even more vociferously because one of their team-mates may have a long throw which could lead to a goal.

At Watford and Liverpool, we didn't worry about long throws because of the quality of the crossing. I was particularly suited to playing on the wing because I cannot kick a ball straight. It always makes me shudder when I watch Ian Rush hitting the ball hard and straight with either foot; I just don't think my ankle, which I damaged when I was younger, could take that. So I always strike the ball with my instep. Running down the wing, the most natural way for me to address the ball with my instep was to swing the left foot across the ball, so imparting curl and lift. A lot of wingers, those with stronger ankles, have to turn their body to deliver a cross. I don't, which gave me an edge because I could cross at speed. But when I played central midfield, I had to turn my body to kick the ball straight. It was useful for free kicks less than twenty yards from goal where I could bend the ball over the wall. But I do not possess the power to blast them from thirty yards like Stuart Pearce does.

Graham Taylor had a theory about left-footed versus right-footed play. He wondered whether I used my left because I kicked better with it or because I was actually right-footed and could balance better on the right. When a footballer kicks with one foot, he balances on the other. It is not clear-cut. I'm left-handed at writing and all racquet sports but right-handed at cricket.

Despite my occasional injury worries, fitness has never been a problem for me. From my early days pounding the streets of London, I have always gone running. During France '98 when I did studio work for ITV, I ran around a park near the television centre in Paris. I have never been fitter. Newcastle recorded the players' fitness levels when we returned and I was among the top three. During the six-week closed-season, I normally go on holiday for a fortnight and then train on my own until pre-season starts.

Undermining the good training was my weakness for junk food. In the past, I haven't been able to keep out of McDonald's or Kentucky Fried Chicken. My story is similar to many in England. It is only recently that professional footballers in this country have become more health-conscious in terms of diet. Eating was never an issue until well into the 1990s, except among a few enlightened players like Gordon Strachan, when players started behaving like athletes and pasta became the staple diet for many. Like many British footballers, it took me time to improve my eating habits. Players can now go on longer because they look after themselves. When I joined Liverpool, we were guided by another set of principles.

outgunned: liverpool '88–89

L iverpool were guided by the preachings and practices of Bill
Shankly, a man obsessed with football and nothing else. His
philosophy suffused not just the Boot Room and the whole football
side at Anfield but the club generally. The commercial dominance
that Manchester United enjoyed in the 1990s could have been
achieved by Liverpool in the seventies and eighties. In that period
Liverpool were even more successful than United are now, winning
trophy after trophy at home and in Europe, year in, year out.
But Shankly would never have thought of exploiting Liverpool's
commercial potential and nor did his immediate successors, most
notably Bob Paisley. Shankly was solely interested in football.
Anfield is not a grand stadium. When I visit Tottenham Hotspur I
walk through tastefully decorated rooms and climb into smart lifts.
White Hart Lane is a lovely stadium. The interior of Anfield is very
basic, functional even, not like Old Trafford, which is staggering
inside and out. The training facilities at Melwood were no more than
average, although they have since improved with a new canteen and
neat reception area. The only thing Liverpool were concerned about
was winning trophies. Impressive architecture or attractive designs
were irrelevant to the club of Shankly.

Belatedly, Liverpool are entering the age of merchandising by profiting from the appeal of Michael Owen and Jamie Redknapp and linking up with Granada, although their club shop remains modest compared with those at Old Trafford, Elland Road and Stamford Bridge. It is unimaginable how many millions Liverpool could have generated when they had stars such as Kevin Keegan and were winning trophies rather than when they were flattering to deceive as for most of the 1990s.

The old Boot Room symbolised Liverpool – unadorned but inhabited by people committed to footballing success. It symbolised Anfield's managerial tradition, the passing down through the years of collected wisdom, from Shankly, through Paisley and Joe Fagan to Roy Evans and Ronnie Moran. Roy and Ronnie originally sat there in the corner of the Boot Room and were then brought into the middle. It was a policy of continuity, stemming from Shankly. I once went into the Boot Room to get a lemonade from the fridge but all I saw were a load of old guys talking rubbish. People have always written that Liverpool's tactics were developed in the Boot Room but once Shankly laid down the ground rules, it wasn't necessary to be in there talking. Everything was known. They really used to go in the Boot Room after the game for a whisky. Visiting managers would stop by for a chat. It was almost the manager's lounge. The mystique that built up around the Boot Room helped Liverpool gain a psychological edge over other teams. Opponents were always worrying about the secrets of Liverpool, rather than thinking there is nothing supernatural about this team.

It was hardly a secret that Liverpool's dressing-room was full of real camaraderie, a characteristic that is easy to develop when the team are winning. This sense of unity and kinship was inevitably going to be strong between 1987 and 1992 because Liverpool enjoyed so much success. There were spells when we didn't win the Cup or the League but such barren patches were brief. Yet only in times of adversity is a team's true spirit revealed. When things were going well, as they did for my first five years at Anfield, of course the players were going to love each other. We'd all be mates, going out together. But when results start to slip, players start blaming each other, whispering behind each other's backs, and dressing-room cliques become more apparent. We never had that at Liverpool in my time.

Liverpool and Kenny Dalglish were obsessed with winning. He was an intriguing manager to work for. I had to be very careful around him and I still am now we are together at Celtic, because he is the biggest mickey-taker imaginable. Kenny is completely different from his public image, loving a laugh in private. He is very guarded with those he doesn't know so I understand why people label him as dour. When he worked for television, Kenny never criticised a player, even a modest professional from Estonia. I don't think anyone in Estonia would hold it against him if the great Kenny Dalglish questioned the skill of a little-known Estonian, but Kenny wouldn't do it. I remember watching him on television when he was in the BBC studio at Euro '96. I was laughing so much because Des Lynam could get nothing out of him. It was so predictable but Des kept trying – 'Come on, Kenny, tell us what you really think.' Kenny did open up a bit, but not much. Among friends and those he trusts, Kenny will be the life and soul of the party. I saw him drunk once at a Christmas party at Liverpool. Someone had spiked his drink. We had to carry him out and Peter Beardsley drove him home.

Kenny is like me. He loves being around footballers. He cannot wait to come into work every day just for the banter. I see that all the time at Celtic. No other form of employment would provide Kenny with the satisfaction that football does. All managers say that nothing beats playing for the camaraderie. Kenny has said it himself. The closest thing to playing is managing and that is one reason why so many footballers go into it. They cannot leave football because football will not leave them. It is in their blood. At Liverpool and Newcastle, Kenny could not detach himself from the playing side because he revelled in the jokes and wind-ups. He always wanted to be in the five-a-side matches as if he were still part of the team itself. The problem is that when a manager reaches his mid-forties, he cannot run around any more, but because he is the manager no one dares tell him. When I was at Newcastle, we used to have a laugh with Terry McDermott about Kenny.

'Why can't Kenny bow out gracefully like you have, Terry?' I inquired. Terry Mac knows he hasn't got the legs any more so he didn't join in the five-a-sides at Newcastle. But there was no way anyone could persuade Kenny that he wasn't the best player on the pitch. Kenny was the most enthusiastic person in training; he tried harder than anyone else, always wanting the ball. That is how Kenny, an ex-player, stayed immersed in the world of banter and camaraderie that he loves. Management is a very lonely job. Even the coaches are closer to the players. Roy and Ronnie used to go out for a drink with the boys at Liverpool. Newcastle's coaches and physios drank with the players. Managers cannot become involved in that. I feel sorry for managers or Directors of Football like Kenny, who find it hard to detach themselves from the dressing-room culture they thrived on as players. Kenny has never got over not being a player any more.

Under Kenny, Liverpool were always in contention for the major domestic prizes. In my first season at Anfield, we won the League but lost the FA Cup final. In my second, 1988–89, the situation was reversed. Arsenal stole the championship from us in the most startling manner imaginable with a last-minute goal on the last day of the season, 26 May 1989. I had not watched the game on television until Sir Bobby Charlton, in his Sky TV *Scrapbook* programme, analysed the game with George Graham, who was Arsenal's manager on that remarkable night at Anfield. Liverpool did not play badly against Arsenal; we moved the ball well but we were over-cautious. We were not the normal dynamic, free-flowing Liverpool. The mathematical equation was supposedly in Liverpool's favour; we needed only a draw or even a 1–0 defeat to give us the championship ahead of Arsenal. Psychologically, having that comfort zone actually inhibited us. We never attacked as we should have. Instances arose during the game where if we had been more ambitious we could have exploited Arsenal's need to push up. We created promising opportunities but never played the killer ball or got enough people in the box. Yet Liverpool were controlling the game; despite the lack of openings, we appeared to be closing in on the double by the minute.

We reached half-time in one piece. We were particularly concentrating on Arsenal's set-pieces because we knew how dangerous a side prepared by George Graham could be in those situations. That was all we were worried about and with good cause. Seven minutes into the second half, Nigel Winterburn sent in an indirect free kick which flew past Bruce Grobbelaar. A linesman flagged and Liverpool protested but I knew Alan Smith had got a headed touch on the ball. Merseysiders still question the goal but it was legitimate. Despite this setback, I believed we would win the championship. Arsenal still required another goal. The second half was footballing drama at its very best.

The match was well into injury time, the Kop was already celebrating and most Liverpool minds were on the double when I decided to show some ambition for possibly the first time in the evening. What I did next cost Liverpool the championship. For some reason, I had wandered over to the right and was in possession. To this day, I do not know what I was doing over there. Arsenal, aware of the ebbing time, were desperate to retrieve the ball, to launch one final attack, so Tony Adams slid in on me. I beat him and carried on towards the corner flag. Here I made a terrible mistake. I should have taken the ball down to the corner and stayed there, running down the clock. But Kevin Richardson came across. Ambition clouded my judgement. I looked at Kevin, a midfielder clearly exhausted and out of position, and felt I could dribble past him. Then I would be in on goal and glory awaited. So I ran at Kevin but as I tried to push the ball past him, he nicked it off me.

So unfolded a chain of events that destroyed Liverpool's double aspirations. The move should never have been allowed to start or develop. I should never have risked losing possession. On gaining the ball, Kevin passed back to John Lukic, Arsenal's goalkeeper, who in those days was allowed to pick the ball up. Lukic quickly threw the ball out to the right to Lee Dixon. Even here, we could have stopped the move. Steve McMahon flew out to try to block Dixon's pass to Smith. Steve failed and was also now out of position. The midfielder whom Steve was supposed to be marking, Michael Thomas, began his famous burst through the middle, running on to Smith's pass. Once again, Liverpool had an opportunity to halt the attack. Ray Houghton was chasing back and closing on Thomas. I only learned this through talking to Chris Waddle at Italia '90. Chris watched the match on television with some friends on a beach in Portugal. As a Tottenham fan, Chris obviously didn't want Arsenal to win, so he was shouting at Ray 'go on, go on'. Ray was catching Thomas, who was dithering. Ray expected Thomas to shoot but just as it seemed he would, he took the ball on another stride which confused Ray, who slowed down and slid in only when the ball was racing into the net. Two-nil to Arsenal and Liverpool's double dream was shattered.

No one at Anfield that night could actually believe Arsenal had won the championship. I couldn't. Even the Arsenal players had disbelief etched on their faces, almost unable to come to terms with the fact that they had overturned the odds in the last minute of the last game of the season. Perhaps if Thomas had scored in the eightieth minute, they would have had ten minutes of thinking 'we've won the League'. But it all happened so quickly; moments after Thomas's goal the final whistle went. The Kop, ever generous, applauded Arsenal. We never saw their players afterwards, although we heard them in their dressing-room which was reverberating with noise. It was great for Arsenal but we really should have avoided it, particularly me. In the dressing-room, Ronnie Moran said to me, 'What were you doing? You should have taken the ball down to the corner flag.' But no one else criticised me. Everyone was too shell-shocked. Besides, the emotion of winning or losing, the very significance of football itself had been placed into perspective by tragic events a month before.

chapter fourteen

hillsborough

The events of 15 April 1989 at Hillsborough made me realise what is really important in life. After each funeral I attended, when another set of parents buried a beloved son or daughter, when another grieving family mourned a relative who died following Liverpool, I would come home and climb into bed with my eldest son, Jamie, just to hold him, just to hear him breathing. We slept curled up together. Jordan, my second son, was just a baby and I would cradle him in my arms. For months after Hillsborough, I couldn't bear to be apart from my two sons. If one of them fell over, I ran across and hugged him, soothed him, showed him my love. Scarred into my mind was the image of those parents who could not hold their loved ones any more, who could not see them smile and grow up. That thought devastated me. So I hugged my children tight.

Before Hillsborough, I had always tried to keep things in perspective but what happened on the Leppings Lane terrraces made me question so much in my life. When I struggled to get in the team at Liverpool and then Newcastle United, I said to myself, 'Does it really matter? I'm alive. My family are alive. That is all that matters.' Hillsborough crystallised my priorities. Football lost its obsessive significance; it was not the be all and end all. How could it be when ninety-six people died, when parents lost children and children lost parents? Bill Shankly's comment that 'football is not a matter of life and death, it is far more important than that' sounded even falser after Hillsborough. Football is a game, a glorious pursuit but how can it be more important than life itself?

Saturday, 15 April 1989 should have been a day of excitement, when a compelling FA Cup semi-final between Liverpool and Nottingham Forest was played at the home of Sheffield Wednesday. I try not to think about the day itself, but I will never forget it. The events were like a nightmare unfolding. I didn't realise anything was amiss on the Leppings Lane terrace until a couple of fans ran on to the pitch shouting, 'There are people being killed in there.' I thought they were exaggerating, like when players say 'that tackle nearly killed me'. I just thought the fans were getting a bit squashed. In those days, with stadiums packed with standing supporters, it always looked cramped. Before Hillsborough, I had often seen fans crushed together but never thought anything of it. I just assumed there were a lot of people in there, having a good time. To me, it might look uncomfortable, but fans used to say they liked the whole atmosphere of being in together, swaying around. In the Kop, people loved being lifted up, their feet not touching the ground as they were carried back and forth in a sea of bodies. That was one of the attractions of the terraces to many supporters.

When Forest won a corner at the Leppings Lane end, I looked into the crowd and could see fans crushed up against the fence, but the enormity of what was happening still did not register. My mind was on the game, on defeating Forest and reaching Wembley. All of Liverpool's players focused on the incoming corner. No one could envisage anything like what was happening, even when it was happening before our very eyes. Even when more fans started spilling out on to the pitch, we guessed they were excited by the occasion. Liverpool had met Forest in the Cup the year before and a rivalry had built up between the clubs. Things had been said which stirred the passions. I actually thought it was a pitch invasion. So did all the other Liverpool players. But Bruce Grobbelaar, who was closest to the Leppings Lane terrace, quickly realised there was something terribly wrong when he went to retrieve a ball and heard fans screaming – 'They're killing us, Bruce, they're killing us.' Bruce shouted at the stewards to do something.

Six minutes into the match, a policeman ran on to tell Ray Lewis, the referee, to halt the game. Lewis immediately led the players back to the dressing-rooms. The scale of the tragedy was still unimaginable. We thought a few fans had been squashed but that we would be playing again soon, once the stewards had sorted out the problem. In the dressing-room, Ronnie Moran said over and over again, 'Keep warm, lads, because we will be going out in a minute.' Lewis came in and said, 'We'll be going out in ten minutes.' So we kept stretching. After a while we heard voices in the corridor, shouting that people had been killed. But the match had still officially to be called off, so we carried on stretching and jogging on the spot. After a while, a few players said, 'Let's sit down, we can't jog for ever.' Some of the players were tiring themselves through jogging on the spot. We were loathe to sit down, though. It was a Cup semi-final and we all worried that Kenny Dalglish might see us sitting there reading the programme and looking bored. We had to be up for the game, so our minds were still on going back out. No one sat there discussing where they were going that night. We had to stay focused on the game. Lewis kept coming in and saying, 'Another five minutes.' Each time, we all got up and started jogging again until he finally came in and said, 'That's it, lads, match off.'

Stories began filtering into the dressing-room about what was happening outside. First we heard that two fans had been killed in the crush, then fifteen. It was impossible to take in. I thought to myself that maybe one or two have died, which was bad enough, but it couldn't possibly be any more. Suddenly the figure jumped to twenty-five. When we heard the voices in the corridor saying fifty people had been killed, we thought someone had got carried away, in the way rumours escalate. One over-excited person says,

'I've heard fifty people may have been killed,' and somebody else passes it on as fact. None of us really knew what was going on.

We showered and hurried up to the players' lounge. Suzy was there, crying her eyes out.

'Some people have died,' she said.

'Don't believe that,' I replied, 'it's just a rumour.'

But Suzy and the other wives knew what had happened. Because the game was not at Anfield, the wives didn't wait in the lounge before kick-off. They arrived and went straight to their seats. They had sat there and watched the awful scenes on the Leppings Lane terrace, the fans coming on to the grass, pleading for help, lifting limp bodies on to the pitch, ripping up hoardings to bear the dead away. The players never knew. We were cocooned from all the horror outside. I was telling Suzy that 'it's not that bad' when I saw the television and realised it was far worse. All the rumours of crushing and deaths became desperate reality when I heard Des Lynam say, 'There's been a tragedy at Hillsborough. There are many dead.' I went numb. I couldn't believe it. Complete silence seized the room. Every face turned towards the television screen. No one sat down. No one spoke. Forest's players were also in the lounge. What could they say? 'We're sorry your fans have been killed'? The fact that they played for Forest and we played for Liverpool was irrelevant. These were human beings who died.

We watched the television for an hour in silence. Many in the lounge were crying. Each of the players wondered whether he knew anyone who could have been in that terrible cage. I had only been at Liverpool for two years and knew hardly any of the fans. It was far worse for the local players like John Aldridge and Steve McMahon. Aldo was very agitated. He was desperately trying to make phone-calls. Eventually, we got on the coach, each player sitting next to his wife, holding hands, still numb and speechless. Everyone drank heavily all the way back to Liverpool. I got completely smashed on brandy. People wept all the way home. All the wives were crying. I was crying. Kenny was crying. Bruce said he was considering quitting. Although I never thought about giving up football despite being filled with guilt afterwards, I understood what Bruce meant. Those Liverpool fans went to Hillsborough to watch us and there we were, stepping on to a luxury coach to go home, and they were being laid out in a temporary morgue. As we travelled back across the Pennines, their mums and dads were making the reverse journey to come and identify their children's bodies. Guilt swirled around my head. Had I been out there on the pitch, and not back in the dressing-room, I would have helped. I know I would have done. I would have done anything, ripped out hoardings to carry the injured to the ambulances, talked to the dying, willed them to live, argued with the police to move faster. Anyone would have helped if they could. I've still not watched that television docu-drama on Hillsborough. I taped it and it sits in a box on the shelf but I still cannot bring myself to watch it. Suzy feels the same.

Back at Anfield, Suzy and I climbed into our car, Suzy drove home and we watched the news on television, tears streaming down our faces. I remember going in and cuddling Jordan. As I took in the television pictures again, all I could see were devastated parents. I kept thinking that could have been my child going to a match on a lovely sunny day, a child brimming with excitement at the prospect of an FA Cup semi-final. How many parents got their children semi-final tickets so they could go to Hillsborough with their mates? And they never returned. I cried and cried just thinking about that tragedy. I held Jordan and Jamie for hours that night and thought about my own family, about what would I do if something like that happened to one of my children on an occasion which was supposed to be joyful. I managed to sleep that night only because I was still drunk. The brandy on the coach did it. The next morning, I couldn't read the papers. The photographs were so horrific I had to put the paper down. I stayed at home with Suzy and the children, thinking how lucky I was to have them. I didn't touch a drop more of alcohol. I didn't need to. I already had a raging headache from the brandy that had been my only chance of sleep.

Initially, I saw Hillsborough from a personal perspective. I just thought how heartbroken I would have been if it had been my child. Over the next few days, my emotions turned to disbelief and concern for the people who suffered. I kept thinking about the events that led to the crush. It would be easy to blame South Yorkshire Police but they never set out that morning to allow ninety-six innocent people to die. They could never have foreseen Hillsborough. No one could. Hillsborough was a tragic accident. I shudder when I hear people blame Chief Superintendent Duckenfield, the man who ordered the opening of the gates leading on to the Leppings Lane terrace. Liverpool fans wanted to get in. They kept asking the superintendent at the gates who radioed Duckenfield for permission. If Duckenfield had known ninety-six people were going to die, he obviously would never have given the order. He probably thought he was doing Liverpool's fans a favour. He was just letting supporters in to watch the team they love. Because Duckenfield ordered the gates to be opened, he was deemed worthy of blame. I thought that was unfair, although perhaps he should have ordered them to be opened earlier.

But Duckenfield's policemen did handle the crush badly. I'm sure they were trained in the correct procedure, but however much preparation a policeman undergoes, he can never be ready for what transpires. No policeman could predict those scenes or his own reaction to them. A friend of mine is an air-hostess and no matter how much training she does in smoke-filled rooms at Heathrow, I would be very surprised if she acted as the text-book dictated should a real emergency occur. Nothing could have prepared those policemen for Hillsborough. Some are claiming compensation for post-traumatic stress disorder. Just because they are policemen doesn't mean that when they encounter a dead body they cannot collapse and suffer like anyone else. Nobody, not even policemen, can prepare for that sort of horror.

I feel no anger towards the ordinary policemen involved at Hillsborough. My sense of outrage was provoked by the top policemen and here Duckenfield was culpable; he and his colleagues should have been far more compassionate towards the grieving relatives. Amidst all the recriminations, the South Yorkshire Police refused to accept any responsibility. Their attitude was disgusting. They should have been more thoughtful, sympathetic and honest than just to say 'it's all the fans' fault'. Listening to the police and all their leaks to the newspapers, Hillsborough seemed to be the responsibility of everyone apart from the South Yorkshire Police.

A story about Liverpool fans nicking money from dead bodies and urinating on corpses was shamefully printed by the *Sun* under that terrible headline 'The Truth'. For the police to manufacture a story like that when people were killed and their families in mourning was disgraceful. Everyone on Merseyside was incensed with the *Sun* calling Liverpool fans 'scum'. The families were outraged. Liverpool Football Club was outraged. The whole city was outraged. Liverpool players continued to read the *Sun* but no one talked to the paper after that evil story. Sales of the *Sun* on Merseyside plummeted.

On the Monday morning, the players went through the papers looking at the awful photographs. The full horror of what had happened became brutally clear. Two girls were pictured on one front page squashed up against the fence. Somehow they lived. We knew those girls. They used to hang around outside Melwood for autographs. I saw one of the girls, Jackie, early in 1999 at the Liverpool–Blackburn game. Jackie was outside Anfield and I had my picture taken with her. Everyone knew Jackie. Players were looking through the papers to see if there was anyone they knew. I'm sure John Aldridge and Steve McMahon, the local boys, did but they dealt with it in their own private way.

Later that day, we travelled over to the hospital in Sheffield. When we got there and encountered row upon row of people in comas, we all felt terrible. The players stayed in groups initially. At Christmas, when a squad goes into the local hospital to visit sick children, the players all stick together. Footballers are generally embarrassed at being fit and healthy and surrounded by the unwell and injured. I always worry about saying something condescending, so I tend to march across and ask a child in a wheelchair, 'How did you lose both your legs?' Children come to terms with things quickly and can talk about it. I love kids. In Sheffield, no one felt like making the first move. We clung together for the first ten minutes, unsure of how to approach beds containing fans in comas. It was the relatives who took the initiative. A father walked up to me and said, 'You are my son's favourite player. Please come and talk to him.' Relatives went up to each of the players and asked them to see their child. We were all hesitant but of course agreed.

I had never seen anyone in a coma before. I didn't know what to say or even whether he could hear me. If the child had been my son, I knew I would have no trouble talking. Eventually, I said something like, 'It's John Barnes here. I'm sorry it happened. Keep fighting. I know you can pull through.' It was the type of line actors say in *ER*. Parents sometimes come to the training ground and ask me to speak into a tape-recorder to send a few words of encouragement to their ill child. 'This is John Barnes here,' I say into the microphone, 'wishing you well, don't give up, we want to see you supporting us again next season.' It wasn't the same at the hospital.

It is amazing what a few words can do. Some of the players started to get a reaction, a flicker of life. 'He moved, he moved,' came the cry from the parents. Families and nurses urged us to 'keep talking, keep talking'. That spurred us all on. It was so important to feel we could actually help. So we chatted away non-stop. Parents told their child, 'John Barnes is here,' and encouraged me with 'Come on, John, talk to him.' I held their hands and just talked and talked and talked, about anything that came into my mind about football, about the club we all loved. Sometimes, after a while, some movement could be discerned in their hands. 'Let him rest now,' the nurse said, more hopeful that the boy would emerge from the coma gradually. I couldn't believe it.

Two fans came out of comas while the players were in the hospital. It made us feel very good. I am not religious in the church-going sense but I do believe in higher spirits, fate and the greater good. It was a very humbling experience. One asked, 'What's the score?'

He saw Aldo and said, 'John Aldridge?! What's going on?' Then he started smiling. He thought Liverpool's players had come to visit him at home in bed. Another awoke with a start and jumped up. Everyone heard the commotion and rushed around the bed. He opened his eyes and saw Peter Beardsley and me looking at him. He couldn't believe it. Neither of them had any recollection of what happened on the Leppings Lane terrace. They had slipped into comas because of the weight of bodies crushing them. Their last memory was of travelling to a football match.

If I had ever needed reminding of the importance of life and family, Hillsborough and events in that hospital ward brought it home to me. I was only there for a short time and found it deeply moving. Most of the parents had been there from the Saturday, waiting for hour after agonising hour. They just sat there, talking to their child, praying their loved ones would open their eyes. The parents were so brave. They were all convinced their children would recover. I know if it had been one of my four children lying there, I would never have lost hope of them coming round. I know my beloved daughter Jasmin and if she were ever in a coma, I am certain she would recover if I talked to her enough.

I feel tremendous respect for the parents of the Hillsborough victims, almost awe. They were so strong at a time when their world was collapsing. The parents saw the players as a means to revive their children. They never blamed us when the child remained unresponsive, still reliant for life on a bedside machine of lights and tubes. We did what we could, but I didn't expect to be a miracle worker. It was incredible when those two boys came round while we were at the hospital.

It was difficult walking past parents whose child was still in a coma. As those two revived, people expected more and more to awake left, right and centre like a nice film where everyone recovers, opens their eyes and says, 'Hi, how are you doing?' But life is not like a Hollywood movie.

After three hours, we climbed back on the bus. It was buzzing on the way home. That visit helped the players so much. We talked about everything that happened at the hospital, about the guy who woke up and asked what the score was, about his ecstatic, emotional parents.

By then, the families of those who had died had started coming to Anfield. Meeting them was an extraordinarily moving experience. Their relatives had died following Liverpool and here they were, almost speechless with disbelief that they were walking into the players' lounge at Anfield. Most were crying. Many said, 'He would have loved to have been here, talking to John Barnes in the middle of Anfield. He will be saying, "I should be there because I love Liverpool."' So many grieving mothers and fathers observed that their lost child would be jealous of them. Not only was I humbled by their emotional reaction to being inside Anfield, I was embarrassed. I didn't know how they would behave towards me. The families could have blamed me. They could have said, 'My precious son came to see you play and now he is dead and you've still got your money, your car and your house.' But none of them did. They were so appreciative of what we did, of how much we meant to their lost loved one. Faced with the bereaved at Anfield, all I could think of was that their relatives died because of us. But the families seemed almost awestruck and deeply grateful. They came into Anfield, sat down, looked at us and said, 'This is the only place we are happy.'

Often, whole families came to Anfield – second cousins, distant nephews of the bereaved, all made the journey. That really brought home to me just how much football means to people in Liverpool. If my son had died supporting Liverpool, I wouldn't have gone to Anfield afterwards. Not a chance. For me, it would be a time for private grieving. If I had lost a child at Hillsborough, I would have blamed the players, not wanted to meet and praise them.

I couldn't believe how strong the families were and still are. When we met them at Anfield, most of the parents seemed to be coping astonishingly well. Maybe privately they weren't. Maybe when they were away from Anfield, they wept uncontrollably for their beloved child taken from them. Maybe at home, with the world shut out, they broke down and cried 'Why, why, why?' I would have done. But whenever I met the bereaved, they were so dignified. The families thought the players were helping them. I cannot state too strongly how much the families helped me. They helped me with my own guilt. Their sons and daughters were there to watch me play. If Liverpool hadn't played Nottingham Forest on that day, their children wouldn't be dead. They died because of Liverpool and I was a Liverpool footballer so I felt desperately guilty. The families' reaction to me eased my sense of blame.

Anfield became a shrine. Hour after hour, day after day people arrived to hang scarves on the Shankly Gates and place flowers or mementoes on the Kop and, when that great stand was full, on the pitch itself. It made me choke with emotion to see the flowers spreading across the pitch, to hear the cellophane wrappers rustling in the wind, to look at the teddy-bears tied to the goalposts, to walk past a dead child's football boots placed there by his grieving parents. The scene was eerie, both sad and beautiful. Cards were left everywhere, pinned to flowers or nestled within a scarf. I read the messages, the words of condolence and support from all corners of the globe, from Australia, Bangkok and China. All the while, a sorrowful stream of visitors walked past in silence, rendered speechless by the sight of all these tributes and the tragedy that elicited them.

The players still went in to Anfield so I saw the carpet of flowers grow by the day, at first covering the six-yard box, then the penalty area, then reaching out towards the halfway line; so much grief and love and disbelief covering Anfield's pitch. Suzy came to see it. Women love flowers and she wanted to read all the cards. The wives were magnificent that week. Suzy was at Anfield for most of the time. Marina Dalglish, Kenny's wife, rang round the wives and asked them to come to Anfield to make it more welcoming for the families. Being involved helped Suzy. She made tea and talked to the relatives. Women are more compassionate than men in sensitive situations. They are used to dealing with children and there were lots of kids there with the families. In the immediate aftermath of Hillsborough, the wives were probably more effective than the players in helping and communicating with the families.

The tributes were not just at Anfield. I walked into Stanley Park and saw all the Everton scarves tied together. They stretched from Goodison Park to Anfield, a symbol of the unity between the two clubs. That was the nature of the rivalry; the relationship between Everton and Liverpool was so different from that between Newcastle and Sunderland or Celtic and Rangers. On Merseyside, families are split red and blue. I was initially surprised by Evertonians' reaction but then understood that many of them would have lost a brother, a cousin or a father at Hillsborough. The coming together of the blue and red parts of the city touched me greatly. Support flowed from everywhere. People travelled from as far afield as Australia to pay their respects at Anfield. All football fans were united in their grief. Even those from Manchester United sent gestures of sympathy. Every fan had reason to mourn. Every fan knew that it could have been him or her on that terrace death-trap. A few politicians appeared at Anfield to pay their respects. I was glad more politicians didn't show their faces. Hillsborough and the grieving process was nothing to do with politicians. If they had turned up, it would simply have been a publicity stunt. Politicians had no right to be present at Anfield.

I had never been to a funeral before. The first one I went to was for Gary Church, in Waterloo on Merseyside. Kenny, Gary Ablett, John Aldridge, Ray Houghton and I went. Liverpool were keen to have at least two players at every funeral. Particular players were requested by some families so some went to more than others. Most players preferred to go together. They felt less awkward. I went to five funerals on my own and three with other players. I went wherever Liverpool sent me, to whichever family telephoned Anfield and requested my presence at their son's or husband's funeral. I drove to Bromsgrove and London, all over the country for the eight funerals. The last one was as difficult as the first.

When we encountered the families in the immediate aftermath of Hillsborough, they were mourning and filled with sorrow. In the week before the funeral they were busy organising the church and all their relatives, which distracted them from their grieving. But on the day of the funeral, all the emotions flooded forth again. Although I had been invited to the funerals, I felt like an intruder. I drove to the house, went in and had a cup of tea in the kitchen whilst the family sorted themselves out before leaving for the church. They usually had grannies or aunties staying, so there was a fair amount of chaos. I just stayed out of the way until somebody said 'come in the car with us' or just told me to see them there, in which case I drove with the procession and parked in a side-road. My instincts were to stand at the back of the church, so as not to bring attention to myself. But the families always insisted I come down the front. I did whatever they wished. I was there to help them. Bruce Grobbelaar did some of the readings at the funerals he attended. I wasn't asked to but I would have done if asked.

Sitting alongside the grieving relatives made me uncomfortable. The mourning was very apparent in church so guilt filled me again. At Anfield, the relationship between player and family had been good and positive, but not at the funeral. Everyone cried. I sat there, listening to the sobbing around me, the sounds of parents breaking down, the feelings of utter desolation sweeping everyone within the church. I relived the emotions of Hillsborough and the days immediately after, the feelings of guilt and remorse and intrusion. I felt I really shouldn't be here in this church, in the middle of someone else's nightmare. Those were the saddest days imaginable and I just sat there thinking the child in that coffin had come to watch me. Then the vicar started talking about the dead child, about how he had set off from home on that fateful day, filled with excitement at the thought of seeing his idols. When the vicar said that the child had ended up dying, the guilt came rushing back into me again. And there I was, sitting in the middle of the child's devastated family, none of whom I knew. The real friends were sitting at the back, they were the ones who loved him. They must have resented my presence, the sight of John Barnes being pushed in as some sort of hero.

Looking around the church or at the wake afterwards, I detected some antipathy towards me. I could tell from their faces which ones didn't want me there, who would not appreciate me attempting to console them. For them, I symbolised the world that claimed their loved one. No one said anything unpleasant to me but I knew from their body language. I understood. I understood them thinking, 'There you are John Barnes, you are going to leave the funeral and go back to your big house and my relative has spent all his money following you and now he is dead.' Each funeral contained some who felt anger towards Liverpool's players.

But generally we were well received at the funerals. When we gathered back at the house afterwards, I wasn't sure how to behave. What do I do? Do I go up and hug them? Do I keep away from them? But a lot were coming up and hugging me. Talking to the relatives was shattering. The stories they told were devastating. Friends or brothers of the dead fan described how they had gone to the match together. They recalled the fateful moment when they became separated in the crush, of the last eye contact or word between them. They related how they found the lifeless body. Personally, I didn't really want to broach the subject of what had actually happened. I thought they might flip and relive the nightmare and go mad. But most wanted to reflect on the events of Hillsborough; it formed part of the healing process for some. The families took comfort from the presence of someone whom their dead child had admired. But I wasn't there to be the families' rock. I don't know whether I would have had the strength to be that anyway. There was a danger that I remained the last link to their son. But no one ever became like a leech. No one ever rang up, although we did meet at the Hillsborough Memorials. It is important to have that link for them and us.

It meant so much to me to be able to help the families, in however small a way. That was why I chose not to play for England against Albania in a World Cup qualifier on 26 April. It coincided with a funeral. People wrote that I was not in a fit state emotionally to focus on an international. That was rubbish. Physically and mentally, I was ready to play. If there hadn't been a funeral on that day, I would have played. The funeral was far more important than an England match. I wasn't making a statement that people were playing football too soon after Hillsborough. It was just a question of timing and priorities.

The funerals deeply affected everyone at Liverpool. Some of the wives and players went round singing or humming bits from hymns because of the number of funerals they attended. I don't know any hymns. It always amazes me when I go to church for the children's carol services, and the vicar says we are going to sing a certain hymn and everyone knows it. I've never heard it, apart from 'All Things Bright and Beautiful'. And there was Anfield filled with the sound of hymns being hummed or sung.

The players discussed funerals after training but wouldn't touch on the emotions involved. As for coping with the continual sight of grieving families, each player handled that situation on his own. None of the players opened up to each other. No one said to me, 'Digger, how are you coping?' and I never asked anyone that question. We all dealt with Hillsborough on our own.

We did talk about some of the funny things that happened. There was one funeral in Kirkby that I went to with Terry McDermott, who comes from around there. The church had a bell-ringer who was only little and about eighty years old. The only way he could pull the rope properly was by jumping off a chair and then climbing back on it. He received word that the coffin was on its way so he started ringing the bell by grasping the rope, standing on the chair and jumping off, standing on the chair and jumping off. But the coffin was delayed for ten minutes. Having started, the old man obviously felt he had to continue. He was soon exhausted. Sweat poured off his brow as he jumped up and down. At first, I managed to control my giggles. I was trying to be dignified because the Mayoress was in front of us. Terry Mac couldn't and he was shaking with laughter. Soon the whole church was laughing. The Mayoress glanced back at us; she looked indignant but after a while even she started laughing. Liverpool funerals are like local weddings; a fight or laughter could break out. During the service, people were lost in mourning. But before and after there was plenty of humour.

Liverpool did not play competitively for a couple of weeks after Hillsborough but we still trained. The players discussed whether it was right to play in the FA Cup final should we defeat Forest in the re-arranged match. We talked about whether to scrap the Cup as a sign of respect for those who died at Hillsborough. But the majority of the families pleaded with us to continue. 'You have to play on in the Cup,' they kept telling us. It was if they wanted to win the Cup as a memorial to their lost children. The players became caught up in the relatives' desire for the Cup to go on. We were determined to go along with their wishes even if some of the players didn't feel like playing sport so soon after so many deaths. But the families made the decision for us. One father looked me in the eye and said, 'You have to go on for my son. He would have died for nothing if you don't play on.'

Liverpool waited the right amount of time. On the Monday after Hillsborough, the families' response was that 'you've got to play for them'. But the club wanted the relatives to calm down, think about it and then decide. This was an emotional period when people may not be thinking clearly. Liverpool did well in not jumping to a rash decision. Everything had to be right for the families. I did not need a recovery period. I did not deserve one. It was the families who suffered, not me. I actually thought I was being selfish in feeling sorry for myself. If the families hadn't wanted us to play again that season, I wouldn't have. But the mood amongst the families was for us to re-start.

Once that was clear, Liverpool organised a friendly match. It would have been too difficult to go straight back into competitive action. We needed a warm-up to sharpen us and to release some emotion. So we went to Glasgow and played Celtic in front of 60,000 people who sang 'You'll Never Walk Alone'. The singing was so moving; the words, and the intensity with which they were sung, told of the support for Liverpool and everyone connected with the club. We were all so proud to represent Liverpool. We were also relieved to be playing again, particularly with a 4–0 win over Celtic. Once we decided to play again, people swiftly re-tuned into football. Our first competitive game back was, fittingly, against Everton on 3 May where again the whole city showed its unity.

Four days after that scoreless draw, the semi-final against Forest took place at Old Trafford. Forest were on a hiding to nothing. If they had beaten us, everyone would have hated them. The whole country wanted Liverpool to win. I think deep down even Forest wanted us to win because Liverpool had to go to the Cup final for their fans. Everton had won the other semi-final against Norwich City and it was as if Forest were intruding on a Merseyside affair. We were determined to beat them and Forest were determined to beat us but the script dictated we had to win. Maybe subconsciously Forest's players felt that as well. I'm sure even the Forest fans were not that displeased that Liverpool reached Wembley. John Aldridge ensured we did, scoring twice in a 3–1 win.

Liverpool versus Everton in the sunshine at Wembley was the best FA Cup final scenario, if there could be one after something so tragic. Everton fans lost family and friends as well so it was a poignant day for them. What a day the final was. Unforgettable. The sun shone, the fans mixed, observing a minute's silence in which you could almost hear the tears drop. Everton fans wanted to beat us, so did their players, and there was real passion but it seemed a family event. The day was very moving but, as a professional, once the whistle goes, football takes over. I couldn't believe it when Everton came back to 2–2 and then Rushie got our winner. At the final whistle, the fans poured on to the pitch, which I could understand. There was some sadness within me that Liverpool didn't get the chance to do a lap of honour because of all the fans spilling across Wembley. I've completed four laps of honour as a loser but never one as a winner. It would have been nice but there was no stopping the fans. As the last seconds of the game ebbed away, I could see the stewards preparing for the fans but they could have called out the Turkish Army without a chance of keeping the fans off the pitch. As I wormed my way out of the crowd, they kept rubbing my head.

Scousers love pulling your hair and rubbing your head. I just went under a sea of people and everyone was going mad so we had to get out quickly and collect our medals.

Hillsborough changed football, ushering in all-seater stadiums. As with the Ibrox disaster, something had to be done. Following the Bradford fire, Hillsborough was the last straw. A tragedy in which ninety-six innocents lost their lives had to occur before the authorities would decide to treat fans better. Although a lot of fans wanted terracing to continue, football decided to improve conditions. I am all for progress anyway. I'm a modern person. I prefer new houses. I want all-seater stadiums, preferably indoor ones where I don't get wet, with nice restaurants and toilets. The Taylor Report, which transformed stadiums in this country, affected the atmosphere within grounds. Some used to be famous for fans jumping up and down and making a lot of noise. That has survived at certain clubs. Now that Anfield is all-seater, I don't think the Kop is necessarily quieter, although the supporters don't sway any more. The Kop has always been sensational with its noise and scarves. The noise is still there at St James' Park on Tyneside. It is deafening at Celtic Park. It depends on the people. Liverpudlians, Geordies and Glaswegians wouldn't keep quiet if they were sitting down or standing up. But many grounds have become quieter. Old Trafford has definitely changed. People who remember Charlton Athletic at the Valley in the 1950s insist the fans made more noise then.

From a personal perspective, Hillsborough made me more sanguine, more appreciative of my luck. For example, I have become a more relaxed driver. If someone cuts me up, I don't get angry. I just think that driver probably has to get somewhere quickly. When my contract was close to expiring at Newcastle, I wondered, 'Where the hell am I going to be next year?' But then I thought, 'Hang on, I've got a house, the kids, health and wealth.' So was it important whether I ever played again? Playing is not everything. There are times when I do worry about stupid things; then I remind myself of the visit to the Sheffield hospital and of people waking from comas. Having experienced Hillsborough and the aftermath, I understood that it was unimportant whether I got an extra year on my contract or more money for endorsements. Early in 1999, I was down in London and took the Underground to go to a restaurant. I saw some people with sleeping bags begging for money. There was I thinking, 'I want to play at Newcastle for five more years. I want Newcastle to pay me more money. I want a nicer car and more clothes.' But when I saw the beggars I asked myself whether I really needed all that extra money. Hillsborough was the biggest reminder of how fortunate we are as human beings just to be alive. I remind myself of that all the time.

Hillsborough was a profound experience, chastening, moving and eye-opening. I became friendly with one of the relatives called Chrissie, whom I used to speak to now and again. We meet the families at the annual commemoration and talk about the child they lost, about how old they would have been, about how much they loved Liverpool. It's amazing to see the families again. Sometimes there is someone there I don't recognise.

'Who's that?' I ask.

'She was a baby at the time,' they reply. Some of them don't even remember the dad or brother they lost. The letters I received were very humbling. Families wrote to thank me for all I had done and I didn't think I had done all that much. All I did was get in a car and go to a funeral. It just shows, any kind word or gesture really goes a long way.

I've heard it said that the public's perception of me changed because of Hillsborough. I don't know how people saw me before, but it upsets me if they thought I couldn't be compassionate. People are not paying me a compliment when they say, 'Weren't you nice during Hillsborough.' Anyway, as soon as I donned an England shirt, they booed me again. I have always kept football matters in perspective. Hillsborough simply confirmed that reality and re-confirmed my love for my family.

chapter fifteen

private life

My wife Suzy does not know much about football. She once watched a match at Anfield and wondered why David James was not in goal for Liverpool in the second half. David was standing in the other goalmouth having changed ends at half-time. Suzy is just not interested. 'But I want to support you,' she says. 'You don't need to, Suzy,' I tell her. She comes occasionally, goes in the players' lounge at half-time and usually stays there for the second half. Sometimes Suzy spends all game in there. 'Why come?' I ask her. 'I don't need you there to support me.' Many footballers' wives engross themselves in football, although they hate it and would much rather be doing something else. I take the children or friends to matches but tell Suzy to go off and enjoy herself elsewhere. Businessmen do not expect their wives to come to the office.

Suzy and I are chalk and cheese. Our tastes in music and films differ. I'm addicted to kung fu movies, always have been. I go out and buy forty at a time, hurry home, lock myself in the conservatory and watch five in a row. The session lasts about seven hours. Suzy goes mad! She is actually very good, just leaving me to get on with it. For me, kung fu movies offer the best form of relaxation, escape even. As a kid in Jamaica, I went with my cousins to the matinee kung fu triple bill at the Regal Theatre in Kingston. When my family moved to London, I found a cinema on the Holloway Road which ran late-night screenings. My mates and I would sit there, loving the whole fantasy element of kung fu plots. It's brilliant when the fighters jump fifty feet in the air and kill ten people with one blow. Afterwards, all the kids used to spill out on to Holloway Road jumping across cars and pretending to do kung fu.

Our heroes were actors like Wang Yu, Chen Sing and the legendary Carter Wong. They were the One-Armed Swordsman and the Flying Guillotine. I love *Iron Monkey 1* and *Iron Monkey 2* but my favourite films are the tales of the Shaolin Temple. A man came from India and taught the monks of Shaolin how to protect themselves against the Japanese and other bad people. I tell my children that I am actually a Shaolin master. My son, Jamie, does karate which is Japanese. A big rivalry exists between karate and kung fu; it's Japan versus China with all the historical edge between the two. When Jamie comes home in his karate suit talking about how his teacher is a black belt, I say, 'Karate is nothing compared with kung fu. Let me show you.' And we watch one of my Shaolin Temple films. My kids love them.

I don't like the Jean-Claude Van Damme or Steven Seagal films. My favourites are the old kung fu films where the lips aren't in synch with the voice, where Carter Wong jumps off cliffs and lives. I almost met Carter Wong once. Kenny Jackett, Luther Blissett and I were having dinner in Hong Kong en route to hooking up with Watford, who were touring China; the three of us flew out late because of the Home Internationals. We were sitting in the restaurant when suddenly this famous figure walked in and I stopped talking. Luther and Kenny looked at me, saw the shock on my face and asked, 'What's the matter?' I couldn't hide my excitement.

'I can't believe it,' I said. 'Carter Wong has just walked in.' Kenny and Luther started taking the mickey out of me.

'What do you mean, Carter Wong?' Luther laughed.

'Carter Wong,' I gasped. 'The greatest! Seriously. He's here. In this restaurant. He's just walked in.'

Luther and Kenny had never heard of Carter Wong. They were not raised on kung fu classics, like I was. I called the waitress over.

'Do you see that man there?' I started. She immediately interrupted.

'He's a very famous actor in Hong Kong called Carter Wong,' she said. I was awestruck. I almost asked for his autograph.

Hong Kong is the home of kung fu films. I played in an exhibition match there once, partly because I wanted to buy some kung fu films. We had a local guy looking after us and I asked him where I could get some videos.

'All the films are in DVD and DVC so you need to go to the distributors,' he replied. 'The distributors are called Mei Wah and they are miles away, virtually in China.'

The journey took ages. He came with me. I realised we had travelled a long way when we were suddenly surrounded by all these people wearing Mao tunics. We went into the distributors' building, found the main office and asked if we could buy some films. I had a huge list and read out the titles. The Chinese took one look at me, a black guy with a huge empty bag, and walked away. They obviously thought I was crazy. I spent a couple of hours in the office explaining what I wanted. Eventually, someone said, 'We don't do videos.' So I bought loads of films in VCD and DVD format and when I returned to England, I invested in DVD and VCD machines so I could watch them.

I don't need to shop in Hong Kong any more; I found a guy in Streatham, south London, who gets me most kung fu videos, all the good stuff and always up to date. Most videos go to Hong Kong, America and now Streatham. My collection of kung fu films is vast; I own hundreds. The quality of recording is terrible on some; a few of the tapes are almost obliterated by sub-titles. Some have four different sets imposed on them – German, English, Mandarin and Cantonese. I've even got one with Arabic sub-titles. The sound and picture can be so poor it gives me headaches, but I always watch them to the end. Any true kung fu fan would.

Suzy is not a fan. The only programmes we agree to watch together are *Coronation Street* and *EastEnders*. Suzy and I have heated discussions on all manner of matters because our views are so disparate. We disagree on most things. I cannot put a finger on what it is we have together but is something very special and unique. It is amazing we got together in the first place.

We met when I was a teenager living in digs in Watford. My landlady, Anne Nicells, looked after lots of young Watford players. The club trusted her. Steve Terry stayed there as well and ended up marrying the girl next door, Tanya Lamont. They had a baby but there were complications and Tanya needed a heart transplant. Then she divorced Steve and married Vinnie Jones. Tanya is best friends with Suzy, whose family, the Bicknells, lived on the other side of Anne Nicells' house. I had noticed three of the Bicknell daughters first before seeing Suzy about four months after moving in. We got talking and started going out together. I found it refreshing that Suzy was not interested in football, that she was keen to be with me, not the Watford Star. Suzy was always very go-ahead, always busy. She worked in a wine-bar, as a secretary, driving a delivery van, anything. We found a flat together when I was twenty-one and Suzy was twenty-three. The following year we had our first child. When Jamie was born, it was the happiest day of my life. I was in Mexico with England and I could not wait to get back home. When we returned two weeks later, I rushed to see Jamie and held him, bursting with pride and love.

Even before becoming a father, I loved children. Growing up in Jamaica, I always baby-sat for my younger cousins. I cuddled them and kissed them. When Jamie arrived, I assumed I would enjoy the kind of relationship I had with my cousins. But the feeling was so much stronger. When I saw Jamie it was love at first sight. I took him everywhere. I checked him every night. This baby-listening device was rigged up next to Jamie's cot and broadcast into the kitchen. I would listen to him lying in his cot, making baby noises. If I did not hear any, I sprinted upstairs and shook him awake just to check he was OK. Jamie was so special. Such warmth stems partly because I come from a very loving family. Even second and third cousins were considered close family. Suzy finds the Jamaican way very different. I treat my third cousin like my sister. There is a far greater emphasis on the family in Jamaica than in England.

Like most Jamaicans, I'm very tactile. I hug my grandmother, my aunts and my friends. In Jamaica, I thought nothing of walking down the street with my arm around my best friend. At school, I had this thing about playing with people's ears. As a twelve-year-old, I sat in class and played with the earlobe of the guy sitting next to me. Once they got to know me, they knew nothing funny was going on. It was just me being affectionate. My daughter Jemma does it now; she often fiddles with friends' ears. She's a touchy-feely person like me.

When Jamie was born, I poured my love on him just as my family showered me with affection. I often curled up in bed with him. I don't love Jamie any more than I love his brother, Jordan, or sisters, Jasmin and Jemma. Suzy and I tell them all the time how wonderful they all are. Our four children are the greatest in the world. It's just that Jamie was such a good-natured little boy. I wasn't obsessed with him because he was the first child. He was genuinely special. No one could wish for a better child than Jamie. He was like the Dalai Lama, so placid, loving everyone, always smiling, never crying, never any trouble, just kissing and cuddling everyone. When Jamie was a toddler, if he fell over and hit his head, like all toddlers do, I would run to him, my heart beating fast, my face full of worry. Jamie was so precious. When he was born, Suzy and I began the whole love affair with family life. When Jordan came along, we started the real parenting thing, immersing ourselves in the practicalities of looking after two children. Then the girls arrived and that was really special. I always wanted a daughter. When Jamie was born, I had actually hoped for a girl. Jamie and Jordan did look like girls because they had long ringlets and were really pretty. When Jemma, my first daughter, was born, we developed a special relationship. I doted on her. We snuggled up together, still do. I sleep with Jemma all the time. 'I'll have the husband tonight,' Jemma tells Suzy. They share me! Jemma becomes quite indignant when Suzy says, 'Daddy is sleeping with me tonight.' We all joke about it and then Jemma gets carried away and starts insisting that it is 'my turn tonight'.

Jemma and Jasmin, Jamie and Jordan are all so different. Jamie is serious, bright and extremely knowledgeable about computers. Of the six of us in the family, Jamie is the most sensible. Jordan is the joker of the family, always telling stories and singing songs. Both boys are very athletic, very sporty, which is a long-standing family trait. Jamie represents his school at swimming, rugby and football. He also held the school high-jump record, and he is so adept at basketball that he needs to play with older boys, simply to give him a proper challenge. Jordan and Jamie attend rugby-playing schools and experience their most competitive football for local clubs. Up at Newcastle, Jamie and Jordan turned out for Cramlington Blue Star. Like all ten-year-old boys, Jamie and Jordan have both talked about wanting to be professional footballers. Jamie understands that he may not achieve his dream; he appreciates that only one kid in a thousand makes it. He loves football but because of the school he goes to, A-levels and university are next on the agenda for him. Jamie now wants to be a psychologist.

Jordan is still at the stage where he is obsessed with the thought of becoming a professional footballer. If Jordan decides football really is his chosen career, I will insist he completes his A-levels while a Youth Trainee at a club. Jordan may even realise his dream one day. He is a very talented athlete and has competed at county level at cross-country, 800m, high jump and triple jump. In 1999, Jordan won five gold medals at the inter-schools level and brought home six cups on sports day at Birkenhead, where he was crowned Victor Ludorum. Jordan really is an outstandingly gifted athlete. But I think he will grow out of his desire to be a professional. Only recently did Jordan realise he could leave school at sixteen. Like Jamie, Jordan thought he had to go to university because that's the kind of academic environment he is in, which I was happy about. Somebody told Jordan he could quit at sixteen, which was music to his ears. He actually loves school and works hard there but Jordan is a bit of a rapscallion.

Jemma was the first girl and has been spoilt. Jamie and Jordan play up to her. Everything is 'me, me, me' with Jemma. She's like a little actress, quoting sayings off the television – 'because I am worth it' is one of her favourites. At six, Jemma pretended to be a Spice Girl, wearing sexy clothes, dancing around in her hot-pants and boots, high heels, make-up and false nails. She was six going on twenty-six. I said to Suzy, 'If Jemma ever goes out dressed like that she is going to be in trouble.' We really worry about that. But if a stranger happens to glance at Jemma she turns shy. When I played for Newcastle, there was a coffee shop in Jesmond where I took the children after school. We knew everyone in there including the lady who runs it. Peter Beardsley goes there with his kids. But Jemma is so coy in public that she wouldn't go to the counter and ask for a packet of crisps. When she is surrounded by her family, she feels as if she is in charge of everyone. If Jamie or Jordan tell her to do something, Jemma replies, 'Who do you think you are talking to? Don't you know who I am?' Jemma behaves like she is the Queen. If she acted like that in public, I'm sure people would look at her and say 'what a spoilt little brat'. But she's not. Our youngest child, Jasmin, is adored by everyone. Everyone naturally panders to Jasmin's every whim. I am always telling Jamie and Jordan to do things for Jasmin. They do because they love her so much. Jasmin is the most angelic and beautiful little child.

The children are good with each other. When Jamie was five, he would help to change Jordan's nappy. When they were slightly older, Jamie got Jordan ready for school every day, even knotting his tie for him. Their alarm would go off and I would come down twenty minutes later to find Jamie and Jordan sitting there, washed and fully dressed, having breakfast.

'I'm going to sneak in there tomorrow morning and see what Jamie does,' I told Suzy one night. Next morning, I peered around the door of Jordan's room and Jamie was in there, getting Jordan's clothes out. When Jordan woke up, he sat on the edge of the bed and held his arms out. Jamie put his shirt on.

'Come on, Jordan, lift your legs up,' Jamie said and put Jordan's pants and trousers on him.

It is a fact of life for footballers' children that they are often uprooted and moved around. When I moved from Liverpool to Newcastle in 1997, Suzy and I thought it would be difficult for the kids to leave their happy environment at school. At their schools in Liverpool, they were all the centre of attention and hugely popular with class-mates. All of a sudden, they were being asked to make a new life in Newcastle. But they took to the change like ducks to water. From the first day, they walked into their new classes, said 'hello' to everyone and sat down. They mix so well. They are such well-adjusted children without a trace of big-headedness. I could not imagine any of them saying, 'My dad is John Barnes, I'm special.' Their headmasters have always said that they are a joy to have at school. Their reports are always positive, praising their behaviour. When I left Newcastle for Charlton, the kids returned to their old schools in Liverpool and were warmly welcomed back.

Before I moved to Glasgow, I always collected the kids from school. The main thing I can give my children in life is a good education. I send them to good schools in Birkenhead and they went to the Royal Grammar School in Newcastle. I want them to know right from wrong, learning from Suzy, me and from their teachers. When they reach sixteen, I cannot do anything else for them. I will love them forever but they will be adults and must make decisions on their own. If they make mistakes, become mass murderers, I will still love them. But they have been given a good grounding. I believe the way parents bring their children up between ages three and ten is vital; after that, parents have no real control over them. Their formative years are crucial. When I look at despots like Saddam Hussein, I am sure his belligerence can be traced back to his childhood. We all have it within us to love and hate, to show compassion and to murder. Personality is shaped by childhood. Prisons are full of forty-year-old child-molestors, rapists and murderers who were misguided and mistreated seven-year-olds. That is why Suzy and I have taken such great care over our children in their early years.

I'm very strict with them; Suzy says too strict. In my own life, I'm probably not as strict as I should be with myself but with my children, as with my football, I'm very strict. Parental authority has to be instilled early. Corporal punishment is something I do believe in. If my children are naughty I will give them a smack. I always have done. Even if their teachers whacked them, I wouldn't mind although I know they don't. In Jamaica, my teachers hit me; corporal punishment was not a sensitive issue there. The only concern would be if parents did not know their children's teachers and the hope is they beat them for the right reasons. I know and trust my children's teachers; beatings do not happen at those schools.

Discipline is important. I shake my head when I hear people say, 'He's only five, let him do what he wants to do; wait until he's ten and then he'll start listening.' That is nonsense. It is too late then. Jasmin gets a smack if she is doing something wrong. She does not understand the situation except that she knows it is naughty because she gets a smack. When Jasmin begins to understand, maybe I won't have to smack her. I would never hit my child hard but a little smack here and there is good for them.

Jamie and Jordan, Jemma and Jasmin mean the world to me. So does Suzy. My wife is very special. She is a real home-builder who sacrifices all her personal feelings and ambitions to look after the family she loves so much. Suzy cannot bear to be away from her children. We married after Jamie and Jordan were born and our honeymoon in Paris was cut short because Suzy missed the boys so much. She had to fly back. They weren't exactly babies either. Jamie was six and Jordan three. Every summer, I say to Suzy, 'Let's go away for two weeks. The nanny or the grandparents will look after the children.'

'No,' she replies, 'I want to be with the children.' The boys and I can go to Center Parcs for four days together but any longer and Suzy becomes agitated.

Suzy doesn't particularly like going to Jamaica. The flight is long, it is too hot when she gets there and air-conditioning is a rarity. Also, Suzy cannot cope with Jamaicans' lax approach to punctuality. She certainly experienced it at our wedding. My family all flew over from Kingston and checked into a hotel in Watford. At 11 a.m. on the day of the wedding, my sisters inquired casually whether there was a hairdressers in Watford. I knew what was coming. I knew that when we got to the church for the 1 p.m. service, my family wouldn't be there. Having their hair cut so late was bound to keep them from reaching the church on time. I just knew it. When I arrived, it was packed inside the church with hundreds outside watching. There were newspaper reporters and television crews everywhere. It seemed everyone was there except my family. My parents, sisters and cousin still hadn't arrived. I was getting nervous because the ceremony had started. As I went up to the front of the church, all of a sudden I heard clippety-clop, clippety-clop, the sound of my mother's and sisters' heels carrying them into the church. That was typical of my family. Jamaicans have a different approach to timing.

Suzy enjoys being prompt. I'm the same now. For Jamaica to be too laid-back even for me is saying something! If people think I am too relaxed, they should go to Kingston. I would find it difficult to live in Jamaica. Maybe when the kids are grown up, and we get a little more relaxed in our old age, we will spend more time there.

Most of my life with Suzy has involved having a little one around. When Jamie was three we had Jordan. Three years later, Jemma came. Then Jasmin. We are always getting up early. Our lives are governed by the children. Jasmin wakes early and we have to come down and feed and play with her. When Jasmin is old enough to get herself out of bed and feed herself, maybe Suzy and I can have lie-ins or go away just the two of us. When we are both in the house and sit down to talk, one of the children will come in or Jasmin will need something. We are not really conscious of never being alone with each other. Besides, it's not a problem because the children are us, our family, our lives. Neither Suzy nor I would ever say or even think, 'The children keep interrupting us.' We understand the responsibility of having children. But I do sometimes feel like a chauffeur. My children have such an active school and social life. From 3 p.m. until 9 p.m., I'm at the wheel of the car, ferrying them all over the place. I start by picking Jasmin up from school, and then it's a mad rush to get Jamie and Jordan to football, ice hockey or basketball and Jemma to tennis or ballet. I drop one off, drive over to the next sports-hall, pick one up or drop another off or just wait for them. I'm happy to do it. Management has placed a greater strain on my time but I still try to do it. That's what my dad did for me. I understand my children have to experience all these different pastimes but sometimes it feels ridiculous.

Occasionally, Jamie will say, 'Sorry, Dad, I forgot I've got to be at roller-hockey in fifteen minutes.' There will be a pause.

'Jamie! Why didn't you tell me before? I've got to go training, I'm not taking you.' But of course I take him and tick him off as I drive. 'You should organise your time better,' I tell him, which is exactly what my father told me. Jamie often doesn't bother with my driving services. He is so used to calling taxis and heading off on his own.

'I'll be back at ten,' he shouts as he heads out of the door to another round of sport somewhere.

We are a strong family. When the *News of the World* twice ran stories about me and other women, Suzy and I were committed enough as a couple and a family to survive. We knew that we loved each other enough to continue. Jamie was old enough to understand what was happening but he was sensible enough to deal with it. I don't think many children would have been rational enough but Jamie was. After living through such testing times as a couple, I don't think there is any way Suzy and I would ever split up. We both understand that. Suzy means the world to me.

the enigma stigma: england

I loathed the England stigma attached to me. I hated it when eight-year-old kids ran up to me in the street and asked, 'Why don't you play well for England?' An eight-year-old cannot understand complex situations but he hears what people say. He listens to his father watching a match and yelling, 'Why doesn't John Barnes play for England like he does for Liverpool?' Children echo their elders without appreciating the significance of the words. When I first went to Liverpool, I heard little kids shouting 'wanker, wanker'. I stopped them and asked, 'Do you know what a wanker is?' Of course, they hadn't a clue. But they hear it. They repeat it. How could an eight-year-old know how I played for Liverpool or England?

But I sympathised with their fathers. I was an enigma in an England shirt. I was inconsistent. I was never as good as when in the red of Liverpool. Circumstances were different, which the press and public failed to comprehend. I believe in fate, so I know I couldn't have done any more for England. I achieved all I could. I was delighted with my England career. Now that is my perspective. If I analysed my career from the outside, I would not be happy. I would say I could have achieved more and never mind the circumstances that England didn't play like Liverpool. I empathise with those fans who booed me and those reporters who wrote that I looked laid-back and that I didn't care. I am more positive about my England contributions than other people are, although there are very few games I really remember. I still cannot believe I played seventy-nine times for England.

From my view, I did not underachieve. It was never going to be possible to score goals like the one in Rio in every international game. I gave all I could. I represented England with honesty and integrity. I never cheated. I always tried my hardest in training and on the pitch. I listen to all the complaints about my career and then I cut away all the nonsense and tell myself that I achieved all I could. If certain things had been different, I would have done better for England. But there were too many obstacles. I did the best I could given the situation. Fans and critics accused Glenn Hoddle of underachieving as an England international, saying he possessed great ability but rarely delivered. Through circumstances, whether managerial mistakes over tactics or whatever, Glenn Hoddle was awarded fewer England caps than I believe he deserved.

In the run-up to the 1988 European Championship, I had been in terrific form for Liverpool. We won the championship and I was voted Player of the Year. I had high hopes for the forthcoming tournament in Germany. Bobby Robson, England's manager, was equally confident about me, saying I could be as lethal on foreign fields as in the League. Bobby imagined me taking on European defenders with the skill and speed I had shown against QPR and Nottingham Forest in the season just ended. But I found England's short, embarrassing stay at Euro '88 desperately stifling because I was marooned on the wing. From my first game at Liverpool, I never saw myself as an out-and-out winger. My views on football changed the moment I put on a red shirt. I felt inhibited out on the wing for England, being told just to stay there and get crosses in. Right-backs are inevitably better at international level and, if I did trouble my marker, the opposition simply put two defenders on me. Euro '88 was miserable. Starved of the ball, forgotten on the flank, it was very difficult to take a game by the scruff of the neck, particularly playing against a team like the Republic of Ireland in the opening match in Stuttgart.

That 1–0 defeat on 12 June was so frustrating. I was shadowed by Chris Morris and scarcely had space to breathe. Ireland dogged us throughout, making it impossible to spend time in possession, to get the ball out to the wingers, to find any room. The match was desperate because the Irish suffocated everything. Our midfielders were unable to find the wingers because they were engaged in a real fight. People argue that you cannot play a composed, short-passing game against long-ball sides like Ireland, Wimbledon or the old Watford but I believe it's imperative to stick to your principles. It's the old DNA thing. What teams must do is play the ball quicker and get into positions earlier to receive the ball. England failed to do that against Ireland.

Euro '88 went from bad to worse. Three days later in Dusseldorf, England met Holland. I was actually quietly confident. The Dutch had decided to use Marco Van Basten and I didn't think he was fully fit. Johnny Bosman had scored at Wembley before Euro '88 when Van Basten was injured but Dutch player power being what it was, the dressing-room demanded Van Basten replace Bosman for Euro '88. I thought how sad and unfair that was for Bosman. Yet Van Basten proved the difference between England and Holland; his hat-trick ensured our humiliating early elimination. He was so special against us. Along with Diego Maradona, Van Basten was the leading light of football in the late 1980s. He was blessed with so many gifts – pace, touch, awareness and, standing 6ft 2in, he was good in the air. He partnered Careca for an Italian League XI versus the Football League in a friendly fixture that I was also involved in. Van Basten stood out then as well.

His emergence, along with Frank Rijkaard and Ruud Gullit, ended a ten-year period when the Dutch struggled by their standards. But inspired by these new stars, Holland were the best team in the world by 1988. Gullit was more dynamic than Van Basten, although he did not possess Van Basten's skill. But with those dreadlocks, Gullit was always going to catch the eye. All of those Dutch players, like Rijkaard, were so aware of what was important for the team. That's the way they are brought up in Holland. They are all great players but their individuality was never expressed to the detriment of the team.

Dusseldorf proved a demoralising experience for England on and off the field. Our fans fought anything that moved. The players never saw the trouble, becoming aware of the skirmishing only when we picked up the papers. International footballers are very cocooned on tours or in tournaments. We remain in the hotel apart from trips to training or the match itself. We only see the fans at the stadium. For the Dusseldorf fixture, England's hotel was miles out of the city centre where the fans had gathered.

I certainly couldn't miss the fans for England's final game of Euro '88. We lost again, this time to the Soviet Union on 18 June in Frankfurt. The abuse directed at me as we came out of the tunnel was unbelievable. Hundreds of England fans chanted 'Fuck off, Barnes'. I stayed pretty sane about the heckling. It had happened before, it would happen again. I came to expect the abuse, even when I played well, because there was a certain part of the crowd who were like that. Maybe they were right-wing. Maybe they were just anti-John Barnes. At Anfield, a section of the Centenary Stand, and a couple of guys in particular, always directed vitriol at me. I was aware of them. However well I played, if I made a mistake I knew the abuse would come flooding forth from the terrace like a broken sewer. Every time I represented England, the booing never surprised me. No matter what happened, it never changed the way I played.

Bobby Robson described me as the great enigma of international football and the biggest mystery of his career. As with everyone else, Bobby wondered why I could be outstanding one week and average the next. The 'enigma' issue is simple to explain. Wingers will always be inconsistent if not utilised intelligently. Bobby used neither me nor Chris Waddle properly. Because England attacked so much through the middle, Bryan Robson scored a lot of goals.

Such tactics were wonderful for a central midfielder like Bryan but useless for wingers like myself and Chris. Bobby wanted me to operate as a winger, beating full-backs and delivering crosses, but that was impossible if I didn't have the ball. I think Bobby wanted wide players more in the mould of Steve Coppell, who was never an out-an-out winger, but he selected me because of my Watford and Liverpool form. England's approach was all wrong.

Chris Waddle and I spent a lot of time at Euro '88 discussing the problem. We shared similar views on the way the game should be played. Chris was such an inventive player. I wished we had been at the same club together. Along with Paul Gascoigne, Peter Beardsley and Glenn Hoddle, Chris was the player I most wanted to play alongside every game. I admired him so much; he was strong, direct and faster than me. People were deceived by his pace. Chris has a languid running style but he really covers the ground. He should have played every game because he was so team-orientated. The work he put in when he went to Sunderland for that short spell in 1997 was phenomenal. It was natural for me to gravitate towards someone like Chris. We were the same age, playing in the same position and both lamenting the lack of a proper structure which would have allowed us to start. Sadly, Bobby appeared to want only one winger, making Chris and I direct rivals, although no animosity pervaded our relationship. I never resented Chris being selected ahead of me. I always wanted to start but never to the extent of hoping Chris fared badly. We shared the belief that standing out on the wing wasn't doing either of us any good. Chris certainly wasn't pleased with the situation. We became soul-mates in discontent.

We bemoaned the fact that Bobby was often being told that our positional similarities precluded us from operating effectively in the same side. Such a ridiculous suggestion really angered me. Those blessed with good technique can play in any position, providing they understand their responsibilities. This nonsensical theory began to surface before the Mexico World Cup and persisted through Euro '88. The classic English disease of pigeonholing players held us – and the team – back. Chris and I were labelled as out-and-out wingers when our career developments proved otherwise. Chris starred as a winger at Tottenham, but on moving to Marseille in 1989 he drifted from wing to wing, played down the middle, moved upfront, came back and collected the ball, and all in all became a much better player. A similar thing happened to me when I went to Liverpool in 1987. We were liberated as footballers. The English often distrusted flair players but the best ones could be accommodated successfully. England did not really have a structure with Bobby.

England lagged behind other teams because Bobby chose players whom he thought were the best rather than working on the way the team actually functioned. Although England were doing relatively well, qualifying for the World Cup finals and European Championship, I never felt we actually performed as consistently as a team like Holland, who profited from a well-established DNA. England experienced bad fifteen-minute spells because we were still a group of individuals, however good, playing to what we thought was a pattern, but without any real structure. Bobby should have decided on the team's structure and then fitted the players in rather than sending out a collection of the eleven best players. Even smaller countries had better organisation. An obvious example were Tunisia who drew 1–1 with England in a warm-up match for Italia '90. Against teams like Tunisia, when we were not obviously the better side, England survived because of a set-piece or a flash of brilliance from one individual. England handicapped themselves by not having the foundations of a proper structure.

Despite being ignored out wide, I could hardly tell Bobby I didn't want to play or that I wanted to move infield. I had a very good relationship with him. Everyone did because he is such a lovely man. He wasn't so much a father figure to me, more a favourite uncle. Everyone really wanted to do well for Bobby because of his likeable nature and the abuse he was being subjected to in the press. Bobby never bollocked anyone. He encouraged me, put his arm around me and emphasised his faith in me.

'The whole country is behind you,' Bobby said. 'I am behind you; we all are.' If I failed, Bobby consoled me, saying: 'I know you have it within you to succeed.' For me, the carrot always worked better than the stick. I found the whole motivational obsession of English dressing-rooms slightly strange and irrelevant. I would rather be left alone. When a professional steps on to the pitch he should not need someone to motivate him. I never did. Professional and personal pride were all the spurs I required.

The sleeves-rolled, clenched-fist style of some players, like Bryan Robson and Terry Butcher, never influenced me either. I have always thought that Bryan and Terry enacted the old Lionheart routine to motivate themselves as much as their team-mates. Terry, in particular, had to get himself psyched up to go out and play. That's fine for him but I'm not a big fan of such an approach. I would rather Bryan, Terry and the other shouters conserved their energy for the match. Games are not won in dressing-rooms. Bryan and Terry were not shouting and clenching their fists merely for effect. It genuinely stirred them up. Unfortunately, some footballers do it purely for effect because that is the way they have been brought up. Many a youngster entering a dressing-room for the first time sees older players headbutting the wall and shouting, 'Come on, let's get stuck into these bastards.' Some youngsters adopt such mannerisms without ever questioning why. There are many players who shout all the old clichés in the dressing-room, but as soon as the match starts they are as quiet as dormice.

Managers tend to like footballers who shout before games. Kenny Dalglish was one.

'Why aren't you making more noise,' Kenny once asked the players in the dressing-room at Anfield. 'Aren't you up for the match?' During my time at Newcastle, I remember Ruud Gullit saying: 'We are a bit quiet in here today.' But I fail to find a problem with quiet dressing-rooms providing players are not silent on the pitch. Some players rant and rave beforehand just to keep the manager happy. I cannot imagine an Italian dressing-room being full of shouting, although I'm sure there would be a lot of talking. I cannot imagine Paolo Maldini slamming doors or screaming for the blood of the enemy. The battle cries heard in English dressing-rooms are senseless. I would laugh inside when I heard a team-mate say of the opposition that 'they will win only over my dead body.' That's such nonsense. No player is going to choose to die for three points. I ignored such dressing-room rituals. I derived my motivation simply from stepping on to a football pitch. I could be lying in the bath reading the programme, talking calmly in the dressing-room and then a few minutes later, when the whistle signals the start, be as motivated as I can get.

Imagine the most animated person, such as Peter Reid. As a substitute, Peter would sit there talking and then, the moment he came on, would become fiercely noisy and committed. That's the right way. Those players who rant in the dressing-room or on the bench simply burn up nervous energy and make themselves tired. It's just words.

chapter seventeen

italia '90:
a summer with gazza

I understood why Chris Waddle shoved a cream-covered birthday cake into Paul Gascoigne's face midway through Italia '90. For the duration of the tournament, Chris shared a room with his fellow Geordie and became exhausted by Gazza, a character as hyper as he is lovable. Chris got his revenge in classic Gazza style. It was hilarious to watch. All the players stood about laughing their heads off as Gazza sat there, covered in sponge and cream. He licked some off his face, then some more. Finally, he spoke. 'Great chocolate,' he said, which made us laugh all the more.

At Italia '90, Gazza usually hung around with Chris and Peter Beardsley. As I spent a lot of time with these two as well, I quickly got to know Gazza. Whatever impression the public may have formed of Paul Gascoigne, at Italia '90 we knew him as a genuinely nice and funny guy, a little boy in many ways. He would do anything for us but was usually a bit manic with it. It was impossible to get angry with him. Characters like Gazza are vital on long trips abroad which can become very monotonous. Even a normal mid-season international can involve a week holed up at Burnham Beeches. Time really drags without jokers like Gazza in the camp.

Gazza, Chris and myself were on England duty once, just killing time in a foreign hotel which overlooked a farm. Our room was twenty floors up and Gazza was hanging out of the window trying to hit the chickens with bars of soap. Suddenly, Bobby Robson walked through the door. Chris and I stood up straight, like naughty schoolboys.

'What are you doing?' Bobby asked Gazza, who continued lining up some poor bantam with a bar of Camay.

'I'm throwing soap at these chickens,' replied Gazza, almost surprised that Bobby should pose the question. Typical Gazza – anyone else would have said something like 'I'm washing my hands'. Gazza's answer was met with disbelief by Bobby.

'You're doing what?'

'I'm throwing soap at these chickens,' Gazza repeated. Bobby joined Gazza at the window.

'Can you really hit them from here?'

'Yeah, of course.'

'Go on then,' said Bobby, 'show me.' Gazza took aim with the soap and scored a direct hit on a chicken. Bobby just walked out of the room, laughing and shaking his head.

Gazza was different from most players. After I'd finished a match or training for the day, I tried to escape from football, ignoring any impromptu kickabouts. I would happily talk about football; Chris and I could always be found deep in debates about tactics at the Is Molas Golf Hotel, England's Cagliari base for the first round of Italia '90. But Gazza is a natural footballer, a doer rather than a thinker who hates discussions about systems.

'Oh you two are always going on about football,' he said whenever I went into his room to talk to Chris. He would turn the music up loud or stick his fingers in his ears and chant, 'La, la, la, I'm not listening. La, la, la.' Chris and I would look at each other and laugh.

Gazza loved football but he never thought about it. He simply did it. He was happiest with a ball at his feet, always staying behind after training. If any of the local kids were kicking about at Is Molas,

Gazza ran out and joined in, showing them tricks, mucking about, trying to hit the hotel windows with the ball, any target. He hasn't changed. Football's his profession, hobby, love – his life.

I don't think Gazza is driven by a desire to please people as many believe. He just tries to please himself. He needs to keep himself occupied. He can't sit still; boredom grips him too quickly. At Is Molas, Gazza would be out in the midday heat playing two hours of tennis with the kit-man the day before a big match, while everyone else put their feet up; or he went sun-bathing for three hours; or he played table-tennis against himself. All these things sap your energy. I cannot remember how many times during Italia '90 I heard Bobby Robson ask, 'Where is Gazza?' The replies were legion – 'playing squash', 'playing tennis', 'playing table-tennis', 'playing volleyball in the pool', 'kicking about with some Italian kids' and so on. The day before England's quarter-final with Cameroon in Naples, Gazza knocked on my door.

'Digger, let's play squash,' he said.

'Don't be daft, Gazza, you have a match tomorrow and I have an injury,' I told him. The injury was only slight and Gazza so persuasive that I agreed. It was like the kid next door coming round for a kickabout. I couldn't refuse. What amazed me was Gazza never got injured playing other sports; he was always diving around the squash and tennis courts, cutting and bruising himself but never sustaining anything serious.

I loved playing football with Gazza, although I could never get the ball off him. He began making an international name for himself on 11 June when we drew 1–1 with the Republic of Ireland. England started Italia '90 slowly and unimpressively. In fact, I felt we stumbled through to the semi-finals. We certainly didn't play well against the Irish. Chris and I both started but Bobby never gave us the complete freedom to express ourselves. I was expected to track back all the time, which inevitably diminished my potency.

Our next game came against Holland on 16 June. The night before the match, some of the players were supposed to have convinced Bobby of the need for a sweeper system. I am sure Don Howe would also have been influential in any talk about tactics. Everyone connected with England remembered what the Dutch attackers had done to us at Euro '88. I was not involved in any discussions with Bobby, whom I always assumed to be a hardened 4–4–2 man. But he changed the formation and Mark Wright excelled as sweeper in the 0–0 draw against the Dutch. Gazza was at his impudent best, even asking Ronald Koeman, 'How much do you make a week?'

Bryan Robson limped out of the game and the tournament, troubled by an Achilles tendon and a toe injury supposedly sustained during training. Bryan actually damaged his toe when he and Gazza were fooling around at Is Molas. Bryan threw Gazza off a bed but Gazza managed to hold on. The bed somehow went full-circle and took the top off Bryan's toe. Gazza started laughing. The rest of us, slightly panicky, surrounded Bryan asking if he was OK. He was very upset. This was serious; England's captain was probably out of the World Cup. For some reason, Gazza couldn't stop laughing, so we had to lock him in the bathroom. 'What the hell are we going to tell Bobby?' someone said. After a swift debate, we decided to inform Bobby that Bryan had been walking across the hotel lawn bare-footed and stubbed his toe on a sprinkler hidden in the grass.

Someone went off to fetch Bobby while Gazza was let out of the bathroom. Bobby arrived and took a look at Bryan's toe.

'How did this happen?' Bobby asked, his face like thunder. Before anyone could speak, Gazza piped up.

'He did it on the bidet in the bathroom.'

'What?' exclaimed Bobby.

'He was trying to wash his toe and caught it,' Gazza explained. Gazza's version was obviously ridiculous. Bidets are smooth and Bryan's toe was a real mess. Bobby looked at the rest of us. We couldn't disagree with Gazza despite the bizarreness of his suggestion.

'Yeah, yeah,' we all said, 'Robbo was washing his foot and slipped.' We all trooped into the bathroom to look at the bidet to see if it was possible. Eventually, Bobby spoke.

'Unlucky Bryan, that was really bad luck.' It was serious for Bryan but that was fate. Bryan wouldn't believe it was fate, but I do.

Bryan's injury let in Steve McMahon, who started in the 1–0 victory over Egypt that sent England through as Group F winners. We had qualified for the knockout stage but without really being convincing. Bobby kept calling team meetings, which Gazza hated. 'Not another meeting,' he moaned. Unable and unwilling to concentrate, Gazza invariably started making noises. It was real schoolboy stuff, back-of-the-class burps and hums. 'Who's making that noise?' Bobby asked, his voice betraying his exasperation. The noises stopped. Bobby continued with his tactical treatise and the noises started up again. Bobby would go off his head. He knew it was Gazza, of course, but he loved Gazza's irrepressible side and just couldn't tell him off. Bobby realised what a talent Gazza was. At times, though, he must have wanted to strangle him because he could be very disruptive. If Bobby conducted a press conference by the side of a training pitch, for instance, Gazza would try to knock the ball into the middle of the reporters, just to make them take evasive action.

By then, England had left Cagliari for Bologna and the second-round match with Belgium. Although we won 1–0, it was a frustrating game for me. I thought I had scored when Gary Lineker crossed and I volleyed in. As I turned away in celebration, I saw the linesman lifting his flag. I knew I was onside, as television confirmed afterwards, but the referee ruled out the goal. Whenever I bump into Belgians who saw it they say it wasn't offside; it was a good goal. I was disappointed because to score in the World Cup finals would have been fantastic. I felt I did OK against Belgium but I injured my groin and had to be replaced by Steve Bull in the seventy-third minute. I watched from the bench as David Platt scored in the last minute of extra time to send us through to the quarter-finals. Platty has always been a dynamic midfielder, running forward and scoring all those goals, but people never remember him chasing back, clearing off the line or making defensive headers.

England were fortunate against Belgium and very lucky indeed to defeat Cameroon 3–2 in the quarter-finals. I started against Cameroon in Naples but was hardly fit. I really struggled before half-time and Peter Beardsley came on for me at the interval. My personal frustration was tempered by the sight of England outlasting Cameroon and reaching the semi-finals.

Speaking to people back home, I became aware that the whole country was obsessed with England's progress, following it avidly on the TV and in the newspapers. England's World Cup song, 'World In Motion', dominated the radio airwaves. Everyone raved about our collaboration with the band New Order, but I thought 'The Anfield Rap' was better. 'The Anfield Rap' involved only Liverpool players so I felt more pride in that than in England's effort. With England, we jumped on the back of New Order, and they probably used us as well; it was World Cup year and they knew the song would go to number one. Only a few of Bobby's squad were actually involved in it. When we were staying at Burnham Beeches a month or so before the tournament, the squad was invited over to a recording studio. Five players turned up – Gazza, Peter Beardsley, Chris Waddle, Des Walker and me. The others ducked out because football songs traditionally had a naff reputation. Four years earlier, England recorded a whole World Cup album. It was daft; we sang 'Viva España' and the finals were in Mexico! The normal routine was for the players to go into the studio for ten minutes, sing appallingly and then disappear while the producer twiddled some knobs and tried to make the record sound OK. Football songs are not greeted with great enthusiasm by players.

Chris Waddle and Glenn Hoddle tried to break the mould with 'Diamond Lights', their attempt at a serious song. But football songs aren't proper songs; they are just FA Cup finalists banging out a record. The agents who organise the players' pool say, 'Let's make a record.' Teams appear on *Top of the Pops* not because the song is any good but because they have reached Wembley, the World Cup or the European Championship finals. With 'World In Motion', there was also a feeling among the players that this was not the squad's song but New Order's. Anyway, when the band asked for some players to attend, only five of us volunteered.

It was a good day, full of laughs, food and drink. At one point, the producer came over and said, 'We are thinking of putting a rap in; just carry on drinking and eating for an hour while the band write it.' After an hour, the producer returned and asked, 'Right, who wants to do the rap?' The five of us looked at each other. It would have defied belief to have any of the three Geordies, Peter, Gazza or Chris, rapping away. That left Des Walker, who wasn't particularly good either, or me. So I did it. The words were pretty meaningless: 'You've got to hold and give, do it at the right time.' What the hell does that mean?! But I'm not an expert on lyrics. I listen to George Michael and love his voice but I never listen to the words. When people say George Michael has written a great song, I can't judge because the words don't make sense to me.

Normally with football songs, no one player takes the lead role; it is a team effort. But my rap on 'World In Motion' ensured I became associated with the record. It was particularly my performance in the video that made people forget about the rest of the England squad. In one respect, those who didn't turn up didn't deserve to be on it, but once the song took off they all wanted to jump on the bandwagon. It was probably just as well they didn't come to the recording studio. I cannot imagine Peter Shilton or Bryan Robson doing a rap. When it came to shooting the video, I was injured so they just filmed the other players in the background singing 'We're playing for England'. But because I performed the rap, they needed me in the video, so they came up to Liverpool and spent a whole day filming me with New Order. That is how I became so prominent in the video.

As everyone back home listened to 'World In Motion', England prepared to face West Germany in the semi-final. I was never going to play; my injury was too sore. Amidst all the patriotic hype, I expected England to lose. The Germans were playing well and England had struggled to the semi-final. But from the first minute to the last, we outplayed West Germany completely. I think that having reached the semi-final made England's players more confident. They were one step from a World Cup final and that made everyone raise their game. The performance was tremendous. Everyone from Paul Parker to Gazza to Gary Lineker was magnificent. That game in Turin was very much like the meeting with Germany at Euro '96 – England's best performance of the tournament but we still went out on penalties.

As the clock ticked down towards penalties in Turin, I became even more convinced the Germans would prevail. England had played so stirringly for two hours but the Germans' reputation for accuracy was well merited. I always thought our five nominated penalty-takers would score and that the shootout would go into sixes and sevens and eights where we might struggle. It started well. Lineker, Beardsley and Platt scored for us with Brehme, Matthaus and Riedle replying for the Germans. When Stuart Pearce stepped up to take England's fourth penalty, I assumed he would score. Stuart never misses a penalty; his left foot is just a hammer which blasts the ball into the net. Yet his shot cannoned off Bodo Illgner, Germany's keeper. Olaf Thon then converted to put the pressure on Chris. I was not worried when Chris walked up. He is very good technically at putting the ball where he wants. But the ball flew over. I couldn't believe it. Chris and Stuart were the last two I expected to miss. There was not a lot I could say to Chris. I muttered 'unlucky' and put my arm around him. But it was really a time for him to be left alone. It was an emotional night all round; no one will forget Gazza's tears when he was booked.

I was amazed by the reception we received on our return to Luton Airport. There were tens of thousands there to greet us as if we had won the World Cup, not come fourth after losing to West Germany in the semi-final and then Italy in the third-place match. All of the squad were greeted almost as conquering heroes, particularly Gazza.

public image

J ealousy dominates English society. Even the most cursory viewing of any of the English soap operas, such as *EastEnders*, *Coronation Street* or *Brookside*, reveals the streak in English society that relishes seeing people struggle. The archetypal American soaps, such as *Dallas* and *Dynasty*, feature rich families. Americans are much more positive. They like to see people prosper. I don't suppose the equivalent of *EastEnders* would be a success in America with all that depression, poverty and everyone losing their jobs all the time. But English people want everyone to feel as bad as they do.

The public loves, perhaps even demands, a press that prints negative stories about famous, over-paid footballers falling over drunk, womanising and not caring about the sport that gives them such a lavish lifestyle. Newspaper editors know what people want to read, and they do not want to learn that Paul Gascoigne is actually a nice guy who does tremendous work for charity (which he does). The public want to read that Gascoigne is out getting drunk, squandering his money and talent. The press simply responds to this deep flaw in the English psyche. Newspapers mislead readers who want to be misled. Stories about footballers clubbing at Stringfellows on a Saturday night rarely mention the rest of a footballer's typical week, training, playing, doing the school run and going to the supermarket. I spend more time in Sainsbury's than Stringfellows. The only consistently positive comment ever written about a footballer is 'he played well'.

No British Prime Minister could have survived as Bill Clinton did over Monica Lewinsky. The general public would have revelled in seeing a person who dared to fly high brought crashing to earth, his wings burned. Perhaps it makes the onlookers' lives more bearable. This trait is peculiar to the English. Politicians have mistresses in France where all the voters care about is whether he performs his public duties successfully. Scandal rages in England over the discovery of a politician's mistress.

Nobody should care about whether I was born in England or Jamaica or whether the players have shared one boozy night out. The revelling in a footballer's trouble stems from the envy felt by a certain group of people. For all its perceived gentrification, football remains predominantly a working-class sport so it is predominantly working-class people on the terraces. A middle-class sport like golf does not attract the same reactions. The public do not want British golfers to fail, or to hear about them getting drunk, yet it seems the last thing an English football fan wants to read is that this superstar is really a nice bloke as well. That would depress them. By catering for this national tendency, the press exacerbates the situation. Many readers believe tales simply because they are there, in black and white, in the newspapers.

The most dangerous time for a footballer is on the eve of a major tournament. The qualification and preparatory matches have been completed, the squad announced. Everyone is waiting to fly out. Interest is massive, newspapers have acres of space to fill but there is little concrete to write about. So before every World Cup and European Championship involving England, minor events during the run-up are exaggerated out of all proportion. Newspapers never waited for us to have a nightmare at the tournament and then criticise us; they laid into us before a ball was even kicked.

The worst tournament for fabricated stories was Italia '90. England had hardly landed in Italy when the newspapers concocted a tale about some of Bobby Robson's players and a hostess called Isabella who worked for the Italian World Cup organisers. The story started when we arrived at our Cagliari base, the Is Molas Golf Hotel, and there was a hostess greeting the dignitaries. One of the players gave her an England pin. We had hundreds of the things to hand out to people in foreign countries. It's good PR. The next day, Bobby walked into the team meeting room and said, 'There's a story in the paper about you lot and a hostess called Isabella. It says some England players were round at this girl's flat, having sex with her.' We all just burst out laughing because none of the players had gone out that night. I laughed loudest because the story was such nonsense.

'Come on, Bobby, they must have named names!' I said amidst more laughter.

'Well, you are one of them for a start,' Bobby replied. The others fell about laughing even more when they saw my jaw drop. 'Don't worry, I'm just joking,' said Bobby.

No names were mentioned in the papers so no one could sue. The players were not worried anyway. We knew this wild party with a hostess never happened. No one did anything; no one had gone anywhere. I heard my name got mentioned in some capacity, although not in print. The hostess received two pins and people whispered that one originated from Steve McMahon and the other from me. My name got thrown into everything. I never even saw the girl. If any reporter had written anything about me he would have received a writ for libel the same day. Incidents like the Isabella story can be harmful to a player's personal life. I never even told Suzy because the story was such rubbish but family and friends can be affected. Relationships can end and families be broken up by newspaper lies.

Even when the stories are true, the press has no right to print them because they have nothing to do with being a footballer. Footballers are no different from anyone else. We are human beings, capable of mistakes. If a couple experience problems in their relationship or a footballer is caught having an affair, that should be a personal issue for the people concerned to sort out, not for the newspapers. Whether it happens to footballers, milkmen or journalists, it's got nothing to do with their jobs. It's life. Why should Paul Gascoigne be considered different from anyone else? Why should I? We are called role models but it is human to err. Because footballers are in the public eye, we get reported on and savaged and the readers are glad because they are jealous. Well-known people are expected to behave like angels, which is impossible.

I have been the target of some horrid articles. The worst was published just after the Isabella story at Italia '90. The *Sunday Mirror* claimed that I couldn't perform for Bobby Robson because he reminded me of my mother who abused me as a child. Inside the paper, they carried a cartoon of me on the psychiatrist's couch. It was pathetic and hurtful. How the *Sunday Mirror* came up with the story is another disgraceful episode in the annals of Fleet Street. When I joined Liverpool three years before Italia '90, I did an interview for a Channel 4 programme called *Network 7*, a chat-show which other sports personalities such as Tessa Sanderson had appeared on. Part of the interview centred around my childhood.

'Your father was in the army, so was he very strict with you?' the interviewer asked me.

'Yes,' I replied.

'Did he discipline you?'

'No, he left that to my mother. All the boys who were naughty in the Caribbean used to get beaten. My mother would whack me with a broomstick.'

Three years later, the *Sunday Mirror* used the quotes with a photograph of the interviewer, who happened to be a psychologist and had once worked in Broadmoor Hospital for six weeks. The *Sunday Mirror* headline screamed: 'John Barnes reveals all to psychologist who works at Broadmoor'. The article started: 'In a private consultation, part of which was screened on Channel 4 . . .' That was crazy in itself. How can a 'private consultation' be shown on public television? The article continued: 'Barnes reveals that his mum used to beat him so that's why he can't play for Bobby Robson, who is too strict with him.' I burst out laughing, although I did phone my mum in Jamaica to tell her about this stupid story.

We thought that was the end of the matter. But just before England faced Belgium at Italia '90, a reporter from the *Sunday People* flew to Kingston and went to my parents' house. When my mother came home from work to watch the first half of the Belgium match, she found this journalist on the doorstep.

'I have nothing to say to you,' Mum said.

'But I have sent my taxi away,' he replied.

'Well, wait on the verandah and I'll call another for you,' my mother said and went inside. She never spoke to the reporter again. He sat on the verandah and presumably disappeared in his taxi. My mother watched the first half of the Belgium game and returned to work.

The following Sunday, the front page of the *People* carried a photograph of my mum looking stern underneath the headline 'Don't Blame Me'. The caption read: 'John Barnes' mum walks out in disgust at son's performance against Belgium.' My mother laughed about it. So did I. My family is above getting worried over such silly things. But such newspaper behaviour is still incomprehensible, having no connection with football or even reality. What are the motives of papers like the *Sunday Mirror* and the *People*? Do they want England to win? Are they attacking me personally? The stories were so obviously ridiculous to anyone who knew me, my mother or even read the words which bore no relation to the headline. 'Barnes reveals all!' What a joke! Unfortunately, some people will not question the story's validity, but they are reading lies.

What can I do? I cannot respond to the newspapers and issue a statement saying 'my mother didn't beat me as a child'. I wouldn't dignify the story or give these journalists the time of day. When I returned from Italia '90, I talked to friends about the *Sunday Mirror* and *People* lies.

'No one really believes these stories,' they argued.

'But these papers are among the biggest selling in the country,'

I replied, 'and people believe what they read.' Even professional footballers, people who have had terrible things written about them, believe what they read in the papers. I admit to falling into the same trap. Countless times I have talked to team-mates about comments newspapers claim they have made. 'I haven't spoken to anyone,' they reply. The power of the media is made even more dangerous by its streak of mendacity.

Most incidents on tours or in tournaments are not worth mentioning but they can get exaggerated ridiculously by newspapers. Footballers have learned they cannot afford any incident, however tiny and innocent.

Newspapers can distort any blameless situation into a damning story. I became sick of having to tell managers, 'Boss, we were just drinking lemonade, we didn't do anything,' and the manager replying, 'Yes, but you know how it is going to be written up.' If an alleged incident happens, we cannot afford to be in a place drinking lemonade. It is so sad because we footballers are losing part of our humanity. Players need to relax but cannot because a quiet soda at the local can be re-written as a hell-raising bender. When England were staying at Is Mola during Italia '90, Chris Woods, Chris Waddle and myself used to walk down to a bar in nearby Pula which we re-named the Pula Working Men's Club. We would have a few drinks, nothing excessive, and take on the locals at arm-wrestling. They were great nights. We were there for an hour at most, no one got drunk and we all returned home safely. I hate to imagine how hysterically the English press would have reacted if they had heard about the arm-wrestling and drinking at the Pula Working Men's Club. The headline would have been: 'Drunk England stars fight with Italians'.

Teddy Sheringham was involved in a daft story before France '98 about being in a nightclub and smoking. He was pictured with a cigarette although he doesn't smoke. Stories like that, and those about the England team's behaviour during and on the return flight from the visit to China and Hong Kong before Euro '96, can unite squads. Collective responsibility represents a great idea for those players not targeted for abuse in the press and on the streets. But the victims are still singled out. Teddy was still slaughtered by everyone. Players will say 'let's all pull together' as long as it's not them. That's human nature. But I still do not understand why the 'incident' that always precedes tournaments must be negative. Why can't the newspapers show a picture of a player doing something positive, like sitting at home with his family? What a nice picture! There he is with his wife and kids, ready to do his best for England. There he is with his mum and dad in a restaurant, talking excitedly about the mission ahead, about how much he wants to represent his country with pride. But the media is not interested in such stories. The public prefer controversy and the press is happy to deliver it. That's the way the English are. On the eve of World Cups, other countries' players go out with their wives, have a drink and it's not a big deal with their press. At the two World Cups I went to, Mexico in 1986 and Italy in 1990, the situation became so fraught that players wouldn't talk to the press. Gazza even threw a drink at Paul Parker for chatting to the press in Italy.

The bad feeling that arises just before a tournament, as the press searches for its 'incident', creates a legacy that sours relations between players and reporters during the event itself. Once the football starts, newspapers are completely behind England, having tried to upset everything beforehand. In Mexico, when Ray Wilkins was sent off against Morocco and England needed to beat Poland to qualify for the knockout stage, all the newspapermen supported us. A lot of sympathy was expressed in the media towards Wilkins. But by then the players were completely distrustful of reporters who had slated us in the run-up to Mexico. The tension continues to this day.

I've been pummelled by the press. So have countless other players. The tacky, untrue stories at the front of papers are generally nothing to do with the sports reporters. But a problem arises when the football hacks come to me wanting stories or interviews, wanting me to help their paper which has just been printing lies about me.

'It's not us,' they cry, 'it's the news guys.'

'I don't care whether it is your news guys or you, it is still your newspaper,' I reply. 'I know you are fine, but how can I help you when the rest of your paper has so maligned me? It's nothing personal.' Gazza even has a contract with the *Sun*. He can give an interview which is splashed across the back of the *Sun* while on the front page he is being pilloried.

I've done exclusive, paid-for stories but that doesn't give the newspaper the right to try to destroy my life by writing lies about me. If a newspaper pays me £10,000, £50,000 or £100,000 for an exclusive, surely they should show some loyalty and not publish rubbish about me. The word exclusive is a joke anyway. I've seen articles about me with exclusive stamped on them when I've just been talking to a bunch of journalists. I have been paid for exclusives before Cup finals but the money went into the players' pool. We deserve to be paid. In England people are glad to see famous people like myself or Glenn Hoddle slammed by the papers. I can just imagine these sad souls saying, 'That Barnes, he deserves to get hammered by the paper,' and, 'That Hoddle, he deserves criticism too.' But it's just jealousy.

I have become very guarded in what I tell reporters. I say things in a way that ensures they are reported as intended. A lot of footballers, particularly those new to the profession, don't appreciate the pitfalls with the media. Their words are twisted by the press, who they then don't want to talk to again. Through experience, some bitter, I have learned what I can say. I stop myself all the time from making comments that could be misconstrued. I often break off a sentence to establish that the reporter realises something was said in jest. I never use irony. Irony doesn't work in print.

The press is not all bad, though, even the tabloids.

Those reporters covering my club career, from Watford to Liverpool, Newcastle and Charlton, have been generally fair and positive towards me. Problems mainly arose for me through my England involvement, and I've suffered really cruel press about my personal life. The front-page personal attacks hurt. Back-page criticism is normally about football; even when newspapers debated my commitment to England or Jamaica, at least the issue was football-related. But I resent the English public's obsession with the lives of famous figures. On the Continent, prominent people are allowed to get on with their lives without this horrific intrusion by reporters and photographers. In England, people want to know everything about you if you are a sporting celebrity. Just before Christmas 1998, there was a headline in the *Sunday Sun* which ran 'Flash Footy Star in £6,000 Wine Bill'. I was still living near Morpeth and every time I went to the Chinese takeaway, I popped in to the off-licence next door. Knowing of my interest in wine, the staff told me of a wine fair being held in Edinburgh. It does not take long up the A1, so I drove up to have a look. The wine fair was very impressive so I ordered some bottles to add to my collection of fine wine. The wine was delivered to me via the off-licence and someone along the way must have tipped off the *Sunday Sun*. Suddenly, my wine-buying trip to Scotland was splashed all over the front page of one of the biggest papers in the north east. I was furious. How could this be front-page news? What had a private trip to do with being a 'flash footy star'? I wasn't being flash. I wasn't doing a promotion about drinking wine. I collect wine so I bought some. Do people really want to read that I've got £6,000 to spend on wine?

Newspapers never look on a footballer's good side. In 1998, I travelled to Burundi as a Christian Aid ambassador to see the crisis between the Hutu and the Tutsis. I organised a match between children of both tribes for the John Barnes Peace Cup but who cares about that? I didn't want publicity and it didn't get much. But if I went out and got drunk tomorrow how many pages would that get in a tabloid? Loads. The public cannot appreciate the number of charity events that players such as Alan Shearer, Ian Wright and I attend because they never hear about it. If they did, perhaps it would go some way towards changing the conception of footballers as self-obsessed, money-grabbing individuals.

I have always laboured under this image of 'John Barnes, the laid-back Jamaican'. If people knew how much I cared maybe I wouldn't have got all that bad press. This perception of me being casual is wrong but widespread. During my spell at Newcastle, I spoke a lot to Temuri Ketsbaia, a Georgian who had a stereotypical image of Jamaicans.

'Ah, you are from Jamaica,' Ketsbaia said, 'always lying on the beach, smoking marijuana, listening to reggae music and having fun with girls and drugs.' Jamaica isn't like that; not the Jamaica I know anyway.

My career was never covered in a racist way. White footballers suffered the same stick as me; Gazza got even more. Andy Cole was known among certain reporters as NWA, Nigger With Attitude. That has nothing to do with Andy's colour but his character. Andy has got attitude. Vinnie Jones is white and he's got attitude but people don't think of him as a right-wing racist.

I have moved into coaching and management knowing how I want to handle the press. If journalists hinder me doing my job at Celtic, I will not help them in their job. If reporters are going to upset me or one of my players, so creating a situation which might make Celtic lose a match, why should I help them with an interview or story? However, I understand that the manager or head coach has to make himself available to the media. Managers should take the pressure off players who don't enjoy talking to the press. As a player, I often found myself walking to my car at the training ground and suddenly being ambushed by reporters. 'Just a few words, John,' they say and all of a sudden I found myself talking. That was wrong. It is not the players' job to deal with the press. I will protect players more than most managers do. As I settle into management, my long-term aim is to attend one press conference before a match, one immediately afterwards and not to talk to journalists outside that. Ruud Gullit did it well at Newcastle. He would talk at the set time and place and then say, 'I'm off, don't be ringing me.' Also managers do need the press to find out about certain situations, perhaps with players at other clubs.

A new breed of young journalists has come on the scene, particularly in England, whom I just don't know. One columnist I respect is Johnny Giles in the *Daily Express*. He knows what he is

Left foot forward: My touch was developed through playing scrimmage, a Latin American short-passing game, as a kid (*Popperfoto*)

Supporting the strikers: I get hugged by John Aldridge after creating his goal at Arsenal in my first game for Liverpool. Peter Beardsley (No. 7) was also involved in the move (*Colorsport*)

Uplifting feeling: Winning my first Championship at Liverpool, in 1988, was special (*Popperfoto*)

Overwhelmed: Arsenal's title-winning second goal at Anfield in 1989 resulted from my mistake (*Popperfoto*)

Red Rapper: 'The Anfield Rap' was a brilliant tune, a rare gem among football songs which are usually rubbish (*Popperfoto*)

Eyes on the prize: When I take a shot such as this one against Crystal Palace in 1995, I try to visualise the ball's speed and trajectory (*Liverpool Daily Post and Echo*)

Shooting star: Steve McManaman's goals in the 1995 Coca-Cola Cup final confirmed to me his brilliance. Jamie Redknapp and Robbie Fowler were also fast emerging talents (*Colorsport*)

French without fears: Eric Cantona, whose late goal defeated Liverpool in the 1996 FA Cup final, inspired a whole generation of Manchester United players (*Popperfoto*)

The worst day of my life: Saturday, 15 April 1989, at Hillsborough (*Colorsport*)

Hillsborough Memorial Service: The disaster affected me deeply. After seeing so many parents lose their children, I cuddled Jamie at every opportunity, such as here in Liverpool's Anglican Cathedral (*PA*)

Never forgotten: Scarcely a day goes by without me thinking of the 96 Liverpool fans who died (*Colorsport*)

Lads together: Relaxing with my best friends Antony, Mark, Len and Lofty in the front

What a night: Newcastle's 3–2 win over Barcelona in the Champions League was one of the greatest games I have ever played in (*Colorsport*)

Down and out of the Premiership: I console Clive Mendonca after Charlton Athletic are relegated in 1999 following defeat to Sheffield Wednesday, my last match as a player (*PA*)

ITV's Euro '96 team: I enjoy my television work and am hoping to continue with it in the future (*PA*)

New Bhoy: I join Kenny Dalglish and Celtic's chairman, Frank O'Callaghan, on my first day at Celtic Park in June 1999 (*PA*)

talking about, but some of these new young journalists think they can produce good stories just because they have been writing about football for a few years. I can appreciate a journalist's writing skills while thinking his article was the biggest load of rubbish ever. Just because a journalist is around football doesn't mean he knows it. Reporters toss out comments like 'Newcastle didn't have any width or penetration'. I would love to get them on the training field and ask what they meant. I suspect they wouldn't have a clue. But it's easy to write: 'No width, no penetration, that's why Newcastle lost.' These journalists spout clichés they don't comprehend – 'They didn't defend as a unit', 'They didn't get enough crosses in', 'They didn't push up as a team'. Such phrases sound good, encouraging readers to think the writer knows what he is talking about. They may have graduated from university, gone on a journalism course and be able to write well but that has nothing to do with football. I used to tell team-mates at Liverpool, Newcastle and Charlton to ignore what was written about them.

I once watched from the stands when Liverpool played Blackburn. I could see everything from runs that players made, to the runs they should have made, to whether a dangerous move was unfolding. My vision was magnificent, but I knew that if I had been down there, on the pitch, right in the thick of it, I would not have been so inspired. Most journalists have never played the game professionally yet they believe they could and so give the world the benefit of their so-called expertise. Reporters criticised Ronny Rosenthal for missing that open goal for Liverpool at Villa Park, but until a journalist has been down there and appreciates how hard and fast football is, they really shouldn't be allowed to judge.

Liverpool once had an exchange with England's cricketers, which involved Darren Gough coming to Melwood and me going into the nets. As with football, anyone watching cricket believes they could do better. I knew I could take catches or hit fours but when Angus Fraser started bowling at me in the nets, off two steps and spinning the ball but with such pace that I couldn't even see it, I realised the gulf between observer and player.

As much as I disliked the press, I would never have gone abroad just to escape the English media. If I had moved to Italy and struggled, the negative press reaction would have been worse than here, although it would have been football-related. In England, newspapers feed off the public's jealousy by finding or creating stories about a footballer's problems. English newspapers are a sad reflection of English society.

I avoid newspapers and radio but I enjoy the company of television people. ITV Sport are good to work for; their main men, Brian Barwick and Jeff Farmer, are nice, easygoing guys who understand if I occasionally pull out of a studio appearance. 'No problem,' Jeff says. Jeff and Brian are football fans and that's the great thing about ITV Sport. They are all sports people, not just television people. Until Des Lynam arrived the chief football presenter was Bob Wilson, a very good operator. During France '98, Bob's daughter Anna was dying of cancer and yet he went into the studio every night, never letting his heartache show, always the professional. I don't think I could have been as brave as Bob was.

In France Bob anchored the studio show with a changing collection of experts, of whom I was one. During France '98, I was based in Paris full time with ITV while Terry Venables, Alex Ferguson and Bobby Robson flew in. Glenn Hoddle joined up after England went out. Glenn was despondent after events in St Etienne but cheered up. ITV's studio is a lively place, particularly off-air. In the studio, Terry is just like he is in real life. On-air, Terry is tremendously professional, but before the cameras roll, he is very sharp, very witty, always trying to get one over on the rest of us. Terry loves to take the mick. For France '98, ITV used a backdrop of the Eiffel Tower. The studio was in Porte de Versailles, which is miles from the Eiffel Tower, so they used a very realistic picture. When Bobby Robson came into the studio the first time, he looked at the window and asked, 'Is that the Eiffel Tower out there?' We all knew what Bobby was trying to say but Terry started to have some fun.

'Yes, of course it's the Eiffel Tower,' Terry replied. 'Doesn't it look like it?'

'Yes, I know it's the Eiffel Tower,' Bobby retorted, 'but is it *the* Eiffel Tower? When you look out there, is it *the* Eiffel Tower?' Terry was almost beside himself with laughter.

'Yes, Bobby, if you look out there you will see the Eiffel Tower.'

That went on for a good few minutes until the programme started.

For me, one of the most enjoyable parts of the World Cup was the half-mile walk back from the studio to the hotel with Alex Ferguson. We covered a lot of England games together and consequently discussed his Manchester United players. We talked about Nicky Butt, a midfielder I really rate. Nicky deserves his place in the Manchester United team. Alex admires him a lot, even though he doesn't play him all the time. I told Alex how well I thought David Beckham and Ryan Giggs coped with the clammy hand of media interest pawing at them. Alex's relationship with his players is exceptional on a personal level, let alone footballing. That's why they have achieved so much. The public may see Alex as a mad jock but he is immensely canny and caring.

With characters like Alex and Terry, ITV's studio is always a fun place. Nevertheless, it can be difficult to develop a rapport with people on-air because of the number of experts who work for ITV. The BBC employ a smaller roster of studio guests, who consequently can get the banter going. Alan Hansen is brilliant at it. Also, their studio discussions are not interrupted by commericals so they can be more relaxed, allowing arguments to develop. Sometimes with ITV, I am told I have twenty-five seconds to deliver a punchy, authoritative verdict covering all the important points – not twenty-six seconds or twenty-four but twenty-five. ITV's staff work under greater pressure than the BBC's. ITV lack the BBC's ability to be spontaneous.

I try to be diplomatic when criticising footballers or managers on television. I don't sit on the fence but I bring some perspective to the analysis of a mistake. I can point out that it is easily done because I have done the same myself. I understand how simple it is to miss an open goal or be in the wrong defensive position. I hate it when former professionals are critical. They should know how easy it is to make a fool of yourself.

Becoming head coach at Celtic has limited my opportunities with ITV but I love heading for the studio when time permits. My role is very straightforward at ITV. All I do is respond to the presenter's questions. I do not envy Barry Venison his presenting job. Barry has to pre-empt situations, portray what's going on and guide the studio debate. As an analyst, I just react to situations. In years to come, I will have to become more polished, particularly as I would very much like to continue working in television, whatever happens in management.

england: life under taylor and venables

Italia '90 and Euro '88 were so disappointing for me that I was thrilled when Graham Taylor, the master-motivator, succeeded Bobby Robson as manager of England. At our first training session together at Bisham Abbey, Graham took me to one side.

'I told you I would make it,' he said.

'What kept you!?' I replied.

I knew Graham would manage England. Graham is very single-minded, which he needed to be to overcome some serious obstacles such as his association with a club like Watford. Lower-division players find it easier to make it with England than a manager. Graham had to leave Watford before he could contemplate any chance of taking over England. Watford's style would never have worked at international level. Graham went to Aston Villa, toned down his direct tactics and Villa finished second in the League. Having achieved success with one approach at Watford and another at Villa, I knew he was right for the England job.

Graham was immediately besieged by pundits clamouring for me not to be included in his first squad, for the friendly with Hungary in September 1990. Newspapers overflowed with specious observations such as 'Graham Taylor is like John Barnes' dad'. Many journalists wrote that 'Graham Taylor is bound to favour Barnes because he used to play for him'. The critics' hostility was as huge as their naivety. If they had managed to curb their bile momentarily and pondered the situation positively, these so-called experts might have remembered that it was Graham Taylor who had brought the best out of me domestically. Surely, then, he had a good chance of doing it again, albeit on a more elevated stage. But people, particularly in England, would rather look at the negative. Anyway, the match came, I beat three Hungarians in the first minute and the boos changed to cheers.

Graham's appointment excited me, particularly when he started talking about my position.

'I have no intention of using you as an out-and-out winger for England,' Graham said. Unlike Bobby, Graham appreciated how my game had changed at Liverpool.

For all Graham's good intentions, it was impossible for me to reproduce my Liverpool form for England. The teams were so different but supporters and reporters do not understand systems. When I heard, 'Why doesn't John Barnes play for England the way he does for Liverpool?' I wanted to scream, 'Well, put clones of Ronnie Whelan and Steve McMahon to my right, Steve Nicol behind me, Alan Hansen, Gary Gillespie or Glenn Hysen in defence, Barry Venison at right-back with Rushie and Aldo upfront.' Or England could have cloned Liverpool's system, but that never happened. Every manager, whether Robson or Taylor, is driven by his own ideas. I just craved more flexibility to move around the pitch. I was so closely marked during internationals that I wanted the licence to wander intelligently, which would confuse the marker. But I was never granted permission to perform my best role.

Playing for Liverpool, I gained possession probably twenty times a game. That was enough to have an impact, either delivering crosses or maybe even a goal. For England, I received the ball possibly as few as six times. Simple mathematics indicated I had less of an opportunity to shine with England than Liverpool. That disparity reflected the dominance Liverpool enjoyed over other teams. England never had that. During all my years representing England, I cannot remember a time when we monopolised possession, which would have allowed creative players including me the chance to show our class. Goalscorers are judged on whether the ball goes in the net. If Gary Lineker did nothing all game, lost possession every single time he had the ball, and then it went in off his shins in the final second, he would have been deemed to have had a good game.

Liverpool were so commanding that although I might lose the ball fifty per cent of the time, I still had ten opportunities to create or score. Enjoying possession was so rare with England, I tried twice as hard to beat two or three players. If I failed, I strived even harder the next time. I became trapped in a vicious circle. Eventually I decided just to do the simple things, but never risking possession entailed passing not dribbling. My England managers, Graham Taylor and Terry Venables, were happy but the public weren't. 'Where is the dribbler of Rio?' they asked.

Nobody was to blame. Every footballer runs into the same problem on moving up from club to international level. I don't know any player who has impressed more for England than for his club. Gary Lineker and Alan Shearer might be exceptions but then theirs is a specialised role, just being expected to score goals. Players become used to their club's style. Imagine John Fashanu moving from Wimbledon to Juventus. It would be quite a culture shock. At Wimbledon, Fashanu proved very effective because they banged high balls up to him. Fashanu would have struggled at Juventus because the Italians play the ball to feet.

Imagine coming from a team like Wimbledon to play for England like John Fashanu did. It was difficult. Imagine coming from Liverpool's pass-and-move into an England team with two wingers. The transition is easier for defenders; a good centre-half or full-back possesses skills which are obviously transferable. Their job is primarily to prevent, not invent and it is easier to be negative. Flair players like myself and Chris Waddle are expected to make things happen.

Defenders also do not get attacked as much at international level as in the end-to-end Premiership. It's most difficult for attacking midfielders like myself to make the jump.

The contrast between club and international football is underestimated. The England team always seemed too obsessed with matching the league tempo, with trying to make something happen within ten seconds of gaining possession, whether it be a cross or shot. That approach is fine for goalscorers but not for the creators. A midfielder whom I deeply admire, Glenn Hoddle, once observed, 'You can get the ball up too quickly at times.' Hoddle's right. Attacking too hastily can mean strikers having to wait for support and probably losing the ball. Mistakes are less costly in the Premiership; if a team squanders possession in a World Cup or European Championship they often do not touch the ball again until it is fished out of the net.

England's chances were inhibited by this fixation for ten-second moves. I hated hearing players shout, 'Come on, lads, we must have a high tempo.' Operating at a high tempo precludes changes of pace. The leading overseas sides, such as Brazil, may play slowly but they have that ability to race through the gears. English supporters do not understand that. They hate seeing footballers dwelling on the ball, going backwards to go forward. Ray Wilkins prospered in Italy but was criticised in England for passing the ball square. At the risk of repeating myself, the best teams and players do not risk losing possession. Most domestic footballers do not understand how they compromise themselves by insisting on a 'high tempo'. All those clichés spouted in the dressing-room about playing at full throttle are rubbish. They might mean something for Wimbledon, because that's the way they play. It is laughable to listen to footballers yelling, 'Let's play with a high tempo and be patient.' How can they? Patience and high tempo are mutually exclusive.

I feel sorry for whoever is England manager: he has to create a side fit for international football's game of patience from members of the high-tempo Premiership. He works with players for a week at most before each match. Only under Glenn Hoddle and before him,

Terry Venables, have England developed a structure which is more suited to the way clubs play. Graham Taylor was trying to create a structure but never got to finish it. England have evolved during the nineties.

Missing a structure during most of my international days, England were never going to get the best out of me. What made me appear even more of an enigma was the ruptured Achilles tendon I suffered before Euro '92. The injury robbed me of my explosive pace and prevented me from playing too often for my mentor, Graham Taylor. It was so frustrating. The injury occurred as I regained fitness following a blighted season. I was working overtime to sharpen up in time for the European Championship. Graham knew I lacked full fitness but he selected me in the squad.

'There's three weeks to go before the first match,' Graham said. 'Get as fit as you can in that time.'

So I travelled with the England players to the training camp in Finland. Every morning, I went running with Trevor Steven and Carlton Palmer. I felt my fitness slowly returning and my confidence growing. Then came the fateful match against Finland in Helsinki on 3 June. In the dressing-room beforehand, Graham took me to one side.

'I want you to play upfront from the start. If you want a rest during the game, come and stand out on the wing. Don't go in the middle if you feel tired; you'll have to run around there.' Graham was determined to ease me back gently. But then the nightmare started. Shortly into the game, I went up to control the ball, landed and felt as if I'd been kicked from behind. As I lay on the ground, I looked up and swore at the nearest Finn, the centre-back Erik Holmgren.

'You kicked me,' I shouted at Holmgren.

'I never touched you,' Holmgren insisted.

I rose gingerly to my feet and tried to walk. Every time my right foot went down, I felt I was stepping in a hole. I could not go up on my toes. It was the strangest sensation; my mind relayed messages that I was walking normally but I kept looking at the ground, wondering where the hole was. The pain was minimal so I kept walking, albeit flatfooted, towards the wing. England's bench probably thought I was having my rest period, as Graham had suggested, although seven minutes was a bit early.

'I have to come off,' I shouted. They did not listen so I hobbled around for five minutes until Graham finally sent on Paul Merson to replace me. England's doctor immediately squeezed my calf to check for a ruptured Achilles tendon.

'I'm afraid it's the Achilles,' he said and organised for me to be operated on the following morning.

As the anaesthetic wore off, my mind filled with thoughts about the future.

'How long do you think I will be out?' I asked the specialist when he came to see me.

'Seven months,' he replied.

My mind began racing again. It was early June and I promised myself I would be playing again around January. On the flight back to England, I conjured up an image of what it would be like stepping back on to a pitch, of how it would be cold so I must dig out my gloves and tights. The moment the plaster was fitted, I asked the doctor, 'How long until I can take it off?'

'A month,' the doctor responded. So I focused on a month's time, getting ready for the plaster's removal. The next advice was that I could start running in a week and begin re-building my fitness. Eventually, I returned to competitive action in November, two months early.

I never, ever told myself that my career could be finished. All I ever thought about was that I would come back better, stronger and fitter. Although I didn't, I told myself I would. Rupturing the Achilles tendon did not affect me in terms of running long distances or once I was in full flight, but it definitely dulled my acceleration. Taking off over the first five yards, I found the explosiveness had disappeared. Having spent so long in plaster, the muscle in my right calf wasted and became smaller than on the left. That muscle never returns. It took me a long time to accept that my lightning burst from a standing start had drained away. Eventually, I had to change the way I played. I could not accept that at first. I don't think the fans ever did.

At least I played again. The doctors informed me that not only had I ruptured my Achilles tendon but that I had also shredded it. If the tendon is only ruptured and torn, the surgeon just stitches it back together. Unfortunately, I shredded it as well which makes it impossible to sew the frayed ends back together. The surgeon trimmed off the shreds before pulling the thick bits together. This shortened the tendon and reduced my flexibility and ability to push off powerfully. When the specialist examined the tendon, he asked me, 'Have you experienced problems with your Achilles before? Because it looks degenerate.' What happened in Helsinki was perhaps inevitable; a weakening tendon was always going to give way at some point. It just required the impact of a violent landing to trigger the rupture.

I dribbled with the ball on my left foot and used my right to push off, which meant it came under greater strain than the left. If I had damaged my left Achilles in Helsinki, I would probably not have lost my explosiveness. The doctors never warned me that I might have lost that surge forever, but I knew the history of Achilles tendon injuries, of how they affected footballers' careers. I realised it was my pushing-off foot that had been harmed. Mark Lawrenson's career at Liverpool was ended by an Achilles injury. Gary Stevens ruptured his and although he played again, he was never really the same. No one is, particularly not a pacy player such as myself. I realised the English public would accept me even less now. By 1992, I had not been dribbling around seven people for a while; now I definitely wasn't going to. But there was still that expectancy from the supporters. I moved into a more central-midfield role, keeping the ball, passing it, playing with intelligence, but people still moaned – 'What's John Barnes doing there? He should be speeding past players out on the wing. If he's not, he shouldn't be in the team.'

That year, 1992, was potentially a very hazardous period. My contract at Liverpool was close to expiring. In February, Liverpool offered me an improved contract but I waited and hoped for interest from overseas. I dreamed of Juventus, Barcelona and Real Madrid. Speculation arose about a move to Real Madrid but it was nothing concrete. Some newspapers linked me with Monaco which was flattering. A few *Serie A* clubs, including Roma, were interested but news of my Achilles tendon injury promptly ended all that. My Italian ambitions died on that pitch in Helsinki.

The situation could have been worse. If the Bosman ruling allowing freedom of movement had operated then, Liverpool could have bidden me farewell at the end of my contract and not paid me a penny; they might have been tempted to release a player who had just been shorn of one of his main strengths. The rules at the time stipulated that Liverpool must offer me the same salary or grant me a free transfer. They were not willing to give me a free transfer, so I was able to stay.

I could have wallowed in thoughts of how brutally unfair life was, but negativity never pervaded my mind. A move to Italy, Spain or France was simply not meant to be. It was pointless moaning about life being so cruel. I accepted the misfortune dealt me by fate. That's my approach to life. I look at people enjoying some apparently undeserved luck and think they must have something terrible lurking within their lives. I also believe they will pay for any luck they do not deserve.

The extinguishing of the Italian light certainly damaged my prospects of performing better for England. *Serie A* would have improved me. Liverpool were banned from Europe following the Heysel disaster, so I never really gained much experience of playing against continental opposition. Facing Giuseppe Bergomi at club level is better preparation for playing him in an international setting than tackling Lee Dixon every week. An England wide player does not encounter many full-backs of Dixon's type on the world stage. Experience of *Serie A* would have taught me more about continental players' strategy, about what they were thinking. For too long, English footballers have thought Italian defenders are superhuman. The mystique arises only because the English have not faced them regularly. Manchester United came up against Italian teams regularly in the European Cup, and eventually acquired the knowledge they needed to overcome Inter Milan and Juventus on their way to winning the Champions League in 1999. Playing against Italians regularly would have made me realise they were actually no better than me, and were just as capable of mistakes and insecurities. Familiarity allows an attacker to exploit defenders' weaknesses.

My return to the international arena following Helsinki came on 17 February 1993 in a World Cup qualifier against San Marino at Wembley. On the morning of the match, I awoke to an unbelievably abusive article about me in the *Daily Mirror*. Jimmy Greaves had been questioning my commitment to England and this *Mirror* article really stirred things up. Tensions invariably arise before England meet one of the minnows of world football; there is a swirl of national introspection with people asking whether England were going to win and if not, why not? Here was a situation where the English sought a scapegoat in advance. The *Mirror* decided I would make a perfect scapegoat because I had joked that I wanted West Indies to beat England at cricket. The *Mirror*'s argument was that here was a man, who wasn't even born in England but in Jamaica, who hoped West Indies' cricketers would defeat England's but was about to represent England at Wembley. The cricket thing was a joke. Whenever the West Indies and England met at cricket, I used to pull the legs of the players at Watford, then Liverpool and England. I was always winding up Bryan Robson, who gets fiercely patriotic. It was nothing serious. I enjoyed the debate such comments fuelled in the dressing-room. I just wanted to be different and also to be supporting the winning team, which the West Indies were at the time. Laughably, the *Mirror* took offence. They wrote that 'how can John Barnes play for England when he wants their cricket team to lose to the West Indies'.

That night at Wembley, England suffered a modest opening twelve minutes against very mediocre opponents. Some of the fans, hyped up but now restless, remembered what was in the *Mirror* that morning. I can still imagine these narrow-minded supporters responding to the newspaper's comments that 'John Barnes wasn't even born in England', that 'he wasn't committed to the cause', that 'he wants West Indies to beat England'. Stirred up, they decided to boo me. I was an easy target because I did not run around screaming and looking like I was giving a hundred per cent. The situation would have been laughable if it had not been so serious. I know black footballers who were not born in England, who probably want the West Indies to win at cricket, but because they charge about, shouting their heads off, clenching their fists and appearing to give everything for the team, the fans do not turn on them. Because I'm perceived as laid-back, it's like I supposedly don't care. So Wembley slaughtered me.

The abuse was deafening. In Frankfurt, it had just been one section heckling me. Against San Marino at Wembley, it felt like the whole stadium was shouting 'fuck off Barnes'. I was glad Graham Taylor didn't substitute me. The flak was terrible but I never hid. I always wanted the ball. I did what I thought was right. I could have faked trying harder by doing what the fans wanted and trying to dribble around opponents. I refused to do that; I passed and did what was right for the England team. The abuse never faded. In 1998, I actually received a letter from someone who had booed me at Wembley. He wanted to apologise after reading a quote from me saying how much football meant to me. I sent him a signed photograph.

Fans are fickle. Two minutes into England's next game at Wembley, the 2–2 draw with Holland on 28 April 1993, I scored from a free kick and the ground erupted into cheers. The very people who had spat vitriol at me two months earlier, who had chanted 'fuck off' relentlessly at me, now sang my praises. From being a hate figure I was a national hero. I understood the hero-villain nature of modern football. I could cope with the abuse because of my family upbringing and my outlook on life. I knew why they were booing. Having read the *Mirror*, the supporters at Wembley for the

San Marino game thought I had no commitment for England. Why should I forgive the foul-mouthed fans for telling me to 'fuck off'? But I put up with it. Many others wouldn't. It did hurt, of course it did, but it would have been far worse if those booing me actually understood football. I don't believe they did. I think many of them booed simply because the person next to them was doing it, the instinct of the herd. Many England fans are too thick to realise what they are doing.

In the dressing-room after the San Marino game, a lot of my England colleagues condemned the booing and expressed their sympathy. Of course, they were relieved it wasn't them being targeted. When England were not living up to the country's massive expectations, somebody was given a hard time. I've been in games where the whole team played badly and one person was being singled out for abuse and I just thought, 'Thank God that's not me.' I would hide away from the situation, go up and put my arm around the player and say, 'it's terrible', secretly pleased it wasn't me for a change.

Graham was angered by the criticism directed at me. He went out of his way to console and encourage me.

'You have to live with the abuse,' he said. 'Don't let it get you down. Keep playing and believing.'

Graham, too, suffered, hounded with increasing venom by the press; the personal attacks were disgraceful. The 'Turnip Taylor' campaign was disgusting. It was so cruel because Graham, whose father was a journalist, tried to accommodate the press. When Graham managed Watford, the press loved him. Everyone loves an underdog and Watford could do no wrong because they ruffled the feathers of the big boys. Graham could be open and honest, just like Joe Kinnear was at Wimbledon. He lost all underdog status on becoming manager of England. As much as Graham wanted to be as frank with the press as he had been at Watford, it was impossible with England. It took him a while to understand that he had to treat the press differently, that he could not open himself up to them otherwise he would be abused. At Watford, his message to the press was 'I'm trying my best, please love me, please come on my side'. He tried that with England and was crucified. Graham is still bitter about his treatment. He is such a patriot that he expects every Englishman to get behind the country. He felt that journalists were Englishmen first and reporters second; he painfully discovered it was the other way around. They were never going to get behind Graham.

Many people thought my international career was over when Graham left, but I thought I would play for England again. I have never lost faith in my ability, even when I couldn't get on the bench at Newcastle after Ruud Gullit arrived in 1998. Reserve-team football was the pinnacle of my competitive week, but I kept telling myself that I was good enough to represent England. Back in 1994, I was excited when Terry Venables was appointed to run the national team because he is an excellent coach, similar to Graham Taylor in his meticulous, methodical preparation. Terry likes people who want to talk about football, who want to understand the game and who can play in a certain way. I knew Terry was strong enough to put me in. Some managers wouldn't have been but Terry could handle the criticism that would inevitably follow my recall.

In September 1994, Terry summoned me for the game against the United States. The tabloids immediately questioned Terry's judgement. 'Nobody likes him – I don't care' read one headline. As well as being a brave decision, it was a decision Terry thought was right. It certainly wasn't favouritism because I hardly knew him. One of Terry's great qualities is that he is big enough to make unpopular decisions. I was determined to repay his faith. I had worked really hard to get fit. Every day I went running up and down the Heswall hills near my home on the Wirral and lost a stone. I had never really had a problem with weight in my career, apart from the usual thing of men hitting thirty. Any excess can become difficult to shed but I became careful what I ate. My fitness regime on the Heswall hills certainly meant I was in good shape for England training.

Back in the Bisham Abbey fold, I was able to watch Paul Gascoigne at close hand again. Gazza is the hardest trainer I have ever seen. His problem is that he does not understand the concept of pacing himself, whether in training or in a match. Gazza gives everything from the start; he began every game at Italia '90 at whirlwind pace and was fit and young enough to maintain it. Six years on, training under Terry, he still started at lung-busting speed despite the fact that he was older and had suffered all those injuries. The day before matches, Terry would organise a practice match and Gazza would be sprinting everywhere in the first five minutes.

'Stop making those runs, otherwise you'll be knackered in fifteen minutes of this match let alone for tomorrow,' I told Gazza. He was just being over-enthusiastic.

People accuse Gazza of not being able to last ninety minutes but he probably runs more in the first hour than many do in the entire match. For the first five minutes of every match, Gazza runs about like an absolute lunatic. In 1990, Gazza had the legs and lungs to maintain it. Nowadays, Bryan Robson uses him in front of Middlesbrough's back-line, getting the ball and passing but not running so much. When we were holed up in an England hotel together, I often felt like giving Gazza some advice, but he never sought it and wouldn't have heeded it anyway. Gazza wants to listen, learn and change his life but he finds it difficult to do.

My seventy-ninth and final England game came alongside Gazza against Colombia on 6 September 1995. I hated playing Colombia because they epitomise the scrimmage approach and it was almost impossible to get the ball off them. I don't think I had a kick in the 0–0 draw. It was not the most auspicious way for my England career to end.

It still angers me that I was labelled lazy as an England international. No player drilled by Graham Taylor could be lazy. Graham would never stand for it. I have always shown a good work ethic, always worked back, always been aware of the need to keep the team's shape. If the opposition's right-back slipped past me and I didn't chase him, Graham would have substituted me. People misunderstood my style. When I ran at defenders, my natural approach was languid and fluid. If the opponent dispossessed me, it appeared as if I was not trying. If I took the defender on in a busy, bustling manner and still lost the ball, everyone praised me for showing such endeavour.

Although I was committed to the team, I can understand why people pigeonholed me as an individualistic performer rather than a team man. Everyone was blinded by that goal in Rio and did not recognise the need for me to change my game in the wake of the Achilles injury. Fans never forgave me for losing the flair. But whatever supporters say, whatever the press write, I know my professional career was marked by intense dedication.

Peter Reid is described as 'a hundred per center' who gave more than Matthew Le Tissier, but Peter never gave more than Matthew. Matthew delivered a hundred per cent of what he could as did Peter. Because of their respective styles, it just looks like Peter did more than Matthew. Footballers do not want to fail so they do everything they can to succeed. Positioning is important too. Matthew can be laid-back playing off the front-line, but if he had gone alongside Terry Butcher at centre-back or Peter Reid in central midfield, he could not look languid.

The accusations of being laid-back irritated me. Those making them wanted to see and hear the commitment, almost smell the cordite. Defeat or a bad performance pained me as much as it hurt Bryan Robson or Peter Reid. Just because the likes of Glenn Hoddle and I never shouted, flew into tackles or clenched our fists like Gazza, didn't mean we didn't care. If Glenn had been born in Spain, France or Italy, the national coaches would have built their teams around him for years. During my era, England appeared more interested in building teams around those who clenched their fists, not those with class in their feet.

The memories of my England career remain special to me. I met some fascinating characters. Glenn Hoddle was such a gifted, intelligent midfielder of marvellous vision who should have won more than his fifty-three caps. Terry Butcher was a great leader and a good defender. For someone so tall and heavy, Terry was quite fleet of foot, which people never appreciated. Terry's Ipswich team-mate, Russell Osman, should have won more than eleven caps. Russell was quick and comfortable on the ball. Dave Watson, at Everton, maximised his potential. Kenny Sansom and Viv Anderson were great attacking full-backs. In midfield, Ray Wilkins, who exuded calm assuredness, and the tenacious Bryan Robson were terrific footballers as well as being really nice people who helped me a lot. They always kept an eye on the younger players. People might think Ray and Bryan were superstars but they were really down-to-earth. Ray and Robbo were the ones I expected to move into management. On England trips, the footballers I gravitated towards were those I respected as people as well as players, Bryan, Terry, Ray and Stuart Pearce.

In attack, one of my favourite all-time players, Peter Beardsley, helped make Gary Lineker click as a goalscorer. Gary was a great finisher. In terms of scoring there is not much to choose between him and Ian Rush. But Rushie was less selfish. He worked hard for his teams, chasing around and dropping back into midfield which Lineker never did. In Lineker's era, England really only had him as a goalscorer so he could afford to goal-hang. But since Lineker, England have enjoyed an unbelievable flood of goalscorers. If Robbie Fowler keeps his head together he could go on to surpass all of them. Robbie is blessed with everything – left foot, right foot, going around the keeper, heading, the ability to score spectacular goals and tap-ins. In terms of natural talent, Robbie is phenomenal. Michael Owen has tremendous pace allied to superb finishing ability. Michael, too, can go on and break all the records as he has done on his way up. Alan Shearer is not particularly tall but he scores with his head, as does John Aldridge. Alan has a magnificent right foot and good technique.

Dion Dublin, Andy Cole and Stan Collymore also impress me as forwards. These are players who, if they had been around in Lineker's time, would have challenged him for a starting place. Now they often cannot even get in the England squad. Ian Wright has just retired but he was a serial goalscorer – left foot, right foot, pace and headers. His infectious character made him invaluable at alleviating the boredom of England camps. I would have loved to have played more alongside finishers like them. But I remain satisfied with my England career, even if most people felt I under-achieved when set against the reputation I built at Liverpool.

from kings to also-rans: liverpool '89–97

Deeply disappointed by the denouement with Arsenal in 1989, Liverpool's players were determined to regain the title, which we did with me contributing twenty-two goals in thirty-four games in the 1989–90 season. I added six more in the FA and Littlewoods Cups. My only real frustration was that I didn't receive the Golden Boot, particularly as I hit a hat-trick on the final day of the season at Coventry City to overtake Gary Lineker. Lineker, who was then fronting Tottenham Hotspur's attack, scored twenty-four of his twenty-six in the League, which forms the criterion for the Golden Boot, so he won the prize. As I have never seen myself as an out-and-out goalscorer, it would have been nice to have been recognised as the leading scorer in the land. Fate decreed otherwise.

I enjoyed playing upfront that season; adaptability has always been a strength of mine. I was basically a creative player who liked scoring, but I never felt the buzz that grabs serial goalscorers. My ego was fed when I shone in a team that didn't play particularly well, but I wasn't satisfied because I craved involvement in a team that was the best, that dominated games. Fortunately, that was a wonderful reality for the first half of my career at Anfield. Ian Rush was my main partner in that prolific season. John Aldridge had left for Real Sociedad. He converted a penalty in the 9–0 defeat of Crystal Palace in September 1989, threw his shirt into the Kop and flew out the next day. Kenny also left Peter Beardsley out occasionally so it was primarily Rushie and myself in attack.

My best game of the season came at Old Trafford on 18 March 1990. I never considered Manchester United as Liverpool's rivals then – Arsenal posed by far the greater danger – so travelling to Old Trafford held no fears. We expected to win. It's difficult for younger players to understand that. United's relentless success throughout the 1990s makes it hard to believe that in the late 1980s they were a good team but nothing special. Alex Ferguson was actually in trouble and speculation persisted that he might lose his job. Try explaining that to someone in 1999 who has just seen United take the treble and Ferguson knighted! Back then, the Theatre of Dreams rarely gave visitors nightmares. It still felt good to score at United because they were a famous club. I scored both goals in our 2–1 win, one of which was a penalty and the other an individual effort. Beardsley passed to me and I eluded Clayton Blackmore and Viv Anderson before slipping the ball under Jim Leighton. United moved Paul Ince across to right-back to keep an eye on me, but in those days Ince was not the influential player he became. It took time for him to settle at United. I think he felt in the shadow of Bryan Robson, although Paul did wonderfully well for them eventually. The biggest memory of that game was that I was supposed to give Ian Rush his first goal against United. We were leading and I was running through, on an angle, and I could have squared the ball for Rushie to score. Unfortunately for Rushie, I was on a hat-trick and tried to shoot in at the near-post but missed. I apologised to Rushie afterwards. I must have been playing in attack too long because I was getting too greedy. Rushie was fine about it.

In helping Liverpool to the title, I became the Football Writers' Footballer of the Year again, beating Alan Hansen by one vote to join

Stanley Matthews, Tom Finney, Danny Blanchflower and Kenny as two-time winners. To be talked about in the same breath as those legends, particularly as none were my contemporaries, apart from Kenny to an extent, made me appreciate what a great honour it was. The Football Writers' award is polled at the right time, towards the end of the season. The PFA award, although more prestigious, is voted for in January and February and most footballers cannot remember August, September or October. The player who lights up Christmas often becomes Player of the Year. Les Ferdinand managed it. Players often only see those they face on matchdays or catch on *Match of the Day*.

We began the 1990–91 season with our usual eagerness but it was to be a sad year with Kenny resigning in February 1991, in the wake of that extraordinary 4–4 FA Cup tie with Everton. I wasn't that close to Kenny so I hadn't seen any signs of him being unwell. Alan Hansen had. Alan and Kenny were very good friends. They lived close to each other in Southport and socialised together. Apart from matchdays and training when Kenny joined in the five-a-sides, I never saw him at all. Besides, Kenny would never have let any illness show. Maybe when he went home he banged his head against the wall, but he gave away nothing in public. Kenny said later that the reason he felt so stressed was because of Hillsborough. I could empathise with that. Stress affects people in different ways. If Kenny insists stress from Hillsborough proved so much he had to resign then I respect that.

Everyone at Anfield was stunned at Kenny's decision to go. Only Alan had any idea that something was wrong. I was one of the last to find out. We were playing Luton Town on the Saturday and I had headed south on the Thursday to stay in a house I still owned in Hemel Hempstead, which was close by. Because of Luton's plastic pitch, which Liverpool hated playing on, we used to train at Kenilworth Road on a Friday to give us some familiarity with the strange bounce. Having only a short distance to travel, I was the first one to arrive that Friday. I was surprised to find a load of reporters standing around in the car-park.

'What are you lot all doing here?' I asked. 'We are only training today. The match is tomorrow.' Almost before I had finished speaking, one of the journalists broke in.

'John, what do you think about the news?'

'What news,' I replied.

'The news that Kenny has resigned.' I didn't believe them. But the Liverpool coach rolled into the car-park without Kenny and the players quickly confirmed what had happened. I was shocked.

Everyone thought and hoped Alan Hansen would take over as manager. I certainly did. He was the older statesman of the dressing-room, hugely popular and highly respected. We all admired his views on football. I thought Alan's appointment would be the natural progression, in keeping with Liverpool's commitment to continuity. I never told Alan that I thought he should get the job. I didn't want to be seen to be sucking up to the possible manager. Alan may have looked at me and thought 'creep'.

Two weeks after Kenny resigned, Alan called a players' meeting at Anfield. The coaches came too. We all gathered in the dressing-room and waited for what we assumed would be a major announcement, the one we had all been praying for. Alan walked through the door and looked around the room at all these expectant faces.

'The board have offered me the manager's job and I've taken it.' Before we could applaud or say anything, Alan, his face a picture of severity, went on.

'Things are going to have to change. I know where you live in Southport and on the Wirral. I know which pubs and clubs you go to. Your drinking has got out of hand and it's going to have to stop. Stevie Nicol, you are not allowed to go out to the pub ever again.' There was silence. Then Alan spoke again. 'Every Sunday after every match, we are going to come in and watch the video of the game. And we will be training every day.' With that, Alan turned round and walked out of the dressing-room.

The moment the door swung shut behind him, everyone immediately started cursing Alan, which happens all the time with managers now but was rare then.

'That's it,' everyone said to everyone else. 'I'm not staying, I'm not putting up with that. We are allowed to have a drink. I'm not coming in on a Sunday.' Alan was slaughtered by each player. But a minute or so later, he walked back in through the door, laughing his head off.

'Only joking,' he said. 'I'm not going to be manager. I'm just retiring.'

Alan never contemplated management. He worried that, like Kenny, he would succumb to the stress. He thought he would not be able to handle the pressure of having to get results when he could do nothing about it except sit on the bench and shout. Alan hated the innate vulnerability of a manager's position, so he avoided management. I accepted Alan's decision although I could not fathom the logic. I would have loved the Liverpool job after Kenny's resignation but I was too young.

Liverpool wanted someone steeped in the club's tradition so Graeme Souness returned in April 1991. I never got on with Souness. Some people thought I tried to undermine him but that was not the case. He and I didn't agree on many issues, particularly in terms of the way Liverpool played, but I'm not a confrontational person. He did criticise me in front of the players – 'You can do so much more,' he would say to me – but I never got in an argument with him. I never questioned him. Souness was not a person I would have a drink with but I had to respect him as a manager. He never saw the best of me. Because of the Achilles injury, I was never able to give him what he wanted. I delivered enough to justify selection but not what he had seen from previous years. That frustrated him. I felt he didn't rate me. But everything Souness did was for the good of Liverpool.

Life was difficult for Souness. He had never managed in England, although he had been a great player there. He had managed in Scotland, transforming Rangers, but no matter what Rangers do, they do not encounter the level of intense competition experienced in England every week. It must be impossible to gain consistency by playing Celtic one week, Arbroath the next. Life was easier up in Scotland. Rangers had only Celtic to contend with, and, to an extent, Aberdeen. Celtic were a better footballing side at the time, but Rangers spent a lot of money to build a winning team with players like Terry Butcher, Graham Roberts, Chris Woods, Trevor Steven and Gary Stevens. Souness recruited Mark Falco, Colin West and Nigel Spackman, who were good players, but they were not the best in England. Terry Hurlock was a decent footballer for Millwall who went up to Ibrox, but I don't think Liverpool or Manchester United would have looked at him. Still Rangers won the League.

Liverpool were the best team in the country when Souness arrived, but the English scene was not as simple as in Scotland. A mass turnover of players was not considered healthy practice in England. Souness got rid of too many Liverpool players too soon. Maybe he thought Ray Houghton, Ronnie Whelan and Steve McMahon were finished, but they each had another two years left in them. Peter Beardsley and Steve Staunton were also sold. Souness clearly made bad errors of judgement. Souness didn't get on with the older players; maybe he believed the senior ones would undermine him, but Ray, Ronnie and Steve were never a threat to the manager. They just wanted to carry on representing Liverpool. All these drastic changes ran counter to Anfield's tradition of continuity, of bringing players in and phasing others out. Souness obviously felt radical steps were required and wanted his own men in.

He did introduce some wonderful talents into the first team, skilful individuals like Steve McManaman, Jamie Redknapp and Robbie Fowler. Liverpool and England have since enjoyed the fruits of Souness's decision to promote these youngsters early. In ensuing years, Liverpool benefited from their early blooding but Souness was not around to reap the rewards. Roy Evans took over as McManaman, Redknapp and Fowler were developing into internationals.

Souness didn't intentionally change Liverpool's style, but the process of dispensing with five players immersed in the Liverpool way and bringing in others, whether home-grown or recruited, inevitably meant an alteration of the playing pattern. It was a problem bedding in so many at once. When Kenny brought me and Peter Beardsley into the Liverpool side, it was a relatively straightforward blending process. There were only two of us to assimilate into the team. Souness over-reached himself. It can take a season for one player to settle in, let alone five or six. The policy of progression was broken. Had Souness adopted a more sensible, cautious approach, the older players would have been phased out as the others matured. During his thirty-three months in charge, Souness sold eighteen players and bought fifteen. Liverpool were in a permanent state of flux.

Liverpool did win the 1992 FA Cup under Souness but the supporters expected and deserved far more than a knockout trophy. I missed the final against Sunderland. The previous Saturday I sustained a slight injury that in itself was not serious enough to prevent me playing at Wembley. In preparation for the trip south, Graeme took us to the Haydock Thistle Hotel for a swim. As we played volleyball in the pool, I jumped up to smash the ball and pulled a thigh muscle. That was it. I was out of the Cup final. Liverpool won 2–0.

Liverpool's decline was not gradual. Our standing dropped swiftly under Souness. From being champions in 1990 and runners-up in 1991, Liverpool slid to sixth in both 1992 and 1993. Allied to poor results Souness's ill-advised decision to do a paid exclusive with the *Sun* about his heart condition on the anniversary of Hillsborough meant he had to go. He was in charge of a team who were struggling so he had to bear responsibility. Souness probably thought Liverpool needed a period of dressing-room bloodshed and transition. I'm sure he could see a great future in McManaman, Redknapp and Fowler. He should have remembered that tomorrow never comes for managers; they must deliver today. In January 1994, Souness was sacked. Some of the players were sorry to see him go. The rest weren't.

Liverpool's decline was not solely Souness's fault. Alan's retirement was a huge blow. As the nineties progressed, other teams improved, becoming more aware of what was required tactically and technically to be successful. Norwich and West Ham were the neutrals' favourites because they sought to play the Liverpool way, passing the ball, but this proved to be the undoing of some teams. Liverpool were the only ones who could truly play the Liverpool way. Teams subsequently realised that it was better to develop their own style. Liverpool were being overtaken.

The board's decision to name Roy Evans as Souness's successor did not surprise me one bit. I thought Roy could possibly have been appointed before, perhaps even as far back as 1985. Roy and Ronnie Moran would have been prime contenders for the position after Joe Fagan went because Kenny was still a player. They were in the Boot Room. Ronnie was more of a coach than a manager so I assumed that, of the two, Roy would be first in line. After Kenny left and Alan removed himself from contention, I thought it had to be Roy. When Souness went, Roy finally got it. Roy never really struck me as an obvious manager but Liverpool's board sought sanctuary in the Boot Room, hoping that a return to the principle of succession from within would restore former glories. Roy understood football. He was immersed in the Liverpool way. But management demands so many other qualities. I questioned whether Roy would be hard enough because he is such a lovely guy.

Roy called me his 'eyes and ears' on the pitch. I played in central midfield for him. With so many youngsters coming in, Liverpool wanted someone older, more experienced and more responsible to play in the holding role so I had moved in from the left. It was important that relative novices like McManaman and Redknapp didn't have anything to worry about. I had never played in the holding position before, although I knew how to do it. I'm not a real tackler but I could keep the ball, talk to people and organise them. Liverpool's holding position suited me after the Achilles injury had removed my old acceleration.

Roy and the players appreciated how my game had to change, even if the fans didn't. Most criticism emanated from my father.

'Why do you just give the ball to McManaman?' he said. 'Why don't you take it on yourself?' I ignored him.

McManaman was the main beneficiary of my passing. I gained a lot of satisfaction from seeing Steve do what I used to do, knowing that I had given him a good ball in the right area of the field. From an attacking perspective, Steve's position was the most important in the Liverpool side. The relationship between him and me was similar to that between Rivaldo and Dunga for Brazil at France '98. Brazil played four in midfield with Dunga and Cesar Sampaio in the centre. Rivaldo and Leonardo were the key attacking midfielders because Brazil didn't play the ball straight to Ronaldo or Bebeto. All Dunga needed to do was get the ball and give it to Rivaldo in an advanced position. Rivaldo would then have a dribble or a one-two, always pushing deeper into the final third. McManaman picked up what that Rivaldo position required so quickly. It became second nature to Steve to find space so he could receive a ten-yard pass in an area where he could cause damage. Every time Jamie Redknapp or I had possession, McManaman made himself available left or right. Steve is a wonderful dribbler, brilliant at exploiting defences' weaknesses, but he needs to receive the ball early. I would tell Jamie and Rob Jones to release the ball quickly, before defenders or midfielders could pick up Steve. Delaying the moment would cut off McManaman's legs.

As a person, Macca is very laid-back. When Terry Venables was England coach, he took me to one side at Bisham Abbey one day.

'Is McManaman bothered? Does he care?' he asked.

'Yes, he does care,' I replied. He does; his relaxed manner gives the wrong impression. I know all about that. Terry told me afterwards that our conversation gave him the impetus to stick with Macca for Euro '96. For a new manager to come in and see McManaman walking around on the training pitch so relaxed, not appearing to listen at all, it was important to be assured the player was committed. I identified with Macca's situation.

One of football's most heated debates centres around which is Macca's best position for England. I hate the description 'free role' because it sounds as if the player wants to be lazy, but I would give Macca that freedom, although it must be allied to defensive responsibilities. Macca should be an attacker playing off the front man, switching between the inside-left and inside-right positions. The team's philosophy would be to get the ball in to McManaman. Some players must be rigid in a team formation but Macca would be my flexible friend. For England in Euro '96, he popped up on the right, the left, everywhere.

Macca won the 1995 Coca-Cola Cup for us with two fantastic goals against Bolton Wanderers. Bolton were a hard-working, efficient side. We weren't playing particularly well but it was a very pleasing result because Bolton had knocked us out of the FA Cup a couple of seasons before. The final looked a bit of a banana skin, but Macca scored one of the greatest goals Wembley has ever witnessed, gliding past Bolton defenders and shooting in. Because of Macca's effortless running style, he doesn't look fast. He doesn't appear to have the more obvious speed of Michael Owen, whose action shows the energy he is putting into running, or someone powerful like Emile Heskey. Steve glides past people and he certainly eluded Bolton's defence. That Coca-Cola Cup final confirmed the emergence of Steve McManaman.

I also kept an eye on Jamie Redknapp, giving him the ball in central midfield and telling him to release Macca with long passes. Jamie is absolutely brilliant. He has always wanted to learn, to improve, to do well. Jamie's a manager's dream. He lives, breathes and sleeps football. He's always first at training and afterwards spends time practising striking the ball, concentrating on developing his technique. Jamie's also a lovely person, which is not surprising because the Redknapp family are all great people. Harry is fantastic. I know his brother Mark, a football agent. Jamie is so important at Liverpool but only recently has the Kop begun to appreciate that. He is good-looking and all the girls used to love him. Liverpool fans thought of him as a cocky kid strutting around town, but Jamie has never been like that. He went through a difficult period at Anfield when he didn't know whether he wanted to stay; the fans criticised him and the team weren't doing well. I used to speak to him about it all the time. But he battled on and has done well. Jamie can become the complete midfield player. I still speak to him most weeks, encouraging him to continue expressing himself with the ball.

There's no one I've met through football who I would class as a friend but Jamie, along with Peter Beardsley, comes closest. Professional football is such a transient profession; it always surprises me when I read footballers naming team-mates as their 'best friend' in programme profiles. I wonder whether they would really call that person up regularly if they left the club. Probably not. At Watford, Liverpool, Newcastle and Charlton, as with every club, we were all thrown together as team-mates. Jamie is the exception. I helped him out when he was younger and I respect him as a player and a person. So I ring him and we talk but mainly on a professional level.

Liverpool employed some very talented footballers during Roy's time. I found Stan Collymore a complex character. He doesn't mean anyone any harm. Stan hasn't got a wicked bone in his body. I'm sure he regrets hitting Ulrika Jonsson. It was very unlike Stan to do something like that. I am sure the way he reacted with Ulrika was stress related. Just because he is highly paid with the whole world at his feet doesn't mean he can't suffer stress like someone stacking shelves in Sainsbury's with four children at home and a mortgage. I believe Stan's stress problems are completely true. That's the way Stan is.

Stan's main problem as a footballer is that he just wants to do what Stan wants to do. When I captained Liverpool, if I told him to do something, he was quite likely to reply, 'I don't want to do that.' Stan wasn't being deliberately selfish. He is too much of an individual to understand what it means to play in a team. Socially, I get on fine with him and he is undoubtedly a great player. But, like David James, he has failed to achieve what he could. Stan bears comparison with Ronaldo. He possesses the pace of Ronaldo, has two good feet and great dribbling ability. But all those attributes are not enough in a team sport. Sometimes it isn't enough to score thirty goals a season. When Stan and Robbie partnered each other, they combined to score fifty-odd goals but Liverpool didn't win the Premiership.

David James was shaped from the same mould as Stan. He could have been more motivated. He was temperamental and very artistic (some of his drawings are superb). James is the most naturally talented goalkeeper in the world. He could be the best by a stretch if he exerted himself. When he was at Watford, he was good because there was more discipline. James didn't get enough discipline at Liverpool and his goalkeeping suffered for it. But there is still time for him and he may shine now that he has moved to Aston Villa. He possesses the potential to be even better than Peter Schmeichel if he discovers discipline in his time-keeping and in his training. 'You've got to apply yourself more,' I told him.

Robbie and Macca are both local lads who became almost soul-mates as well as social mates. They both lived on the Albert Dock and had the same friends, so it was natural for them to hang around together. People claimed Robbie followed Macca blindly, almost copied his every move like an impressionable younger brother, but I think that was unfair on Robbie.

Robbie and Macca, Jamie and David, Stan and Jason McAteer all had the 'Spice Boys' label loaded on to them. The 'Spice Boys' criticism was purely down to the players not being successful. The press thought the reason Liverpool were not winning trophies was because the players were going out modelling all the time. Ryan Giggs and David Beckham model clothes and they have won the European Cup. The press hyped up this 'Spice Boy' abuse to explain why Liverpool weren't doing well. It made good headlines but it was unfair. Apart from Gazza, I cannot think of a footballer who trains harder than Jason McAteer. He did some shampoo modelling and was slammed for it. All the players tagged as 'Spice Boys' loathed it. Accusations of not caring about Liverpool, of being obsessed only with money, women and modelling, were far from the truth.

We have it within ourselves to be compassionate or evil, to be good professionals or jack the lads depending on our upbringing. Adulthood is shaped by youth; the twenty-five-year-old footballer is moulded by the environment he experienced as an apprentice. Manchester United's young players could have been 'Spice Boys' but their early days ensured they remained disciplined. Alex Ferguson taught all these great young kids how to be model professionals. They were taught how to behave. I take the same approach with my children. They are not inherently different from their peers. If my sweet children were moved on to the roughest council estate and allowed to run wild they would turn out completely differently. My discipline, like Ferguson's with his young players, has worked. My children are impeccably behaved. If Ryan Giggs, David Beckham, Paul Scholes or the Nevilles had been at a different club they may not have become the impressive, disciplined set of players and people they are now. Giggs, Beckham and the rest learned good habits as teenagers so that by the time they were twenty-one, Alex could leave them to do whatever they want. He trusted them. A sense of professionalism had become deeply ingrained. I had no problem with the Liverpool players modelling but I was concerned with their time-keeping, their lack of respect and casual attitude in training. The 'Spice Boy' abuse was cruelly overdone in the media but we definitely needed more professionalism and discipline in training.

As Liverpool meandered, my frustration mounted. I ranted and raved at the players to get them going. I wasn't really concerned with my own job; driving the team obsessed me now.

'You are spending too much time and energy on doing everyone's job for them instead of concentrating on your own,' Roy and Ronnie Moran told me.

I became intense and dissatisfied about practices at Liverpool. Steve McManaman is a great player but not a great trainer. No matter how little Macca does in training, he can go out and perform on the Saturday. Unfortunately, others see Macca's approach to training and copy it but then they cannot deliver on a Saturday. Jamie was fine; he always wanted to work. Robbie and Stan Collymore were not the best trainers but they scored goals. Once Liverpool allowed such a situation to develop, it was downhill from then on. It became a big problem when players were saying, 'If certain players are not training hard, then I'm not.' Melwood was turning from a training-ground into a playground.

The predicament was seen most alarmingly in the five-a-sides. When Ronnie Moran first started coaching at Melwood, he placed a lot of restrictions on players, insisting every play was one-touch and that players had to be over the halfway line to score. Problems occurred when more and more youngsters pushed through and players came in who hadn't been brought up the Liverpool way. Liverpool's training principles became diluted, compromised even. Ronnie demanded the players play one-touch or two-touch. The sign of a good team is when they play two-touch in training when they don't have to. Players' natural instincts are to take more touches. As soon as a coach shouts 'all in', allowing as many touches as they like, all the players say, 'thank God for that', knowing they can dribble. At Liverpool in the early days, I can't remember Ronnie ever needing to say 'two-touch'. We just did it instinctively, keeping the ball moving with one or two touches, finding someone, getting the ball back. That disappeared during Roy's time. Training became a real problem. I used to have meetings with Roy about goings-on at Melwood.

'We've really got to get training sorted out,' I often told Roy. It was pure frustration on my part. I was so excited about this Liverpool team. I looked at talents like Jamie, Robbie and Macca and felt we could be the best side in the country. Liverpool didn't know why they weren't the best around, but I did. We were inconsistent because we trained inconsistently. There were days when we trained well and because of the quality available we looked good on the field. During the past few seasons, halfway through the year everybody would be saying, 'Liverpool are going to win the League, look at the way they play.' Then all of a sudden, with ten or so games to go, Liverpool slipped up.

'We're inconsistent,' I told Roy, 'because of our training.' Roy agreed with me.

'Yes, you're right, we have to be more professional in our attitude and in our time-keeping,' Roy replied.

I was fortunate. I had kids to drop off at school each morning so I was in training early every day. Maybe if I was single, I would have come in late as well. Some people may call lateness a 'little thing' but all these 'little things' add up. Too much indiscipline crept in.

'We have to stamp it out,' I pleaded with Roy.

I also suggested to Roy that Liverpool needed to develop a playing pattern that everyone understood. It was not enough to say 'give the ball to Macca'. We had to play without Steve at times. We needed to work on patterns of play. Functional work, learning how to move as a team, can be very boring. But Bill Shankly needed time to lay the foundations of the Liverpool way.

Roy hailed from the old school; he probably felt we didn't need to practise patterns of play all the time. He probably thought we just needed to carry on with the five-a-sides and that would be good enough. It had worked under Shankly, Paisley, Fagan and Dalglish. But it wasn't good enough now. Football had changed. Liverpool had changed. Continuity had disappeared from the dressing-room; in the past, the older players showed newcomers the Liverpool way in training. Players have to fear they will be made accountable for their actions. I would come away from training, climb in the car and think that Roy had to become tougher. But the players would have seen through it. Managers have to be true to themselves. Arsène Wenger doesn't shout at people. Alex Ferguson does. It is in their character. Ronnie Moran ranted and raved at the players. But the tone has to be set by the manager.

Roy's team were often criticised in the press. Liverpool were slaughtered for wearing those cream suits to the 1996 FA Cup final when we lost to Manchester United. I didn't like the suits, but I was over-ruled in the dressing-room. However, it was ridiculous to suggest Liverpool were beaten by United because of some cream suits. People just wanted to slate Liverpool for being flash, for being 'Spice Boys'. We succumbed to United because they boxed us in. It's a classic United ploy when they are faced with three central midfielders. I spoke to Alex Ferguson about it some time afterwards and he was aware going into that final that Liverpool often outplayed them, even though United often won. United had these two flying wingers and that gave us a lot of room in central midfield. For that final, Giggs and Beckham tucked inside, which meant we could get the ball to our full-backs but not to central midfield where they were stifling us. We couldn't play. United didn't create many chances because their wingers operated inside. United didn't play particularly well either, but Eric Cantona scored and that was it. The result is everything.

Cantona had been very quiet throughout the match. That didn't surprise me; he was usually quiet against Liverpool. Whenever I watched him against other teams, Cantona was always brilliant. Liverpool closed him down. The effect the Frenchman had on United was sensational. Cantona was primarily popular at United because he made them successful. Time after time, Cantona was the match-winning catalyst, but he was so much more than that. He made his team-mates feel great. Giggs, Beckham and Butt were inspired by playing alongside him. It must have been like being in the same team as Diego Maradona. Chelsea are a big example of that – Michael Duberry and Jody Morris improved when they started playing alongside Gianluca Vialli and Gianfranco Zola, two brilliant professionals. Cantona also had a fantastic attitude to training and United's young players picked up on that. His influence at United far surpassed what he did for them playing-wise.

In August 1997, I was given a free transfer by Liverpool, which angered me. Roy had bought Paul Ince to play in central midfield but I wanted to stay and fight for my place. I felt I was good enough to be playing in Liverpool's first team. When I still wasn't being selected pre-season, I began to worry. I wanted to know what Liverpool thought of me, so I went in to see Roy. I never requested a free transfer; I simply inquired whether Liverpool would be willing to give me one, which was different.

'Yes, Liverpool would be willing to give you a free transfer,' Roy replied.

That told me I was not wanted at Anfield any more; even if two important central midfielders, Ince and Redknapp, were injured Roy was still prepared to let me go. I obviously had no future with Liverpool. If Liverpool had refused me a free transfer because they needed cover for Ince and Redknapp, I would happily have stayed. But it was made plain that under no circumstances would I be needed at Liverpool. It hurt me bad because I regard Liverpool as home. My family base will always be on the Wirral. I wanted to be with Liverpool for the rest of my career. Liverpool were my club, and they pushed me out of the door.

I should have seen what was coming the previous season. I was substituted against Manchester United on 19 April at Anfield and that was one of my better games of the year. I even scored in a 3–1 defeat but everyone cheered when I was replaced by Patrik Berger. Liverpool fans never really accepted me for just sitting in midfield, prodding and poking the ball rather than flying down the wing as before. At the time, everyone insisted that Liverpool required a ball-winner. The fact that we were playing teams off the park but losing the odd game was overlooked by the fans. If Liverpool had won that United game, we would have been in with a chance of challenging the Premiership leaders in the remaining three fixtures. The Kop never appreciated that. People kept on about Liverpool needing a ball-winner. So I was sacrificed. Roy called me into his office after the United game.

'You are not going to play next week against Paris St Germain,' Roy said. Liverpool trailed the French 3–0 from the first leg of this Cup Winners' Cup semi-final and Roy had decided something desperate was required. 'I am not going to play you because we are going to bypass midfield and just get the ball forward quickly,' Roy explained. 'I am going for an aerial bombardment so we don't need any passers in midfield, just runners and fighters.'

I understood Roy's logic and Liverpool battled to within a goal of the French team but still went out. I still felt I would get back in the side. I was ignored for the Spurs game, then the Wimbledon one and only came on as a sub for the final fixture of the season at Sheffield Wednesday. That draw meant Liverpool finished fourth and not second. Newcastle got into the Champions League ahead of us and Arsenal on goal difference. It was a disappointing end to another season of under-achievement. I hoped Roy would address the way we played, because we had performed badly. At the start of pre-season, he said, 'We've got to get back into the passing way.' That is what we should have focused on because we were the best passing team in the country. We should have developed what we had at Liverpool.

I realised my days were numbered. I accepted Roy's suggestion that I visit Amsterdam for a week to look at the way Ajax trained and coached. Roy was not thinking it might help Liverpool, just me. Ajax's training academy, 'The Future', made a big impression on me. No matter how young the Ajax players were, they were so in tune with the Ajax way, sacrificing personal glory for the team. Ajax's principles are driven by respect. Players such as Ronald De Boer were always punctual for training because Ajax's philosophy was that he should be no different from an unknown eighteen-year-old player. Ronald De Boer was a superstar at Ajax but he set an example of team responsibility.

I returned to Anfield from Amsterdam knowing I was leaving. I never accepted Liverpool's obsession with recruiting a ball-winner.

'Why do we need a ball-winner if we keep possession?' I said to Roy. 'If we don't give the ball away, we don't need someone specifically to win it back. We should be concentrating on not losing the ball.' But Roy was set on Ince.

I ran into Incey earlier that summer when Mark Wright and I flew to Hong Kong for a game against Inter Milan. We talked about Liverpool, about the problems with discipline, about what Liverpool had to do to become successful again. 'As senior players, it's up to us to sort the youngsters out,' was Ince's response. Incey is a winner; he's got a good attitude. He was very optimistic and arrived at Anfield with the right intentions. He thought he could come in and sort things out at Liverpool. 'It isn't as simple as that,' I told him. I knew it wasn't just a case of buying a combative midfielder, mixing him in with creative players such as McManaman and Redknapp and Liverpool would automatically win the Premiership. The ethos was lacking towards training. Paul felt his arrival would be the answer. But nothing has changed or improved.

It is sad to see what has happened at Anfield. I still believe Liverpool are the only club who can challenge Manchester United long-term. Arsenal have done so in recent years but they lack youthful replacements for their ageing players. Arsenal cannot rely solely on French purchases and many are unproven. Arsène Wenger was lucky with Emmanuel Petit and Patrick Vieira. The challenge to United must come from Anfield. I still love Liverpool so I hope they turn it round. Hopefully, it won't take that long.

frustration: newcastle united

U nwanted by Liverpool, I initially aimed to rebuild my career at West Ham United. I spoke to Harry Redknapp, West Ham's manager, immediately after the first game of the season, when Ince took my place against Wimbledon on Saturday, 9 August 1997. Harry was very keen on me coming to Upton Park and talked enthusiastically about how he could see me fitting in. I was excited by the prospect of joining Harry at West Ham, so I told him what I wanted financially.

'I'll talk it over with the board and get back to you,' Harry said. On the Monday, Harry called back and explained West Ham had never paid a player what I was seeking.

'But Harry,' I replied, 'you normally pay millions of pounds for players in transfer fees before even reaching the salary. I'm available on a free.' Besides, I wasn't asking for extortionate amounts. Harry went back to talk to his directors again. Phone-calls went on all day and into the evening. I like and respect Harry a lot which probably explained my impulsive desire to resolve the situation quickly. I admire the way West Ham play under Harry. I appreciate his ideas and could see myself at Upton Park. At 7 p.m., Harry called again and said West Ham were prepared to offer virtually what I wanted.

'I'll get a train down tomorrow,' I replied and put the phone down. Within five minutes the phone rang again. It was Kenny Dalglish.

'Digger,' Kenny said, 'I didn't know you had a free transfer.'

'I have,' I replied, 'and I have just got off the phone to Harry Redknapp. I'm going down to see him tomorrow.'

'Hold on,' said Kenny. 'Come up and talk to us at Newcastle.'

'I can't, Kenny, I've got to see Harry.' Kenny started being persuasive.

'Digger, we are in the Champions League. Newcastle are a great club with great fans; you would be leaving Liverpool to come to a club as big.' I told Kenny I would think about it. I couldn't decide. I sat there, turning over the two options in my mind. I thought at least I should go and hear what Kenny had to offer, so half an hour later, I phoned up Peter Storrie, who was West Ham's chief executive at the time.

'Peter, I'm sorry but I've got to go up and listen to Newcastle.' Peter was upset.

'No, you can't,' he said. 'You said you were coming to us.' It was a difficult situation.

'Peter, you can hold me to that because I said I was coming down,' I replied, 'but it wouldn't be fair to West Ham if I came down without even giving myself the opportunity of talking to Newcastle. I could sign for you, play for you but you wouldn't really have me because I would be wondering "what if".'

Peter was annoyed and rightly so. I also felt awkward and embarrassed but I had to be true to myself, so I apologised to Peter and travelled up to Newcastle the next day. I decided immediately that Newcastle was the place for me and signed a two-year deal on 13 August. I really shouldn't have talked to Kenny but Harry understood. Every time I see Harry now I apologise, but he appreciated what an opportunity Newcastle represented at the time. Their situation was full of promise for the season. I had never been able to play in the European Cup during my time at Liverpool because of the Heysel ban. It had always been my ambition to experience the greatest club competition of them all, to pit my wits and skills against the best players in Europe. I thought everything would go well at Newcastle. I had no inkling how badly things would actually turn out.

Newcastle's pre-qualifying commitments for the Champions League meant we fell behind in our Premiership games. We beat West Ham 1–0, and I scored which made me feel even worse about Harry. But I realised this Newcastle side were not playing the kind of football I liked. I envisaged problems even when Newcastle lay sixth in the Premiership despite not playing well. In the dressing-room, the players kept saying, 'If we win our two games in hand we can go top.' That refrain lasted until October. Then it was, 'If we win our two games in hand we can go fifth.' After Christmas, it was obvious we were in trouble. Eventually, we finished only four points above the relegation zone.

Newcastle's fans stayed with the players throughout, never getting on our backs, always willing us on. The passion of the Geordies is unbelievable. These Newcastle supporters had not had any success to savour, simply false dawns and shattered expectations, but they waited and hoped, sang and dreamed. That anticipation, togetherness, fervour and love of the club, even in bad times, was awesome. Newcastle treated the fans to some dreadful, dour, uninspiring performances and yet they never wavered in their commitment to the team. They are special fans.

During my latter years at Anfield, Jamie Redknapp and Steve McManaman stopped going out in Liverpool when the team struggled. They would just get too hard a time from the fans they met on the streets, in the clubs or restaurants. That would never happen on Tyneside. Newcastle players can walk around anywhere; the fans just love them and would stick by them whatever happened. The Toon Army knows the players are trying their best for their beloved Newcastle United. Even when we were at our most unadventurous, I never experienced or sensed any aggravation or intimidation from the fans. We were playing badly but the fans kept coming up to us and saying, 'If we don't get success this season, don't worry, we will get it next year.' The Geordies will always be behind the players.

I often spoke to Newcastle's coaches, Alan Irvine and Tommy Burns, about the need for more pattern-of-play work but we didn't have enough time to do it. Alan and Tommy were good coaches. Tommy had so much experience and knowledge from his days managing Celtic and the players respected him. Alan is a very good coach who impressed me when I was in Newcastle's firsts and reserves, but he did not win over all Newcastle's main players. He probably generated the best response from Newcastle's youth team. That is normal; first-team players have less to prove so are less likely to sweat their all for a coach they scarcely know. Alan is a lovely guy who is happier working with youth players.

Newcastle's assistant manager was Terry McDermott. He was brilliant, basically there for a laugh and a joke, always messing around. Kenny told Terry Mac to take the reserves for training once.

'I'm not taking the bloody reserve team!' Terry Mac laughed back, as he loped off to the reserves. He started with the warm-up. 'What do you want to do?' he asked of the players. 'Oh, just stretch your legs.' Terry was a good buffer between the players and Kenny. Kenny was the straight man while Terry used to smile and gee up the players. Terry Mac was very important for Kenny as he had been for Kevin Keegan, offering light relief from the day's pressures. He now performs a similar role for us at Celtic.

I should have realised that Newcastle's season was going to be painful. The team lost Alan Shearer in a pre-season match at Goodison when he slid in to play the ball and badly damaged his ankle. Some people wrongly suggested that Alan's physical style of play contributes to the number of injuries he sustains. The one at Goodison just proves how unfortunate Alan has been. There was no one near him. Alan very rarely gets hurt by players kicking him. He is so strong that if there is physical contact with anyone else, they are the ones who suffer. If Alan had been fit all season, rather than returning only in January, maybe things would have been different. Newcastle would have had a target to aim for, an obvious magnet for our forward moves. Shearer's importance to a team is incalculable. Blackburn's 1995 Premiership trophy was rooted in Alan's presence and his partnership with Chris Sutton; all the other players worked for and towards Alan.

Alan reminds me of John Aldridge but stronger. Neither was blessed with obvious talents but both were supremely effective goalscorers. Alan is not particularly quick but he usually reaches balls clipped over the top. He is not particularly tall but he scores frequently with his head. He's a nightmare to defend against because if a cross comes in, he will be there. For someone who isn't particularly skilful, Alan can drop his shoulder and drill a thirty-yard right-footer past a keeper. He's very clinical at hitting the target. In Europe, people say Alan Shearer is not a forward with the finesse of a Filippo Inzaghi or Alessandro Del Piero but Alan will always guarantee his team a steady supply of goals.

Alan is as strong mentally as he is physically. He is a single-minded character who will always prove people wrong, particularly those who claim he is finished. Neither injury nor criticism can keep him down. As a player, his physical strength is his greatest asset. Alan manhandles centre-halves, even though he is not particularly big. He can cope with the ball being hit long to him; even with two centre-halves up his back, Alan will always bring the ball down. Unfortunately, Newcastle were so geared to playing this way that they failed to develop other avenues. For the first half of the season, we didn't have Alan yet we still sought to get the ball forward quickly to the centre-forward. We moved from back to front too hastily.

When fit, Alan likes the ball early and because he's a very strong character, Newcastle players became fixated with whipping the ball up to him. This line of attack, pretty much Newcastle's only one, was riven with flaws. Alan's not going to beat three players and score. His style is to lay the ball off to Keith Gillespie, but problems arose here as well. Keith is a good winger who can deliver great crosses, but what if he was injured or the left-back had the beating of him? Newcastle's strategy revolved around Keith crossing from the by-line towards Alan, or set-pieces. That was fine if everyone was fit and on form but it didn't account for injuries or people leaving. With Alan injured, we needed Les Ferdinand to fill his role but Les was sold to Tottenham. The seeds of a sorry season were already being sown.

No Alan, no Les but Newcastle still had Tino Asprilla, one of the most extraordinary players I have ever met. The Colombian is a lovely person, a great character, the life and soul of the party. Like some other foreign players, Tino spoke English when he wanted to. When things were going badly he was like Manuel from *Fawlty Towers*. 'Que?' Tino would say. 'Que? I no understand.' Tino was often hilarious. At one of my first training sessions, Kenny was working on a free-kick routine without Tino, who was injured. Suddenly Tino burst from the club-house wearing flippers and goggles and waddled on to the pitch, pointing at everyone and shouting in Spanish. Everyone burst out laughing. That was typical Tino. As a player, Tino reminds me of Stan Collymore – a maverick blessed with great skills, and not a team player at all. Of course, Tino helped Newcastle to a certain extent. There were times when we were without Alan and under pressure and we just gave the ball to Tino. He would do something brilliant with those outrageous ball skills or simply allow us to catch breath. As I've said elsewhere, players such as Tino and David Ginola, who can do something by themselves, are what teams need if they don't have a real pattern. When Tino played we were glad for him that we didn't have any method or strategy or pattern as a team. We just gave the ball to Tino and he produced something out of nothing.

He certainly did with his famous hat-trick against Barcelona in the Champions League at St James' Park on 17 September 1997. I have always loved Barcelona and the adventurous way they play with fabulous footballers such as Luis Figo and Luis Enrique. The game was billed as Newcastle United against Barcelona but in reality it was Keith Gillespie and Tino versus Barcelona. The rest of us simply accompanied Keith and Tino that wonderful night. Keith gave Sergi, Barcelona's left-back, the biggest roasting I have ever seen anyone inflict on an opponent. Sergi isn't slow but I don't think he had ever come up against someone who was so confident in his own pace. Early in the match, Keith got the ball and I wanted him to pass it inside.

'Keith, why are you going to kick the ball forty yards and chase it when you are already giving Sergi five yards?' I said to him. 'You are never going to catch him.' Keith ignored me and just took off past Sergi like he wasn't there. He kept doing this, humiliating the Spaniard throughout the first half.

Keith is blessed with a special talent; if a manager wants an out-and-out winger, Keith is among the very best around. He's the nicest person imaginable unless he has one drink too many and then volatility rules. Keith's basically a mad Irishman. He was young when Manchester United used him in the Andy Cole transfer and, overnight, he found himself removed from the protective clique of young players at Old Trafford. Keith was left to his own devices at Newcastle and fell into trouble, notably with his gambling. Now that Keith is back with Brian Kidd, Blackburn's manager who kept an eye on him at Old Trafford, he should flourish again. Brian should be able to control and nurture Keith because he brought the best out of him to begin with.

Keith made the goals against Barcelona, delivering perfect crosses for Tino, whose movement was marvellous. Tino terrorised Miguel Nadal. The Spanish centre-half is a big guy but that did not seem to bother Tino, who scored two headers and a penalty to give us a 3–0 lead within fifty minutes. Then Barcelona gave us an almighty pasting. Luis Figo was sensational. I remember trying to get near Ivan de la Peña in midfield but couldn't. The angles Barcelona's players made, the way they accepted and moved the ball, the way they supported each other, the positions they took up were all from another planet. Luis Enrique and Figo brought Barcelona back to 3–2 but we held on for a fabulous result.

Barcelona showed enough of their class in the second half to make us wary of travelling to the Nou Camp on 26 November. They outplayed us there, which was not reflected in the 1–0 scoreline; Josep Guardiola typified how football should really be played. Barcelona fans loved de la Peña and were shocked when he was sold to Lazio but Louis Van Gaal, Barcelona's coach, realised how important Guardiola was to the team in those days. Guardiola played the midfield holding role, keeping moves simple and quietly dictating the tempo. Guardiola has no obvious talent but he is so influential. I thought Barcelona would win the Champions League the year we played them and again the following season, 1998–99, but Manchester United put them out. Newcastle played Barcelona at the right time when Van Gaal was trying to combine his Dutch recruits with the Latin players already at the Nou Camp. The Brazilian, Rivaldo, was particularly disappointing against us at St James' Park, just standing out there in the left-wing position. After that season, Rivaldo enjoyed a slightly freer role as Manchester United discovered.

That night at St James' proved the highlight of the Champions League for us. We lost home and away to PSV Eindhoven, which effectively ended our hopes of qualifying from Group C. Out of Europe, sliding in the Premiership, our only hope of silverware was the FA Cup. Unfortunately, that run to Wembley made us unpopular, particularly because of the Stevenage Borough affair in the fourth round. The whole episode was so silly with Newcastle complaining about Stevenage's facilities and Stevenage being rude about us. I was unimpressed by the attitude of both teams. If a non-league club want to conduct themselves in a tacky manner, fine, but a Premiership club should not respond. Newcastle should not have reacted to Stevenage's petty comments. Both clubs behaved like a pair of spoiled children. Bitter rivalries should be conducted with peers, not a club four divisions below. Tensions between Newcastle and Manchester United or Newcastle and Liverpool are completely understandable. Kevin Keegan's 'I'd love it' rant at Alex Ferguson was fine. They are on the same level. Newcastle and Stevenage weren't so Newcastle should just have ignored it.

My approach was to let Stevenage spout off with whatever they liked. It was their big day. Newcastle should never have risen to the bait and provoked any animosity with Stevenage.

The match was a great occasion for Stevenage and their fans. It seemed the whole town was down Broadhall Way. There was little aggravation on the pitch; any enmity was confined mainly to comments in the newspapers. Stevenage's players irritated us afterwards when they bad-mouthed Alan Shearer. 'He's nothing special,' said one Stevenage player of the England captain. If any trouble was going to kick off between the players, it would have been during the replay at St James' Park. Stevenage should have showed some respect. Alan Shearer deserved Stevenage's respect for his achievements within football. Stevenage's comments about Shearer were pathetic but we didn't need to respond to them. Newcastle should have been more dignified. I didn't voice my concerns about Newcastle's attitude to Kenny because it wasn't my place to do so, but I did do a piece for the Stevenage programme, congratulating them on getting so far and wishing them well.

Newcastle's season was scarred by poor PR. The club had to endure the Douglas Hall and Freddie Shepherd scandal when the pair of them were recorded making controversial comments about Newcastle women, shirt prices and Alan Shearer. Their words were reported in the *News of the World* but such stories do not affect players at all. In the dressing-room, everyone took the mickey out of Alan who had been called Mary Poppins and boring by Hall and Shepherd. Alan wasn't bothered or upset. He laughed about it himself. For Christmas, the players bought Alan the video of *Mary Poppins*. He kept getting called 'boring' by the players. But we already knew that about Alan!

We had to be careful what we said to the press about the scandal, which in private was a source of amusement. We all knew how tiny, meaningless things could be twisted out of proportion. The *News of the World* story was such an obvious set-up anyway. Hall and Shepherd kept making all these bizarre observations which must have been prompted. The undercover reporter probably said something like, 'What are the women like in Newcastle; some of them must be rough?' eliciting the reply, 'Oh yes, some of them are dogs.' That appears in print as 'all Newcastle women are dogs'. I found the whole situation laughable. At the same time, the Hall-Shepherd scandal was quite scary. I thought about how many times I have sat in a room with mates and said all manner of things about people. I would get slaughtered if such slurs came out publicly.

I objected to Newcastle supporters saying, 'We don't mind Hall and Shepherd saying these things about over-inflated shirt prices, but don't rub it in.' Hall and Shepherd weren't rubbing it in. They thought they were having a private conversation. The one rubbing the fans' noses in it was the *News of the World*. The newspaper implied that Hall and Shepherd were saying these horrible things about the fans publicly and laughing at them openly, which was far from the truth.

Our image was being tarnished, we were falling in the Premiership and we had virtually stumbled our way through to the Cup final with uninspired wins over Everton, Stevenage, Tranmere Rovers, Barnsley and Sheffield United. I hoped we would defeat Arsenal at Wembley but I never expected us to. Arsène Wenger's side had battered us in the League. They were a class apart in terms of attackers and organisation. Against opponents of Arsenal's calibre, Newcastle needed everyone to play out of their skins. No one did. We were also hamstrung by our approach. Caution had characterised Newcastle's football all season. It was impossible for us suddenly to be flamboyant. Our plan against Arsenal was to keep it tight and snatch victory. Some people suggested we should have paid special attention to Marc Overmars, Arsenal's flying winger, who scored the first goal in our 2–0 defeat. I disagree. Whether the attacker was Overmars, Nicolas Anelka or Christopher Wreh, we should have played in such a way that defenders instinctively covered each other. Newcastle were punished for not practising patterns of defensive play. If Alessandro Pistone had been covered, one of our centre-backs would have moved across to deal with the ball played over the top to Overmars. But no one did, Pistone was caught out and Overmars sped on to score a goal we should never have conceded. It was so straightforward; the ball was even played straight, not from a diagonal. We had plenty of time to organise ourselves. There should have been cover. But we defended badly and there was no way back after that. Overmars' goal killed us because it settled Arsenal down. Had it been 0–0 for a long time, anything could have happened, but after Overmars scored, Arsenal played us off the park. Anelka's goal came from another through ball and just confirmed Arsenal's superiority. It was a disappointing way to end a frustrating season.

I wished I had been more selfish that season and not been so prepared to sacrifice myself for the team. I talked often about the situation with Ian Rush, who was experiencing a similar problem at St James' Park. Rushie and I had been brought up the Liverpool way of working for the team but, as we got older and found ourselves in this disjointed Newcastle side, we began thinking we had to be more selfish. But neither of us could. Even in training, Rushie and I needed to be completely involved, completely committed. Ian was thirty-six years old and should have been conserving his energy, instead of chasing full-backs. He should really have taken the difficult decision to leave the full-backs and save his breath for Newcastle's next attack, but he couldn't. He had to chase them. Ian Rush embodies real team play. Most players get more selfish as they get older. Rushie didn't; in the end, two footballers moulded by Liverpool's team ethic became angry with themselves for being unselfish. It was a sad, frustrating situation.

Kenny lasted only two games into the following season, 1998–99. The timing of his dismissal surprised me. Over the summer, Newcastle's board allowed him to spend a lot of money on World Cup players like Dietmar Hamann and Stephane Guivarc'h. Newcastle were unbeaten, drawing with Charlton Athletic and Chelsea. The timing was incredible as was the manner of Kenny's sacking and Ruud Gullit's arrival. Kenny was very hard done by. I know results are everything but a board usually sacks managers before the season, at Christmas or at the end of the campaign, not two games in.

Everyone in the dressing-room was shocked and disappointed at Kenny's dismissal, particularly as the board handled his departure so disgracefully. On the morning of Kenny's sacking, the players read in the papers that he would be going although Kenny didn't know. He was on his way to training when Graham Courtney, Newcastle's press officer, phoned him up and informed him he had been sacked. We heard the news confirmed on the radio at lunch-time and never saw Kenny again. Regardless of what Newcastle's board felt about him, he deserved to be treated with more respect. The style and timing of Kenny's sacking shouldn't happen to any manager, whether it be Kenny Dalglish or the manager of Rochdale, Hartlepool or a non-league side.

Kenny had been assailed with criticism, particularly during the previous season's Cup run, but much of it was unfair. Kenny is driven by the Liverpool code that the team is everything; so he looked for people who played for the team, not themselves. The individuals he sold, Tino Asprilla and David Ginola, weren't team men. I thought Kenny's approach was correct, but it would have taken years to change the club's attitude. Under Kevin Keegan, Kenny's predecessor, Newcastle fielded great individuals without playing that well as a unit. Tino, Ginola and Les Ferdinand could perform even if the team weren't playing well, but that is not a recipe for success. To win consistently, a group of players must blend seamlessly. Ajax managed it because great individual talents like Edgar Davids, Patrick Kluivert and Clarence Seedorf all grafted for the team. Kenny was moving Newcastle from Keegan's celebration of the virtuoso to an emphasis on the collective. Kenny needed to change the philosophy, and that does not happen overnight. What Kenny could, perhaps should, have done was keep the mavericks like Ginola at the club, so keeping the fans happy, while he rebuilt slowly. It would not have suited Newcastle in the long run but Kenny might have lasted longer. Newcastle fans loved the Ginolas and Ferdinands and the cavalier football of Keegan. Having made his decision to change things around, Kenny needed to be successful quickly because the Toon Army was never going to fall in love with his more utilitarian methods.

Kenny had to buy because Newcastle's youth policy was dead. Kevin didn't bring any kids through. That's why Darren Huckerby and Alan Thompson left. There was no system in place at St James' whereby youngsters were groomed for the first team. It was the opposite of Ajax's smooth development programme. Newcastle had become obsessed with buying individuals rather than working on promising youngsters like Robbie Elliott. Huckerby couldn't see himself getting into the first team so he moved on. Under Kenny, Huckerby would have been given a chance.

Those newspapers that had trailed news of Kenny's sacking also announced Ruud Gullit was taking over. The following day, the papers claimed Gullit was possibly going to Tottenham. Having offloaded Kenny, Newcastle's board really would have had egg splattered on their faces. Ruud was in a marvellous negotiating position. After the fiascos of Stevenage and the *News of the World* revelations, Newcastle needed someone with a good media image. Such a PR-conscious credo, driven by the money-men who increasingly dominate football, is not necessarily right. If a manager is good enough, it doesn't really matter whether his name is familiar to those who run PLCs. Gérard Houllier, Liverpool's manager, is highly respected within football but hardly known outside because he never played at the highest level. Arsène Wenger was not a big name in England when he became Arsenal manager. Newcastle and Chelsea went for famous figures because their boards felt that a heavyweight would ensure the initial support of the fans. If things went wrong under the well-known manager, the board could say, 'At least we tried, at least we thought big.' Imagine if they had employed a nobody and things hadn't gone right. The fans would have accused the board of lacking ambition. But Ruud had a good track record at Chelsea. He was high profile and available.

Two days after Kenny went, Ruud walked through the dressing-room door and said, 'I'm the new manager.' Whenever such dramatic changes occur at clubs, each player wonders whether he is part of the new man's plans. Although I was disappointed for Kenny, I had to think about myself, be a professional and live with the hand fate had dealt me. I aimed to get wholeheartedly behind Ruud and hoped he would do the same for me. My professional pride and innate commitment meant I would perform. I never felt any bond with him because of his colour. No cultural link existed between us like that between Ian Wright and myself. I've worked more with Ruud than Wrighty but I feel closer to Ian; we have things in common. I didn't have that with Ruud. But then no one had much in common with Ruud.

It was difficult for those players Kenny signed, Guivarc'h, Hamann, Rush, Stuart Pearce and myself. Those brought in by Kevin Keegan, such as Rob Lee, also had doubts. Everyone in that Newcastle dressing-room wanted to know where he stood. Ruud and I both worked at the World Cup for ITV but had no real contact. We just dashed in and out of studios. Although I didn't know him, I admired what he achieved as a manager with Chelsea. His approach to playing the game echoes mine. Under Kenny, I had not played regularly so I thought Ruud's arrival could be the break I needed. Suddenly, I became very optimistic about my future at Newcastle. How wrong I was. Ruud was cold, almost dismissive towards me. We would pass each other in the corridor at St James' or at the training ground, say 'good morning' and that was it. Ruud was not one to sit and talk and be friendly. I didn't expect him to be personable with me because we had worked together at the World Cup. I just think Ruud is very much a loner, completely different from Kenny, who would want to joke and laugh with everyone.

Ruud kept himself to himself, which is unnecessary for a manager. Some managers are more detached than others who can carry on playing cards with the lads. It depends on the individual. I think Ruud was hurt by what happened to him at Chelsea where he was eased out; he felt badly let down and betrayed by a lot of people at

Stamford Bridge. His Chelsea experience definitely made him very cautious of people. Ruud had also been treated badly at AC Milan towards the end of his career in Italy. It seemed they didn't want him so he moved to Sampdoria, did well there and was bought back by an embarrassed Milan. Ruud has experienced a hard upbringing in football. With the Dutch squad at the European Championships in 1988, there were a lot of opinionated, awkward players and Ruud, who has always gone his own way, was very sharp, barking at them to do this or that. He does not treat people nastily on purpose. That's just the way he is. Some footballers need a supportive arm around them, a reality that Ruud fails to appreciate. He wants to get reactions from players so he abuses them verbally. Initially, that was not a problem with me because I do not need soothing words of support to make me perform. My ego is not fragile. If Ruud wanted to be critical of me that was his decision. The reason I became disillusioned with Newcastle and Gullit was only partly because I was being overlooked. What irritated me was that I was ignored for the wrong reasons. I excelled in training, and Newcastle were hardly setting the Premiership alight without me. At one point, Ruud had used thirty players and I hadn't been on the pitch once. I never knocked on his door to complain. I wanted to make my point on the training pitch. I was always among the best trainers, but Ruud refused to notice.

I don't know why he was so unfair towards me. Maybe he felt I was a threat although I never had any intention of seeking the manager's job at Newcastle. Ruud probably has a set, unresponsive attitude towards senior professionals who want to go into management. He may have reflected on how Gianluca Vialli replaced him at Chelsea and wondered about a similar coup occurring at Newcastle. Yet neither I nor Stuart Pearce, who was experiencing the same problems, undermined Ruud. Although Stuart and I each had one eye on management, we were both more interested in playing then.

Gullit sat me on the bench and ignored me. When Newcastle met Blackburn Rovers in the fourth round of the Worthington

Cup on 11 November 1998, the game went into extra time and cried out for someone experienced to keep possession in midfield, but he snubbed me. Even with penalties looming, Ruud refused to send me on. It was inexplicable because I'm a penalty-taker. I took them for Liverpool in big Cup matches, at all sorts of venues and they never scared me. Ruud should have introduced me in time for the penalties, particularly as we didn't have that many penalty-takers. We had young Aaron Hughes, who missed as we lost 4–2 on spot-kicks. That sort of pressure shouldn't have been placed on Hughes. I also experienced Ruud's dislike of using me at Anfield when Dietmar Hamann was sent off; three substitutes were used and I wasn't one of them. It was farcical. Alan Shearer dropped back into midfield into a position that was made for me while a forward came on. It happened against Charlton, when Nikos Dabizas was red-carded and we needed an extra midfield player. Alan shuttled back and another forward came off the bench. I found it strange that Ruud felt I had nothing to offer.

Although there were brief moments when I became depressed, I was strong enough to cope with such obvious rejection. A lot of Newcastle players found Gullit's way difficult because they wanted to be loved. I am certain the same problem existed at Chelsea. He came from the Continent where players are used to going to a club which is not doing well, playing for a period and then leaving. They would never expect to feel part of the club, the city, the community; their relationship is purely financial. But anyone who pulls on the black-and-white shirt of Newcastle acquires an immediate affinity with the city. It is difficult for English players when they are treated as coldly as Gullit treated them. They think, 'I'm being shoved out of the door here but this is my club, my people, I know everyone from the tea-lady to the chairman.'

In Europe, players move too frequently to build up any empathy with a club. When Gullit returned to the San Siro after a year at Sampdoria, no one thought anything of it. Players are transferred between AC and Inter Milan. They are professionals, chasing the riches, businessmen in boots. This detached approach means players in Europe can handle going to a club and being ostracised by the manager. It's no big deal. They just head to another club. Gullit's distant style of management would not be an issue in Italy. Players in England, even if they are not in the first team, want to feel part of the whole enterprise. English footballers need to know that the manager still wants to talk to them. Gullit doesn't do that.

The players in Newcastle's dressing-room couldn't understand this unfeeling attitude. Many didn't take to that type of managing. Most of Newcastle's squad would have preferred a more hands-on manager, one who actually communicated with them. The best managers, such as Alex Ferguson, talk to those players who they are not picking. They offer words of encouragement – 'Get your head up in training, try hard and maybe you will be in next week.' Even if the manager is lying, at least the player is relieved to have some rapport. That never happened with Ruud. He just said, 'You're not playing this week,' and that was it. He doesn't give players much encouragement, much hope of being picked if they train hard.

Ruud doesn't just ignore people outside the dressing-room, he even ignores some of those on the inside. On the night before a match, Ruud would call Gary Speed and a handful of other players into his room and tell them what he wanted from them during the game. He often wouldn't talk to them Monday to Friday unless there was something specific he needed to say to them professionally. There was no contact on a personal level. That is common practice with managers in Europe. Arsène Wenger and Gérard Houllier are honourable exceptions, more experienced with the human touch, but they come from France, which is different from Holland and Italy. Gullit was moulded at AC Milan, which was then the best club in the world with the leading players in Gullit, Frank Rijkaard, Marco Van Basten and Franco Baresi. Milan were such a professional, successful club that no one thought there was anyone there who might need encouraging. The attitude was, 'You are a man. I attack you verbally. You come back at me and we get on with it.' It was very cold.

Arrogance characterised Gullit as a player and as a manager.

All the great players possess a certain arrogance and Gullit was one of the best, even becoming World Footballer of the Year. He was tough and single-minded, not really listening to people. His attitude seemed to be, 'I'm the best in the world so why should I listen to you?'

When he strolled into St James' Park, the feeling was that Gullit had little cash to invest in players. He needed to sell to generate spending money. That was why Gullit criticised the team and players so regularly. He clearly knew some would be sold or he wanted to force them into demanding transfers. It was a dangerous tactic because Gullit had to rely on those players for a while. I couldn't understand the approach. English players don't respond to being criticised publicly by their manager. Resentment fermented in the Newcastle dressing-room about Gullit's comments. He kept saying, 'This is Kenny's team, it's poor but I'm stuck with it.' Well, he knew the team when he came. We were Gullit's players because we worked for Newcastle United. Like the other players, I had to respect Gullit because Newcastle put him in charge. In return, he should have respected me and the other players because we played for the club he managed. The relationship between Gullit and the players became fragmented which affected the atmosphere at the club. There was so much tension and, in the end, I was glad to get out of Gullit's territory. If the results had been better, he could have got away with his criticism. Success overrides everything. No matter how offhandedly the players were treated at AC Milan, they were still winning so it wasn't a problem. In England, players have to feel the manager is behind them. We never had that with Gullit in my time at Newcastle.

Given time, Newcastle should achieve things. I would look around the dressing-room and see all those international players. Shearer is the complete English centre-forward. Steve Howey is a great centre-half. Stephen Glass has done well. He came in from Aberdeen, nobody knew a lot about him but he really impressed me. Garry Brady from Tottenham shows promise. Didier Domi, whom Gullit brought in at left-back, is excellent. Temuri Ketsbaia has great dribbling ability, which is why the fans like him. Temuri is a throwback to Kevin Keegan's time in his individuality. Kenny didn't particularly utilise Ketsbaia's unpredictable talent, which the fans couldn't understand. In Ketsbaia, the Toon Army saw a David Ginola-type footballer, one capable of firing their imagination. Ketsbaia's a great player but if a team has a pattern, he can confuse things.

Ruud was very much a systems man; he wanted a pattern of play. Every day in training we worked on getting into a pattern, mainly defensively. As I was leaving the club, Newcastle were trying to cultivate a 4–4–2 style of play. It was very boring developing the pattern, hour after hour in training, but it improved the co-ordination of the team defensively. Offensively, Newcastle still relied on Glass or Nolberto Solano crossing to Alan, but Ruud was putting down foundations, organising the defence and then allowing the players to use their imagination when Newcastle had possession.

Ruud was unfortunate that Duncan Ferguson injured himself shortly after arriving from Everton. Duncan is always going to be a handful for opposing defenders but people do not appreciate his many strengths. He is great in the air, very quick for a big man over a long run, with a fine touch. He thrives on crosses from the by-line but he is skilful on the ground. Duncan is very good at running off the ball or speeding at defenders with the ball and hitting the target. He's very direct. Duncan and Alan could form a devastating partnership which could terrorise defences. As a person, Duncan is like most Scotsmen, he likes a drink. He is the life and soul of the party. Everyone loves him. Duncan is not the shyest person in the world. He likes to be with the guys, going out, enjoying the *craic* and the camaraderie. He reminded me very much of Maurice Johnston when Mo came down to Watford. They both enjoy a good time.

I never got a chance to play alongside Duncan. I realised I had no future at Newcastle. My poor treatment by Gullit was exacerbated by the club's behaviour. I was awarded an MBE during my time at Newcastle so I asked Ruud whether I could have a day off to go to Buckingham Palace, not that Gullit would know what an MBE was.

'Fine, no problem,' he said. It was a big deal for me but not for the club.

'Where's John?' people asked on the day I had gone to London.

'He's gone to Buckingham Palace,' replied those who knew.

'Oh, OK.' Nothing was really said by the club. There was a small mention in the programme. That was not a problem; it was a personal thing anyway. But I became livid at Christmas 1998.

When Stuart Pearce got his MBE, Ruud called a meeting and we all trooped upstairs to the dining-room, wondering what it was all about. All of a sudden the chairman, Freddy Shepherd, walked in, holding up a black-and-white Newcastle shirt with MBE, PEARCE and 3, Stuart's number, printed on the back. The chairman had clearly realised it would be good PR with the players. The players' committee of Alan Shearer, Rob Lee and Pearce had been at the chairman's house recently for a garden party when someone mentioned Stuart's honour. So the chairman decided to come down to training and make a presentation. A cake was brought out for Pearce and Ruud gave him a present on behalf of the staff. Rob Lee, the captain, stood up and congratulated Stuart on behalf of the players. Pearce responded, thanking everyone, but all the while, the players were stealing embarrassed glances. They could not believe that my MBE had been overlooked by Newcastle.

'Am I black or something?' I asked, trying to make a joke out of the situation, but the club's dismissive attitude angered me. Alan apologised to me.

'Sorry, Digger,' he said. 'The chairman heard of Pearcey's MBE and decided to do something.' I was still fuming. It was definitely time to leave.

into the valley

I had become a forgotten man at Newcastle United. People thought I had either retired or was sidelined by some debilitating injury. I could have stayed at St James' Park and picked up the money but that is not my style. I just wanted to get playing again, to hit a pass and create a chance. I was offered the opportunity by Alan Curbishley, one of football's nicest, most open managers and quite a contrast to Ruud Gullit. Charlton, too, were different from Newcastle, more in keeping with my first club, Watford.

The Valley was such a happy, friendly place; Charlton buzzed with a real family feel. Everyone got on well from the stewards to the groundsmen to the playing and office staff. All of Charlton's employees were so polite. Friends who came down and watched me said Charlton reminded them of Watford, a club famed for being welcoming and community-minded. Stewards showed them to their seats, had a chat, a joke and a 'how are you?' on the way. Such common courtesy is rarely experienced in the Premiership any more. Watford do it but then Graham Taylor expects such politeness. The people at Charlton are similarly cordial and civilised.

Hanging in the secretary's office at the Valley are pictures of Charlton's three legends, Sam Bartram, Derek Hales and Rob Lee.

I knew Rob well at Newcastle and he always spoke fondly of his first club. Rob's positive comments about Charlton were soon confirmed to me after I signed on a free transfer on 8 February 1999. The atmosphere at the Valley was fantastic. When I met the other players, it was impossible to sense that Charlton were actually struggling in the Premiership. They had just suffered a sequence of terrible results yet in training everyone was brimming with enthusiasm. Laughter pervaded. No one ever argued. At some clubs, discord can arise between those in the team and those who feel they should be. Unity reigned at Charlton because all the players knew how much Premiership status meant to the club and to themselves. Many of these players had been used to the lower divisions and were desperate to stay up; they could not imagine undermining team spirit.

Keith Jones and Neil Redfearn are tremendous professionals. After training, Keith, Neil and the other Charlton players always stayed on for extra shuttles, sprints and shooting practice. Curbishley's players were some of the most dedicated professionals I have ever encountered. They trained like they played, with one hundred per cent commitment. Curbishley demanded nothing less. Because he was so popular, the players sweated every ounce for him. Curbs, as everyone calls him at Charlton, really impressed me. He's similar to Kenny Dalglish in that he defends his players publicly. Players respond to that. Charlton's players would do anything for Curbs. Before I joined, I discussed the team with him.

'The players are really hard-working,' said Curbishley. 'When they haven't got the ball, they fight unbelievably hard to get it back. But when they do have the ball, they still rush around. We need a bit of composure on the ball.' My feelings on a team's DNA meant that a side must adhere to a set way of playing. So I said to Curbishley:

'The composure you want from me must be a theme throughout the team,' I said. 'There's no point in me coming to Charlton and just putting my foot on the ball and everyone else running around. The team have to be on the same wavelength.' It didn't work out that way but that was the initial plan. As much as Curbs and I hoped

Charlton would be calmer and more thoughtful in possession, when a team are down in the relegation zone, the pressure affects players during the heat of matchday. As positive as they were in training, Charlton's footballers tended to hurry too much during matches, as if slightly fearful.

Results did improve briefly. Psychologically, it must have helped Charlton to have a player of my experience simply being present at training. I made some joke in the club programme that since I'd been at the Valley Charlton had picked up nine points and I had hardly played. Although I didn't play much, only 451 minutes in total, I was closer to seeing action than at Newcastle so it was a positive period for me. I needed to improve my fitness after so long in the cold at St James' Park. I had played only five reserve matches all season so I gratefully seized on any opportunity. My short Charlton career began in the reserves, a 5–4 Avon Insurance Combination defeat by Cambridge United at Welling United's Park View Road ground. Afterwards, I rushed to Wembley for England's friendly with France where I was working for ITV. It was quite a contrast but I needed matches, even reserves ones.

I wished I could have played more for Charlton; I had two starts and ten substitute appearances. At least I was involved in every matchday squad, which was far more than happened under Gullit. Five days after signing, I came on against Liverpool at the Valley. We scored, won 1–0 and things appeared to be picking up. It was brilliant for me personally because I love playing against Liverpool, against all my old team-mates and friends, even putting one over on them. Charlton were probably lucky because Jamie Carragher never deserved to get sent off but the points were hugely welcome. We then travelled to Pride Park. Mark Kinsella hurt his shoulder early on so I came off the bench to play a part in a 2–0 victory. The team seemed to be on a roll.

Frustratingly, Charlton's momentum slowed. We drew at home to Nottingham Forest, a game we should have won. We kept missing chances, although at least they were being created, which had been Charlton's main problem. In the dressing-room afterwards, everyone kept saying, 'We hope we don't pay for missing those chances.' Charlton didn't; a team never get relegated because of one game. The damage is spread over the season. But Charlton had definitely hit a lull. The lost opportunity against Forest was followed by defeats to Coventry and Chelsea, and a draw at Leicester. Now Charlton weren't creating chances so Curbs changed things, giving me a start at West Ham, where we won 1–0. The mood was so positive afterwards, we felt we could escape.

'If we have a half-decent run-in,' said Curbs, 'we'll stay up.'

Unfortunately, we took only one point from our next four games. We played well in the first half at Middlesbrough but went 1–0 down and the confidence drained from us. Charlton had reached last-throw-of-the-dice stage. It was time for the midfield battlers. I didn't start a game after that.

'I've got to put the scrappers in now,' Curbs told me. He wanted to batter opponents physically. Personally, I felt a team always need a touch of quality. Charlton managed to draw with Leeds but lost heavily to Spurs and Everton. A subsequent point at home to Blackburn was never going to be enough.

Hope still flickered. On 8 May, we visited Villa Park for an extraordinary, rollercoaster match. I sat on the bench, enthralled at the unfolding drama. We kept scoring and then Villa did. We listened to what was happening elsewhere, to other results that would affect us, but nothing could really distract from events at Villa Park. It was so emotional. We were down to ten men when Danny Mills scored to give us a 4–3 victory. It was like a fairytale. It was a lovely sunny day and I was only disappointed because I couldn't go back on the coach. I had to go back up to Liverpool. I'm sure the boys were lively on the bus south.

The last day of the season dawned and the odds were stacked against us. Forest and Blackburn were already down. It was between us and Southampton. We prayed Everton would beat Southampton but we had to do well against Sheffield Wednesday. Wednesday are not a bad side; they had some good, composed players including Wim Jonk and Benito Carbone. They kept the ball well, ensured it wasn't the high-tempo game we wanted and quickly silenced the Valley crowd. The atmosphere was flat for long periods but then Charlton's fans started going mad. News was transmitted from the stands that Southampton trailed Everton. Many Charlton fans had radios with them. The great escape was on. But the rumour which spread so rapidly among the fans proved to be false. Maybe it was designed purely to gee the players up. We played poorly against Wednesday, who won 1–0. Southampton beat Everton anyway.

Everyone at Charlton felt deep disappointment. It had been a great adventure in the Premiership but they just lacked that bit of finance and guile to stay up. As the commiserations continued, I pondered what my own future held. I didn't realise it at the time but my playing career was over. I would have loved my final match to have involved scoring the winner in the European Cup final rather than twenty-nine minutes of a game that resulted in relegation. Since then, I have often been asked, 'Are you sad you have played your final match?'

'No,' I reply. 'Life goes on.' I was sad to leave school but there were new challenges ahead. I always believe better things lie ahead. It would only have been sad had I been twenty-seven not thirty-five when I hung up my boots. I do miss the competitive edge of playing, the banter with the lads, but I was glad I ended when I did. I didn't want to fade away. Some keep going – Peter Beardsley turned out for Hartlepool United in the 1998–99 season because he loves playing football. He cannot think of anything else. Everyone in football says nothing beats playing but the next best thing is managing. It was time to find out.

chapter twenty-three

paradise gained

C eltic have always impressed me. Even as a Liverpool player
visiting for testimonials, I admired the famous stadium filled
to overflowing with impassioned support. Celtic Park is the best
ground in Britain; probably only Old Trafford on European nights
comes close for atmosphere. Some stadiums are big but not grand.
Celtic Park is both. Ibrox appears nice architecturally but is smaller,
less substantial in size and noise. Whomever Celtic are playing,
however the team are doing, the ground is packed with 59,000
singing, flag-waving supporters. In terms of fan base, Celtic are
a bigger club than Rangers. When Celtic dominated football in
Scotland, Rangers suffered poor crowds; but even when Rangers
were in the ascendancy, Celtic always heaved with sell-out crowds.
Celtic fans are very much like Newcastle's – they flock to the
stadium in their droves week in, week out, craving success. Celtic
are a sleeping giant ready to be awoken.

The offer to become head coach of Celtic came as a real shock.
After the season finished at Charlton, I sat back and pondered
my options. I thought I was going to carry on playing so I kept
myself in shape by running every day, although I hoped the
right management or coaching position might materialise. I looked

around in England. Sheffield United were the only club I spoke to. I had an interview but it was difficult to tell who was in charge at Bramall Lane. Someone there wanted Adrian Heath and I never heard from them after the interview.

I carried on seeking managerial or coaching opportunities but I never thought of Scotland. Funnily enough, someone rang and mentioned that the Aberdeen post was coming up.

'That could be a possibility for you,' he said.

'Never in a million years,' I replied. 'There's no point in me wanting to be an ambitious coach and going up to Scotland unless it is to Celtic or Rangers. And that's not going to happen.' Those were my very words. A few days later, Kenny Dalglish phoned.

'Digger,' said Kenny, 'I've become Celtic's Director of Football Operations and we need a head coach. Do you fancy it? If you want it, it's yours.' Coming from anyone but Kenny Dalglish such words would sound a bit offhand, half-serious and not very definite. I still had doubts.

'Are you serious? Is this going ahead or not?' I asked Kenny.

'Of course it's going ahead,' Kenny replied. 'I told you it was. Do you want it?'

Of course I did. Celtic are a massive club with ambitious people on the board. I went and talked to Allan MacDonald, Celtic's chief executive. Apparently, the board were impressed by my determination in the interview. I am very passionate about football. People often say, 'Oh, I didn't expect you to be like that.' A preconception, or misconception really, has persisted about me not caring about football because of the way I played. People saw me running down the wing, beating full-backs and laughing if I got kicked. They saw me refusing to retaliate, rant or rave, which is what English footballers are supposed to do to show you really care. But I do care and people are shocked when they hear me talk ardently about my profession. Kenny knew of my passion for the game. Celtic's board swiftly discovered my desire to succeed as a head coach. They offered me a three-year contract which I signed immediately.

On Thursday, 10 June, I flew to Glasgow for the inaugural press conference with Kenny. I was met at the airport and driven to Celtic Park, slipped in the back entrance and waited for the press conference to begin. It seemed to go on for ever before an audience of TV, press and radio. Loads of fans congregated outside the front entrance so Kenny and I went out to meet them. It was a lovely sunny day, which helped. There would not have been so many fans if it had been raining, I joked to Kenny. He and I waved and chatted for five minutes and then went back inside.

Pre-season training was still some weeks off so I resumed my holiday and visited my sister in America. The one Scottish newspaper I found in Florida was the *Daily Record*, which reported that a lot of people were very sceptical about my appointment. They had every right to be. I was an untried, untested commodity and turning round Celtic represented a huge task. The doubters didn't know me; they had no reason to believe I could come in and revive Celtic. I understood the misgivings of those who argued that the job should have gone to an older, better-known manager. But I have never lacked confidence in my ability. Kenny had faith in me. I only got the job because of Kenny.

But although I was new to management, I had eighteen years' experience of other people's management. I watched how Graham Taylor, Kenny, Graeme Souness, Roy Evans, Ruud Gullit and Alan Curbishley managed. Simply through keeping my eyes and ears open, I couldn't help but learn about the managerial trade, about what it takes to mould a successful team. Watching and listening, I gained an understanding of the importance of man-management, of defending players in public and of building a DNA. People forget I was schooled under Graham Taylor, who is second to none in terms of organising and coaching. Watford were always so well-prepared. As a twenty-three-year-old at Liverpool, I absorbed advice and developed my own ideas. My style of play meant people never realised I possessed an analytical side. They thought John Barnes ran on instinct not methodology.

People see the commitment of Vinnie Jones or Peter Reid, real hard-tackling, barn-storming midfielders, and assume they will make good managers, rightly so in Peter's case. But they never know until they are tried. Flamboyant footballers such as Chris Waddle and Glenn Hoddle were never considered to be managerial material. 'They won't make managers because they just play off-the-cuff football,' ran the critical line of argument. Such a stereotype is one of the reasons why so many eyebrows were raised when Celtic moved for me. It doesn't worry me at all.

As a young head coach, I know I can turn to Kenny for advice and have done so already. I would be daft not to, given that Kenny has been in management since 1985 and won championships with Liverpool and Blackburn. Of course I ask him about players. Picking players is Kenny's strongest point; he can look at a footballer and see his potential. At Newcastle, Kenny was criticised for some of his purchases, but they were all good players if maybe not totally suited to Newcastle. Jon Dahl Tomasson is now back in the Danish squad and has just won the League with Feyenoord. Andreas Andersson scored against England in Stockholm. Kenny knows good players.

As Celtic's head coach, I am the sole person responsible for the first team. I decide which players I want to buy, such as Eyal Berkovic, and the general manager does the negotiating. I organise the tactics and prepare the team. The shaping of Celtic's first team is a hundred per cent up to me. If the first team struggle, Celtic's fans should turn on me not Kenny. Celtic's new set-up is very continental. Kenny has nothing to do with the first-team football, apart from joining in five-a-sides now and then. As usual, he cannot keep away!

Kenny's position is a long-term one.

'How long have you signed for?' I asked him. He didn't answer and no one really knows. We think it's about fifty years! It is a huge job. Kenny's task involves overseeing the overall development of Celtic Football Club. He is busy with the Academy, getting the infrastructure of that right. Kenny's presence will ensure Celtic develop good players. His reputation and stature as a player and a manager will attract the top-quality kids. Parents know Kenny will look after their children. He always stands by his players, to the detriment of himself at times.

Kenny's success with Blackburn's youth set-up proved his capabilities; inspired by such a famous and attentive manager, Rovers produced talents like James Beattie, Marlon Broomes and David Dunn. Kenny brings kids up the right way, developing the player and the person. Under Kenny, Celtic's Academy boys will learn to show respect and humility. They will understand that the key element required to become a successful footballer is discipline. Kenny will demand that. He will spend a lot of time with them, ensuring they acquire good habits. They are in good hands.

Helping Kenny to bring the best young players to Celtic Park is the experienced figure of Dr Jozef Venglos, formerly manager here but now Celtic's European scout. With the market opening up wider by the season, Venglos's European knowledge, expertise and stature is going to be very significant. He will be based in Prague, keeping an eye on developments in his home country. Many good young players are emerging in the Czech Republic. The country will be in the EC soon and will prove a major watering hole for ambitious clubs like Celtic. Venglos can send the best our way.

Rangers have shown the importance of recruiting the right players. They bought Brian Laudrup, for instance, who could win a game almost by himself. Rangers always had better individuals than Celtic so they tended to prevail. But in the last few years Celtic have invested in outstanding players, such as Henrik Larsson and Alan Stubbs, so challenging Rangers' monopoly on the talent coming into Scotland.

I want to develop a DNA at Celtic. I don't want to rely on one individual; if the team's superstar leaves, the team must be able to function. I want good players committed to keeping the shape of the team. We must compete against Arbroath as we would against AC Milan. I used to think about this when I watched Brian Laudrup play for Rangers. If he got the ball against Arbroath, he would beat five opponents and score, grab a couple more and Rangers were delighted. But Brian Laudrup would never be able to do that against AC Milan. Rangers should have done better in the Champions League than they have; they need to play the same way all the time.

Before I joined, I remember watching games involving Celtic and Rangers in which the players took up bad positions. They do it because they haven't paid for it against weaker opposition. We must maintain the same level of concentration whoever we are playing. There is an element of playing against yourself. My sister is an accomplished squash player, even to the point of representing Jamaica. Recently she started playing against Carlos, her new husband, and her standard dropped to his.

'Because you are playing Carlos,' I tell her, 'you try fancy shots. And you will still beat him. But when you play against Jamaica's number one, you will find it difficult to drag your level back up. You need to play the same way against Carlos and maintain your standards.' Football is exactly the same. I want Celtic to play the same way all the time. That's where Scottish teams have fallen down in the past.

Old Firm matches offer little preparation for Europe. Celtic find it impossible to keep their composure against Rangers, and vice versa. For some years, the derby game was all Celtic had to fall back on, with Rangers dominating the League; so Celtic tore into Rangers with an unbelievable intensity. It was similar to when Everton faced the vastly more successful Liverpool. Personally, I would settle for losing four times to Rangers but winning the League.

Rangers' recent dominance, seen in ten of the last eleven title races, means that managers at Celtic are granted little time to get things right. The demand for instant success from Celtic fans is relentless because of Rangers' pre-eminence. So managers have come and gone; I am Celtic's seventh coach or manager in the nineties. Changing managers too often causes problems with any team. Alex Ferguson needed time to build Manchester United into the most powerful side of the nineties. It's a vicious circle. Unless you are given time you are not going to achieve success, but unless you start winning you are not going to be given the time. It's catch-22.

Comparisons have already been made between me and Liam Brady, who arrived at Celtic Park with a famous playing pedigree. Liam Brady may have been a successful, skilful left-footed player but comparing us is fatuous. I find it astounding that people believe that because two men had similar international playing experiences their managerial careers will echo each other. Maybe I'll be the new Jock Stein. Who knows? Comparisons are daft. I have to be me and be allowed to manage my way. I have to be judged on what I do and not be judged on comparisons.

People may question whether I am tough enough. I am. Before taking the Celtic position, I planned to make players aware of what is required of them. If they don't understand, they won't play. That is not being tough; that is just being very clear and comprehensive in explaining what I want. Being tough is pointless if managers do not explain their decisions. I would never tell a player, 'You are being left out but I'm not giving you a reason why.' Players appreciate they have to make sacrifices.

Everyone says it's a long-term job turning Celtic around. It may prove to be so, but when Kenny signed Peter Beardsley, Ray Houghton and me at Liverpool we promptly won the League and should have done the double. When Kenny went to Blackburn, he achieved promotion and the Premiership title very quickly. We shouldn't become obsessed with time. Reviving Celtic might take one year or three. This is my first managerial job and it's a high-profile, high-pressure one. I would love to be successful and stay at Celtic for a long time. But who knows?

Whatever happens at Celtic, one job I will never ever take is that of England manager. Such a statement will never come back to haunt me. It is the 'impossible job' of Graham Taylor's famous description. England coaches never face a level playing field. With a club, there is a local situation where the city loves the club and manager or the fans love the club and manager. With England, no matter how well they have been doing, the moment the team hit a dodgy time, it is difficult to regain the fans' respect. The England team are never the manager's; they consist of players lent by other managers. I would want the players to understand what is required of them and that is impossible with England. Paul Scholes is a Manchester United player who turns out occasionally for England. The national coach cannot put together any long-lasting system in the England team because players get injured, hold different ideas or are simply set in their club ways. Five days, often fewer, is simply too short a period in which to teach a different philosophy.

The presence of so many obstacles restricting national coaches makes me even more impressed with France's achievement at the 1998 World Cup finals. In the wake of Euro '96, Aimé Jacquet worked overtime at moulding a team. Jacquet made the players understand what he wanted. Apart from Zinedine Zidane, France were full of structure-minded players who appreciated their roles. Even a flair player like Zidane knew what he had to do for the team. France's success is mirrored in Arsenal's midfield – Emmanuel Petit and Patrick Vieira are not flamboyant players but they work brilliantly for the team. Zidane gave France that extra dimension. But France are an exception. Otherwise, no manager of a leading nation has the time, support or patience around him to develop a team and a structure as Jacquet did. Jacquet was afforded the time because France had done too little for too long, even missing out on the previous World Cup finals, USA '94. Not having the time would frustrate me so my managerial career will be spent exclusively at club level.

Even before joining one of the great names in world football, I had determined to steer clear of the lower leagues. In 1998, I read John Barnwell, of the League Managers' Association, inferring that former players who want to become managers should learn the ropes in the Second or Third Divisions. I really disagree with that. I felt so sorry for Chris Waddle, who went off to Burnley and struggled there. Just because someone is young, does not mean they should serve an apprenticeship miles from the top level. Chris and I do not know about life in the Second or Third Division. We are used to working for the leading clubs and being with the country's best players. If Chris was asked to manage Manchester United, Liverpool, Arsenal or

Chelsea, I am positive he would do a good job, given his knowledge of teams and strategy. Chris would be successful at a better club than Burnley. They dragged him down to their level. I wanted to go in at a high level and that is why I jumped at the chance to join Celtic. Managing big clubs does not scare me. Whether it had been Celtic, Manchester United, Juventus or Real Madrid, I would have felt comfortable with the challenge.

David Platt prepared for management by taking time off, travelling around the world to learn at various clubs and also working with England's Under-18s. Only then did he feel ready for Sampdoria, briefly, and Nottingham Forest at the start of the 1999–2000 season. That was David's approach but I could not do that. Each individual must decide what is right for him. Some former professionals might climb on the managerial ladder at Darlington or take an FA coaching badge. I bumped into Nigel Spackman at the World Cup in France and asked him about the problems of management.

'I found it very difficult at Sheffield United,' Nigel said, 'because I just wanted to be on the training pitch but I had to talk to the chairman, be on the phone all the time and meet people.' I am not cut out to be that type of manager, involved in all levels of the club, distracted by daily details that really should not concern a football man. The only way a modern-day manager can achieve success is if the team are successful; the only way the team can be successful is if the manager is on the training pitch with them. Fortunately, the structure at Celtic ensures I spend most of my time on the training ground. I admired Glenn Hoddle's approach at Chelsea. He saw himself as the coach, concerned only with building a team on the training ground to win on the Saturday. Like Marcelo Lippi, Nevio Scala and Giovanni Trapattoni, I believe the best coaches are those who spend most time with players. Everything else is secondary. As long as the team are winning, the board of directors will be happy.

Many of the managers I consulted advised me to get a good coach when I started. 'You will not have enough time yourself on the training pitch,' they kept telling me. Such comments went in one ear and out of the other. This current Celtic team are representing me and expressing my philosophy, so I am going to make sure I have the most input. That means doing all the coaching. I will never be swayed by others as a manager. I will always be my own man. 'You have to show your colours,' is a motto I read in a Dutch coaching manual, meaning that a manager must be himself. There is no point me trying to copy Terry Venables, Graham Taylor or Louis Van Gaal. I respect their methods but I will manage my way.

I hope my appointment at Celtic will remove the glass ceiling that many black coaches and players feel restricts their managerial ambitions. People point to Ruud Gullit as a high-profile black number one, but he is perceived as a foreigner rather than a black person; he comes from Holland, he's quite exotic, he played for AC Milan. My situation is completely different. I am a former England international, mainly educated in England. A black Englishman becoming head coach of such a heavyweight club as Celtic is significant for black people within football and in society. We know we can contend with the best physically; we can also do it intellectually. Unless we can be accepted intellectually, we will never be accepted in society. I was so happy when Chris Kamara was doing well at Bradford and I wished he had stayed longer in the job. Luther Blissett is on Watford's coaching staff; he is flourishing as a coach but it's important to be number one.

Black coaches speak a lot about their frustration at not being given the opportunity to rise further. I played alongside Cyrille Regis for West Brom against the Reggae Boyz and we talked afterwards about the problem. Many black players become youth-team coaches, number threes or twos, such as Viv Anderson at Middlesbrough, but few reach number one. It is a sore point with a lot of them. It's not the chairmen holding them back; it's football and society. People will think this of Cyrille: 'He was a great player and has a lot of good ideas but it will be difficult for him to be number one.' A stigma remains.

Cyrille and other black coaches talk about the number of jobs they have applied for but not even had a reply, let alone an interview. The vacancies were not at Premier League clubs but at Nationwide level, even down in the Third Division. Former England internationals and current coaches have not had the courtesy of a letter back and ask themselves why. I always said to myself that if I got an interview, I stood a good chance. But these guys aren't getting answers. I made tentative inquiries about some jobs and was ignored. It can't be because of this laid-back perception that people have of me; they will have seen me on television, making sane analyses of games, but inquiries about vacancies went nowhere. It makes you think.

Whenever I talk to other black coaches, I always argue a counter-point. A whole generation of black footballers, who were at the forefront of playing, are now of an age where they are moving from playing into management. If there are few black managers in ten years' time, that will be the time to ask questions. I hope Celtic's decision sets a trend and that the glass ceiling has been smashed.

I want to leave you with a little saying, told to me by a friend, that sums up my professional and personal philosophy on life: Don't pray for a better wind because the wind blows on us all, but prepare a better sail.

career record

John Barnes

(John Charles Bryan Barnes)

Born Kingston, Jamaica, 7 November 1963. Joined Watford July 1981 from Sudbury Court (Middlesex League). Won FA Youth Cup winner's medal 1982. Transferred to Liverpool June 1987 for £900,000. Won First Division Championship medals 1988, 1990; FA Cup winner's medal 1989; League Cup winner's medal 1995. FWA Footballer of the Year 1988, 1990; PFA Player of the Year 1988. Football League XI v Italian League XI, Naples, 16 January 1991. Free transfer to Newcastle United August 1997. Free transfer to Charlton Athletic February 1999. Head coach of Celtic June 1999.

SUMMARY OF APPEARANCES AND GOALS

Season	Team	Lg	G	FA	G	LC	G	EC	G	CW	G	UE	G	OC	G	U–	G	In	G
1981–82	Watford	36	13	3	–	5	1	–	–	–	–	–	–	–	–	–	–	–	–
1982–83		42	10	4	1	3	–	–	–	–	–	–	–	4	2	3	–	4	–
1983–84		39	11	7	4	2	1	–	–	–	–	6	–	–	–	–	–	8	1
1984–85		40	12	2	–	5	3	–	–	–	–	–	–	–	–	–	–	11	2
1985–86		39	9	8	3	3	1	–	–	–	–	–	–	–	–	–	–	5	–
1986–87		37	10	7	3	3	1	–	–	–	–	–	–	–	–	–	–	3	–
1987–88	Liverpool	38	15	7	2	3	–	–	–	–	–	–	–	–	–	–	–	11	3
1988–89		33	8	6	3	3	2	–	–	–	–	–	–	2	1	–	–	5	3
1989–90		34	22	8	5	2	1	–	–	–	–	–	–	1	–	–	–	11	1
1990–91		35	16	7	1	2	–	–	–	–	–	–	–	1	1	–	–	7	–
1991–92		12	1	4	3	–	–	–	–	–	–	1	–	–	–	–	–	2	–
1992–93		27	5	2	–	2	–	–	–	–	–	–	–	–	–	–	–	6	1
1993–94		26	3	2	–	2	–	–	–	–	–	–	–	–	–	–	–	–	–
1994–95		38	7	6	2	6	–	–	–	–	–	–	–	–	–	–	–	5	–
1995–96		36	3	7	–	3	–	–	–	–	–	4	–	–	–	–	–	1	–
1996–97		35	4	2	–	3	–	–	–	7	3	–	–	–	–	–	–	–	–
1997–98	Newcastle U	26	6	5	–	3	–	5	1	–	–	–	–	–	–	–	–	–	–
1998–99		1	–	–	–	–	–	–	–	–	–	–	–	–	–	–	–	–	–
1998–99	Charlton Ath	12	–	–	–	–	–	–	–	–	–	–	–	–	–	–	–	–	–
	Totals	586	155	87	27	50	10	5	1	7	3	11	–	8	4	3	–	79	11

Headings: League; FA Cup; League Cup; European Cup; Cup Winners' Cup; Uefa Cup
Other cups: 1982–83 Football League Trophy; 1988–89 Charity Shield, Mercantile Credit Trophy (1 goal); 1989–90 Charity Shield; 1990–91 Charity Shield (1 goal).
Under-21 appearances: v Denmark, Greece, Hungary
G=Goals
Note: All appearances include those as substitute.

FULL INTERNATIONALS

1982–83 N. Ireland (sub), Australia (sub), Australia, Australia

1983–84 Denmark, Luxembourg (sub), France (sub), Scotland, USSR, Brazil (1 goal), Uruguay, Chile

1984–85 Egypt, Finland, Turkey (2 goals), N. Ireland, Romania, Finland, Scotland, Italy (sub), Mexico, W. Germany (sub), USA (sub)

1985–86 Romania (sub), Israel (sub), Mexico (sub), Canada (sub), Argentina (sub)

1986–87 Sweden, Turkey (sub), Brazil

1987–88 W. Germany, Turkey (2 goals), Yugoslavia (1 goal),

Israel, Holland, Scotland, Colombia, Switzerland, Eire, Holland, USSR

1988–89 Sweden, Greece (1 goal), Albania (1 goal), Poland (1 goal), Denmark

1989–90 Sweden, Italy, Brazil, Denmark, Uruguay (1 goal), Tunisia, Eire, Holland, Egypt, Belgium, Cameroon

1990–91 Hungary, Poland, Cameroon, Eire, Turkey, USSR, Argentina

1991–92 Czechoslovakia, Finland

1992–93 San Marino, Turkey, Holland (1 goal), Poland, USA, Germany

1994–95 USA, Romania, Nigeria, Uruguay, Sweden

1995–96 Colombia (sub)

index